CU00794411

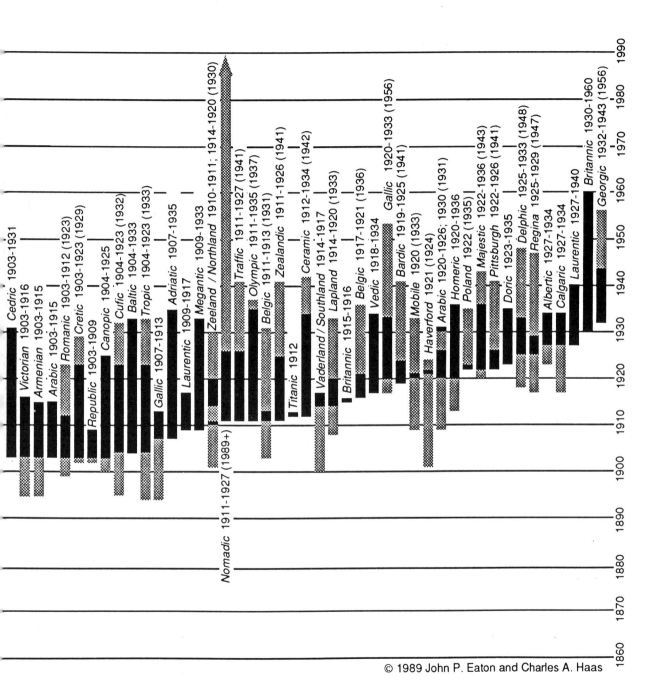

© 1989 John P. Eaton and Charles A. Haas

FALLING STAR

FALLING STAR

Misadventures of White Star Line Ships

John P. Eaton &
Charles A. Haas

Patrick Stephens Ltd

By the same authors:
Titanic: Triumph and Tragedy
Titanic: Destination Disaster

British Library Cataloguing in Publication Data

Eaton, John P.
    Falling star.
    1. Shipping services. White Star Line,
    history
    I. Title II. Haas, Charles
    387.5′06′01

ISBN 1-85260-127-2

Patrick Stephens is part of the
Thorsons Publishing Group

Printed in Great Britain by The Bath Press,
Bath, Avon

10 9 8 7 6 5 4 3 2 1

CONTENTS

ACKNOWLEDGEMENTS

This book is the product of many people and institutions saying 'yes' to sharing information, photographs and talent. Their kindnesses have contributed so much to this work.

Our very special gratitude to Sheila Macbeth Mitchell, *Britannic* survivor, and Annette R. Wolff, *Laurentic* survivor, for their unique eyewitness accounts and warm hospitality. We gratefully acknowledge the considerable contributions of David Hutchings, Michael V. Ralph, Edward D. Walker and photographic miracle worker Eugene A. Shenesky, Jr. Thanks, also to Susan Brubaker, Corinne Cebello, Chris Pagoulatos and the Atlantic Mutual Insurance Company, home of a splendid maritime archive.

We are grateful for the cheerful expertise and unstinting assistance of Laura Brown, Steamship Historical Society Library, University of Baltimore; Joel Buchwald, National Archives, New York Branch; Richard Hill and Catherine Marquard, New York Public Library; David Hodge, National Maritime Museum; Paul J. Kemp, Imperial War Museum; Michael McCaughan, Ulster Folk and Transport Museum; Janet Smith, Liverpool Central Libraries; Charlotte Valentine, Mariners Museum, Newport News, Va. and the competent, helpful staff of the British Library's Newspaper Library, Colindale.

For untangling Washington red tape, we sincerely thank New Jersey Congressman Dean A. Gallo and his capable assistant Betty Denecke. Our deep appreciation to Martin Bayerle, Bruce M. Booth, Thomas Decker, Shelley Dziedzic, Sanford Feld, Michael Findlay, Robert Fivehouse, George Gootblatt, Evelyn Hammaren, Darren Huber, Arnold Kludas, David Kreines, Russ Lownds, Denise Morris, Victor Userowicz and Mrs. J.H. Walmsley. We thank our publishers, Patrick Stephens, Ltd, Thorsons Publishing Group, for their understanding, patience and many kindnesses.

To our respective employers — the St. Luke's-Roosevelt Hospital Medical Center and the Randolph Township (New Jersey) Board of Education — and our supervisors, Ann Dreyfuss and Ronald E. Lucas, our gratitude for steadfast support and interest. And to Beatrice V. Haas, who has shared love, concern and her home through creation of three books, we express our admiration and love.

John P. Eaton
New York City, NY

November, 1989

Charles A. Haas
Randolph, NJ

FOREWORD

For centuries the seas and rivers of the world have been the major highways of communication between peoples of many nations and, as such, have inevitably been the scene of countless maritime accidents caused by collision, grounding, capsizing, fire or conflict — even by complacency. Most of these accidents have been of a minor nature and are largely forgotten, but a very few have been counted amongst the most tragic occurrences ever to have befallen mankind.

That venerable British steamship company — the White Star Line — was not immune from such misfortunes and, during the years of its existence, suffered many vicissitudes. Indeed, included in the company's annals was that most famous of shipwrecks — one which remains to this day the epitome of the Western Ocean disaster — the tragedy of the *Titanic*. Inspired by their exhaustive research into that most unhappy of liners, John Eaton and Charles Haas have rediscovered some of the other unfortunate occurrences that befell a few of the other ships of the White Star Line, incidents which over the intervening years have been forgotten by time, locked away in volumes of dusty records.

Some of these stories make emotive reading — but in all can be traced Man's fight against the sea as he struggles to keep open and safely maintain his peaceful lanes of commerce and communication.

I am pleased that some of these stories of White Star have now been brought together into one book. Far from deterring the prospective voyager, the re-telling of our forefathers' experiences — some of which caused the creation of legislation to improve maritime safety — can only show how today's seaways have been made safer highways on which to travel.

David F. Hutchings
Lee-on-the-Solent
Hampshire, England

AUTHORS' INTRODUCTION

For the landsman, shipping is filled with glamour and excitement. Ships, great and small, ply steady paths through summer heat and winter storm, between exotic ports. Fascinating sounds and sights accompany midnight departures and morning arrivals. History preserves the shipping traditions that capture public imagination. Through them, vessels, officers, crew, entire companies acquire traits and personalities which become reasons for using — or not using — their services. Each voyage differs from those of any other ship, for each vessel bears a unique character that fascinates: luxury combined with utility; honourable employment in war; distinguished service in peace; reliability; longevity.

Accompanied by objective statistics and specifications, such character forms the basis for a company's existence in a highly competitive industry conducted for profit. A year's extension to a ship's life, a day saved on a voyage, a few hours' difference in departure or arrival can change loss to profit, or profit to loss.

Britain's White Star Line was fortunate to own several vessels whose character and reliability place them high on mythical lists of great ships: *Germanic* of 1874; *Cedric, Baltic* and *Adriatic* of 1903, 1904 and 1907, respectively; the esteemed *Olympic*;

passenger-cargo vessels such as *Gothic* or *Suevic*, long-lived under White Star's own flag or those of other companies. Other White Star vessels, while prominent in shipping histories, had careers shortened by disaster or war: the great *Oceanic* of 1899, *Naronic, Britannic* of 1914, the ill-fated *Titanic*.

Throughout the fabric of White Star's story also are threaded many incidents — some important, others insignificant — reflecting pressures to which company vessels were subjected daily. Largely forgotten today and frequently overshadowed by major mishaps, these perhaps more faithfully depict the company's daily operations than do the bolder strokes of major disaster.

Although many disasters were avoidable, most incidental accidents were not. Responding to competitive pressures, *all* companies drove ships and crew to the limits. In sending out its ships to battle storm and time, White Star was not unique among the shipping conglomerates of its day. For three full generations its ships plied routes encircling the world. Telling of great success and abysmal failure, its story represents a microcosm of all major nineteenth and early twentieth century shipping companies whose fortunes rose, reached their zeniths, then descended...

White Star. Bright Star. Falling Star.

CHAPTER 1

Royal Standard, 1864

GOLD . . . AND ICE

When H.T. Wilson and James Chambers, owners since 1857 of the White Star Line, decided in 1863 to add steam-powered vessels to their clipper fleet, they turned to Palmer Brothers & Company of Jarrow. Constructed at Palmer's Tyneside yard, their vessel was 225 ft long, 40 ft wide, and had a moulded depth of 20 ft 6 in. An iron hull enclosed two decks and five holds. The 2,033 gross ton, 1,598 net ton vessel had three masts and carried full sails. A two-cylinder, 165 horsepower steam engine provided auxiliary power, turning a single screw. She provided accommodation for 40 cabin passengers and 800 steerage.

Launched in August 1863 as *Royal Standard*, the ship spent six weeks fitting out at Jarrow before going round to her new owners at Liverpool. Her trip around England's south coast from Jarrow showed the new vessel to be fast and comfortable. The Liverpool press described *Royal Standard* as '...one of the handsomest and most completely equipped steamers afloat. Her saloons are spacious and handsomely furnished with every requisite for the voyage, including piano, library, etc., and [the ship has] every necessity for the safety and comfort of passengers of every class.'

Founded by Henry Threlfall Wilson and John Pilkington in 1845, the White Star Line had been carrying emigrants and cargo between Liverpool and Melbourne, Australia since 1852. Homeward bound, the company's clippers carried some export cargo: whale oil, seal skins, wool. But the principal commodity from the Antipodes was gold and White Star Line vessels brought back many shipments of the precious yellow metal from Australian fields to English bank vaults.

Under command of Captain E.J. Allen, former master of the company's sail vessel *Shalimar*, *Royal Standard* departed Liverpool 23 November 1863 on its maiden voyage to Melbourne, Australia. White Star's first steam-powered voyage was touched by tragedy as Captain Allen died on the outward run, and he was succeeded by G.H. Dowell, under whose command *Royal Standard* departed Melbourne on 21 March 1864 for the return leg of her maiden trip.

As usual she carried gold — 19,521 ounces, more than a half-ton — in her vault. She also carried a full load of standard cargo and twelve cabin passengers.

The first two weeks of the return voyage saw light and variable winds but the ship made good progress and Captain Dowell anticipated a passage to Liverpool of less than 65 days. Sails were in constant use, and the machinery, when required, 'worked admirably'.

Fourteen days out of Melbourne, however, an incident occurred which almost ended the voyage, indeed, the ship itself. In a dispatch to his employer later published in Liverpool's *Shipping and Mercantile Gazette*, Dowell described what occurred:

'...On the 4th April at 11 am, being then in lat. 54 50 S., long. 145 27W., with screw triced up, royal and mizzen topgallant sails stowed, the ship suddenly came into a dense fog; at the same moment the look-out sang out, "Broken water ahead".

'The next moment saw a large iceberg close under the starboard bow, and all that human power could do to prevent a collision was done, but we were too close to clear it. The helm was immediately put hard a-starboard; called all hands and braced the yards sharp up,

Left *The White Star Line began as a fleet of Wilson and Chambers' sailing ships, bound for the gold fields of Australia. Among them was the namesake vessel, the clipper* White Star *(Authors' Collection).*

Below *Day of peril — On 4 April 1864, the homebound* Royal Standard *collided with an iceberg in the South Pacific (Illustrated London News).*

bringing the ship parallel with the berg on its weather side, but she would not lay high enough to clear it, and to stay her was impossible.

'The sea gradually settled her down upon it, and as the sea on the port side knocked her against it, so the rebound of the sea knocked her hull away from it by going under her bottom, thus bringing the yards in contact with the berg. Before they broke they struck the berg several times, bringing down large masses of ice on the deck.

'At last the main and mizzentop masts snapped at the top, bringing down the yards, masts and gear belonging to them, and breaking the truss heads of the lower yards, the ship forging slightly ahead. Her foretopgallant mast, jib-boom, foretopsail yards and stunsail boom then went, and all the gear, damaging all the sails more or less.

'The resistance, having gone from aft, brought the ship's upper work in contact with the berg, smashing the starboard lifeboat and davits, stove in [the] starboard quarter in several places, smashing in the Captain's room, seriously damaging the ship's chronometer and instruments, lifting the poop deck beams 12 inches, and damaging the entire cabin, and another heavy crash split one upper plate amidships.

'At this time destruction seemed inevitable; but as the ship slowly forged ahead under her main and foresail, hope still remained. At last the end of the berg came into view, and we forged clear.

'I immediately ordered the pumps to be sounded in all the compartments, and found the ship was not making any water whatever. At the same time [I] ordered steam up, and the screw to be lowered. Steam was got up and engines [were] at work in less than three-quarters of an hour.

'The berg appeared to be enveloped in a dense fog and upwards of 600 feet high. In the immediate vicinity and surrounding the vessel were several others of similar magnitude. [We] proceeded under steam and arrived at Rio Janeiro [sic] 9th of May. Will take in 350 tons of coal and proceed on the 12th.'

Captain Dowell subsequently reported that his ship had scraped along the berg's protruding, flint-like edges for almost thirty minutes, moving forward a half mile. Since the ship was not damaged below the waterline, few repairs were needed in Brazil. On 19 June *Royal Standard* arrived back at Liverpool.

Early in 1864 White Star Line's owners had joined with the Black Ball and Eagle Lines to form

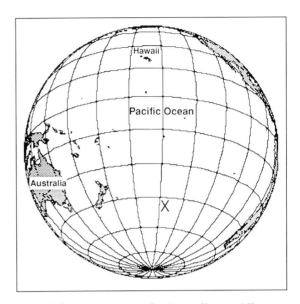

a single large company, the Australian and Eastern Navigation Co, Ltd, for trading between Liverpool and Australia. As one of the new company's three steamships, *Royal Standard* played an important part in the plans but capitalized at £2,000,000 in 40,000 £50 shares, Australian and Eastern soon found itself in difficulty. Rumours swirled of shady dealings, allotment of shares to preferred clients and large amounts of stock being held by company directors in minor company employees' names. An investigation by the Stock Exchange Committee resulted in the plan's termination.

But in May 1864 — even as *Royal Standard* was on her perilous maiden voyage — a new company was formed with the same board of directors and the same capital: The Liverpool, Melbourne and Oriental Steam Navigation Co Ltd. A lack of public confidence, engendered by the earlier scheme's collapse, prevented the new endeavour from proceeding beyond initial discussions. Borrowing and mortgaging its assets to enlarge its fleet, White Star Line found itself seriously in debt. A second steamship, the 620-ton *Sirius*, had to be sold upon delivery. In December 1865 James Chambers resigned from management, and H.T. Wilson took on a new partner, John Cunningham. *Royal Standard*, meanwhile, had completed a second round voyage to Melbourne, this time without incident.

The former steamship Royal Standard *was converted to sail in 1868* (State Library of Victoria, Australia).

A March 1866 bank failure further imperiled company finances. In the hope that some of the lucrative North Atlantic trade might be captured, *Royal Standard* was sent on a voyage to New York, departing Liverpool on 23 May. It, too, was a failure and *Royal Standard*'s next voyage departed Liverpool on 27 September for Melbourne. White Star's mortgages had been assumed by the Royal Bank of Liverpool. In October 1867 this bank too was forced to suspend business, one more in a series of banking and commercial disasters rocking Britain. An audit uncovered a £1,168,000 deficit,

of which Wilson and Cunningham (the White Star Line) owed £527,000.

Late in 1867 the company's assets were sold, and on 18 January 1868 the partnership was dissolved. Following her disposal, *Royal Standard* was converted to a sailing ship and purchased by a Liverpool syndicate that included Wilson and Chambers. *Royal Standard*'s career, which began so spectacularly, ended inauspiciously on 10 October 1869 when she was wrecked on the Brazilian coast near Cape St. Thomé.

But the White Star Line survived, if only in name: among the assets sold were the company's good will and its flag, a red swallow-tailed pennant with a white star. The purchaser was a 31-year-old Liverpool shipowner, Thomas H. Ismay.

Accidents and incidents

In service spanning almost three generations, White Star Line vessels made hundreds of voyages

to six of the world's seven continents. The vast majority were utterly without incident, providing safe, comfortable transportation to millions of passengers. As with any far-reaching endeavour, however, risk was inevitable, and White Star ships were involved in their share of misfortunes, ranging from scraped paint to the unspeakable tragedy of *Titanic*.

'Accidents and incidents' chronicles day-to-day events involving White Star ships. Drawn from marine insurance archives, it offers a portrait — one not always found in newspaper headlines — of a major shipping company's vibrancy and vulnerability.

7 October 1871	White Star's steamer *Baltic* struck the French brig *Confiance*, at anchor off Sandy Hook, New York Harbor's entrance. *Confiance*'s foremast was carried away and a lifeboat was stove in. She began to take on water, and was towed to the Atlantic Dock for repairs.
23 November 1871	Inbound from New York, *Atlantic* collided in the River Mersey with the steamer *Alexandria*, inbound from Alexandria. Both vessels were slightly damaged.
26 December 1871	*En route* to New York from Liverpool, *Oceanic* encountered heavy gales and high seas that broke three of four propeller blades. Sails were raised, but squalls and gales shredded them. On 8 January, *Oceanic*'s lookouts spotted a brig flying her American flag upside-down, a distress signal. The *Mountain Eagle* was sinking, with decks about a foot under water and seas washing over her. *Oceanic* lowered a boat and removed the captain and crew, who had been in waist-high water for 24 hours without food.
15 October 1872	In Liverpool's Crosby Channel, *Atlantic* collided with and damaged the *Wisconsin*.
18 October 1872	Leaving the Harland and Wolff shipyards in Belfast after handing over to White Star, the new *Celtic* grounded on the mud in Belfast Lough and remained there for one tide.

CHAPTER 2

Atlantic, 1873

OF COAL AND CALCULATIONS

Any of several dates might be considered the modern White Star Line's beginning. On 18 January 1868, the White Star Line of packets was forced into bankruptcy, and soon thereafter 31-year-old shipowner Thomas H. Ismay purchased for £1,000 the defunct company's name, house flag and good will. On 30 July 1869, Ismay's partner George H. Fletcher finalized a contract with Harland and Wolff for constructing White Star's first four steamships. On 6 September 1869 the Oceanic Steam Navigation Company, Ltd, White Star's official name, was registered with £400,000 in initial capital.

One year later, on 27 August 1870, its first new steamship, Harland and Wolff yard number 73, was launched at Belfast. The £120,000 liner was given the company's name, *Oceanic.* Her pioneering lines virtually rewrote textbooks on passenger liner design.

Oceanic's deck houses were joined together and extended to the ship's full width, then covered with a light iron deck, creating a sheltered promenade deck. The best accommodation was amidships where rolling and engine room sounds would be less noticed, instead of aft where tradition normally placed them. Her 80 ft by 40 ft dining saloon spanned the ship's entire width, allowing the seating of all saloon passengers at once and in individual seats. Men enjoyed a smoking room instead of having to go on deck with their cigars while innovative electric buttons summoned stewards and stewardesses.

Many first class cabins had fresh running water replacing the usual jugs. Cabins were far larger than any afloat, and almost all first class cabins had portholes twice the usual size. Open railings replaced the more usual solid bulwarks, allowing the rapid clearing of any seas shipped aboard. At the same time *Oceanic's* slim hull lines permitted higher speed with lower fuel consumption. Providing 166 first class ('saloon') berths, *Oceanic* also offered accommodation for 1,000 emigrants. Unmarried male steerage berthed forward, while aft was the married couples' and single women's accommodation. Stout iron bulkheads separated steerage from first class.

Many thought *Oceanic* and her sisters would sail to Australia and New Zealand, as had the old White Star Line's sailing ships, but instead they were placed on the highly competitive North Atlantic route where Guion, National, Inman and Cunard ships were well established. *Oceanic* began her maiden voyage to New York from Liverpool via Queenstown on 2 March 1871. It was hardly an auspicious beginning with just 64 passengers booked for her 1,166 berths. The voyage was further marred when crankshaft bearings overheated and she turned back to Holyhead, Wales before returning to Liverpool for repairs.

On 26 November 1870 a second ship, *Atlantic,* was launched. Within twelve months, sister ships *Baltic* and *Republic* and the slightly larger *Adriatic* and *Celtic* also joined the fleet. Together they could maintain a regular weekly service to New York, departing every Thursday. Generally identical to *Oceanic, Atlantic's* passenger accommodation was even more splendid. As one contemporary periodical wrote:

'The interior decorations are on a most magnificent scale.... The [saloon's] lounges and fixed seats are upholstered in crimson velvet; the [wall] panels are damasked with white and pink and the pilasters, brackets and cornices are of teak, picked out with gold. The bed hangings of the staterooms and sleeping berths, which are large and commodious, are of green rep [corduroy], and the apartments are in all respects elegant and complete.'

Atlantic was handed over on 3 June 1871, and three days later departed Liverpool on her maiden voyage. Philadelphia minister A.A. Willits wrote on the trip:

'The splendid accommodation of the ship, the charming weather, the distinguished and talented character of the

company on board, and the novel instructive and delightful entertainments in the saloon every evening during the passage have together made this a most remarkable and memorable voyage; so much so, that many gentlemen on board who have crossed the ocean repeatedly, declared they had never seen anything comparable with it before, and that it really initiates a new era in ocean navigation.'

Another passenger wrote:

'We have a host of little comforts, some of which are not to be had in a first-class Swiss hotel. We have a good piano, and a real library of books, a smoking room, a barber's shop and a ladies' room... The crew is perfect...'

New York newspapers published a White Star sailing schedule showing Atlantic'*s final eastbound voyage* (Authors' collection).

Ole Nilson purchased his ticket for Atlantic'*s disastrous voyage in Christiansand, Norway on 12 March* (National Archives).

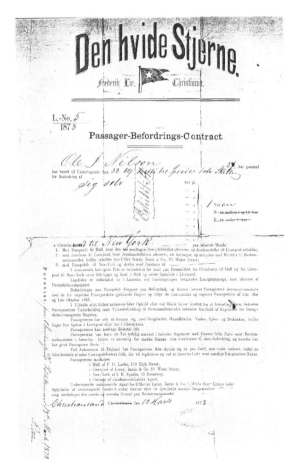

FALLING STAR

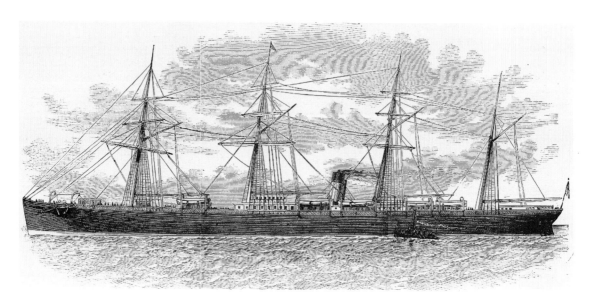

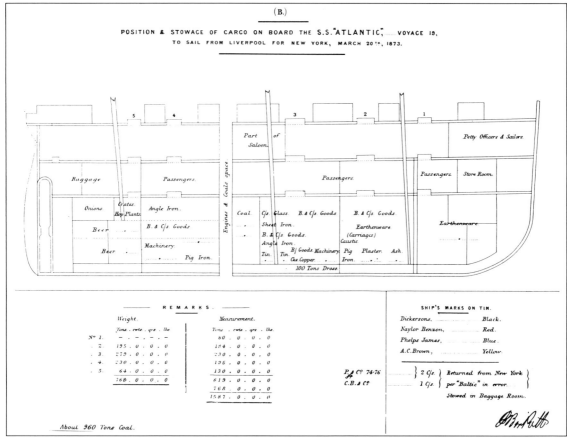

Left *The graceful lines of White Star's early sailing ships are reflected in* Atlantic*'s port profile* (Library of Congress).

Below left Atlantic*'s cargo stowage plan shows the distances passengers had to climb during the ship's evacuation* (Liverpool Central Library).

Right *James Agnew Williams, 33, commanded* Atlantic *on her fateful voyage* (Library of Congress).

En route, America's Independence Day was celebrated with ceremony — and calamity. While firing Fourth of July salutes from *Atlantic's* signal gun, a quartermaster so badly injured both hands that amputation was necessary. The accident contrasted with the company's avowed penchant for safety. White Star commanders were to follow specific transatlantic routes 'generally acknowledged to constitute the safest and most reliable courses for all seasons of the year.' Company rules detailed every ship operation with safety in mind. Each ship had seven strong iron watertight bulkheads. *Atlantic's* ten lifeboats, with a capacity of 600, exceeded legal requirements by more than 50 per cent.* The new ships were surveyed by the Underwriters' Registry of Iron Vessels, assuring integrity.

In November 1871, *Atlantic* experienced a close call. Sailing from Liverpool to Queenstown on her sixth westbound voyage, she was proceeding slowly off the Skerries when Inman's *City of Paris* began overhauling her at high speed. As the Inman ship drew ahead, she cut directly into *Atlantic's* path, passing just 150 ft away. Thomas Ismay immediately wrote to William Inman, protesting to him about the 'unwise and hazardous course' steered by the *City of Paris*.

In late 1872, White Star announced that *Atlantic* would make a January 1873 sailing to Valparaiso, Chile on a new South American steamship service but poor bookings led to the cancellation of the voyage and the steamship service, though their sailing ships continued South American calls.

*In a practice continuing until *Titanic's* disaster, lifeboat accommodation was based upon tonnage rather than people on board. Yet in 1872 alone, some 1,148 British ships were lost, and 2,073 crew and 105 passengers were killed.

After eleven voyages *Atlantic* entered a Liverpool drydock for her three-bladed propeller to be replaced with a four-bladed one to minimize the vibration and blade fractures that had plagued her and her sister-ships.

Voyage 19 began routinely with requisite preparations as White Star's superintendent engineer came aboard to measure coal remaining from voyage 18. He accepted the 132-ton estimate of *Atlantic's* own engineer, then ordered 860 additional tons of mixed Lancashire and South Wales coals. By the time the 863 tons arrived the ship had consumed twelve more tons in port and sixteen tons of the new supply somehow was diverted into White Star's Liverpool tender *Traffic*. Nevertheless, when *Atlantic* sailed, she carried coal within thirty tons of capacity.

The £16,000 ($80,000) cargo — machinery, earthenware, beer, copper ingots — came on board and was carefully stowed under Board of Emigration supervision, as were her provisions. On Tuesday 18 March *Atlantic* anchored in the River Mersey, awaiting her crew, the delayed remainder of her coal and her passengers.

Commanding her a second time would be James Agnew Williams. At 33, Williams held an extra master's certificate. After commanding several Guion Line ships he had been dismissed in 1871

FALLING STAR

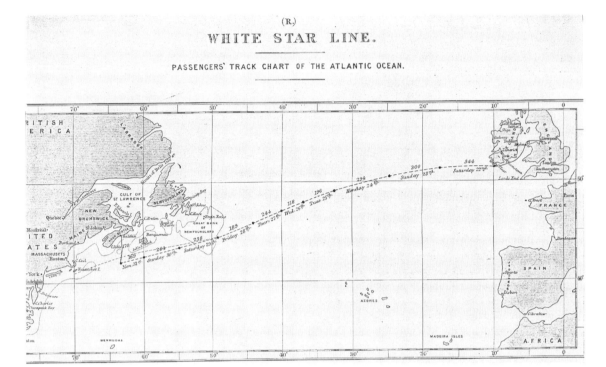

A White Star track chart signed by Atlantic's *Captain James Williams shows the ship's daily runs and the northward course diversion of 31 March* (Liverpool Central Library).

after a passenger alleged insobriety. Joining White Star as a second officer, he had been assigned to *Republic*, and during a gale-lashed Atlantic crossing in February 1872 had been badly injured when a lifeboat broke loose and crushed him, twice breaking his left thigh, dislocating an ankle and fracturing several ribs before two seamen snatched him from further injury. He recuperated for several months in a New York hospital. The experience earned Williams a strong recommendation from Captain Digby Murray and after three voyages aboard *Celtic* as chief officer he was named *Atlantic*'s master.

Passengers began arriving aboard *Traffic*. They paid £27 round trip, first class or as little as £6 6s for a single steerage ticket. Fine print on their contract noted that: 'Passengers are liable to be rejected if, upon examination, they are found to be lunatic, idiots, dumb, blind, maimed, infirm or above the age of sixty years... or any person unable to care for himself without becoming a public charge.' Steerage passengers supplied their own bedding, plate, mug, knife, fork, spoon and water can.

An immigration inspection, a crew muster, a stowaway search and a perfunctory lifeboat drill completed pre-departure activities. Shortly after 3.00 pm on 20 March 1873, anchors were raised and *Atlantic* began her nineteenth — and last — voyage.

At a brisk 13 knots, the ship crossed the Irish Sea and arrived at Queenstown at 9.00 am on 21 March. There, four more saloon passengers, 143 adult steerage, twenty children and eight babies came aboard. *Atlantic* was about two-thirds full: there were just 35 in first ('saloon') class, but 776 steerage and a crew of 141. In all, 952 were officially on board, including almost 200 children. There also were fourteen stowaways whom pre-departure searching had failed to disclose. Ordered to perform various on-board tasks, they frequently refused; some were later suspected of rifling crews' quarters.

18

As the ship moved westward, there was every indication this voyage would prove equal to that which had inspired Reverend Willits two years earlier. With ideal ventilation, ample food, attentive service and comfortable accommodation, it was easy to see *Atlantic*'s success in her passengers' eyes and words. Sunday March 23, clear and bright, was highlighted by divine service. At noon, the crew practised lifeboat drill. The ship completed some 300 miles that day, down slightly from Saturday's 344, but still averaging a respectable 12.5 knots.

Soon, however, the weather began to deteriorate, and by Tuesday a full gale from the southwest pounded the ship. As *Atlantic* struggled onward at reduced speed — 8 knots on Tuesday, and less than 5 knots as the storm worsened on Wednesday — the ship began rolling considerably. Seasickness was endemic, particularly in steerage compartments. Children's laughter was replaced by crying and their parents' comforting words.

Waves began to mount, and the ship shuddered as several struck her upperworks, smashing a wheelhouse window, destroying lifeboat 4 and damaging number 10. Barrels of salt fish and potatoes stored on deck were washed overboard. Tuesday's run was a meagre 196 miles, while Wednesday's was just 118 miles as Captain Williams further reduced speed to minimize passengers' discomfort. As howling headwinds continued, steering gear failed and emergency hand gear was used until repairs could be made. Thursday's run was up to 244 miles, but Friday's brief sun sighting indicated slippage to 189 miles.

After eight days at sea, Captain Williams began to become concerned about coal expenditure. Calculations showed *Atlantic* was burning 70 to 75 tons of coal per day, or about 580 tons thus far. Chief engineer John Foxley estimated some 319 tons remained. Williams did not react beyond posting the estimate in the wheelhouse.

The storm subsided slightly on Saturday 29 March, but the ship managed only a 238 mile run as Williams ordered coal conservation in the engine room and galley. Sails were raised, but less than a day later several were torn to shreds. Foxley now expressed serious concern about coal supplies.

Monday 31 March began with light headwinds, a slight swell and Captain Williams preoccupied with coal supplies. As passengers assembled for breakfast he asked Foxley to assess carefully the bunker contents. The barometer was beginning to fall again, indicating further bad weather, and Williams wrestled with the prospect of further days at sea, dwindling food supplies and a powerless ship.

At noon three officers took a sun sighting. *Atlantic*'s position was 41° 39'N, 63° 55'W, or 460 miles east of Sandy Hook, New York Harbor's entrance. At 1.00 pm Foxley reported that just 128 tons of coal remained. Williams weighed the evidence. Said Foxley, 'The Captain... was afraid that we might get within about 80 miles of Sandy Hook and the coals would be expended at about that time'.

As the Atlantic *canted over after impact, hundreds of steerage passengers struggled to reach the upper decks* (Library of Congress).

White Star's regulation number 37 required captains 'to pay special attention to daily consumption and remaining stock of coal'. Regulation 2 commanded that 'Whilst they are expected to use every diligence to secure a speedy voyage, they must run no risk which might by any possibility result in accident to their ships... The Company... looks for such speed on various voyages as is consistent with safe and prudent navigation.' But then there was the ignominy of being the first White Star liner to run short of coal...

Soon after 1.00 pm Williams reluctantly altered course for Halifax, Nova Scotia, some 170 miles north, where additional coal and provisions would assure *Atlantic*'s safe, if not timely, New York arrival. He plotted a course to a point five to seven miles east of Sambro Light, landfall point for Halifax. It didn't take long for passengers to notice the course change but few complained.

With ample coal to reach Halifax, speed was gradually increased. At noon her speed was 9 knots; by 11.30 pm with sails reefed, it was almost 12 knots. The afternoon's weather was moderate, with occasional rain and southeast winds. Several sightings assured the ship's officers that *Atlantic* remained on course. Williams ordered sounding leads readied and anchors put over the bows, ready for dropping.

By 10.00 pm the weather had again turned foul with heavy rain. At 11.50 pm, Third Officer Cornelius Brady calculated that *Atlantic* had run about 122 miles toward Halifax. Before retiring, Williams made another slight course correction, then ordered Second Officer Henry Ismay Metcalf to keep a sharp lookout for ice and for Sambro Light. If visibility deteriorated or the lighthouse was sighted, Williams was to be called immediately. At the latest he was to be awakened at 3.00 am, when he would anchor and await daylight before navigating Nova Scotia's treacherous coast into Halifax. Going to the chartroom, behind and below the bridge, he asked his steward to bring him hot cocoa at 2.40 am.

In the *Atlantic*'s boiler rooms, the night watch performed routine maintenance work that included cleaning several fires. In doing so they provided more steam and higher speed. But officers of the watch were unaware of the power surge... At midnight Quartermaster Robert Thomas became concerned when he learned Sambro Light still was not in sight, for he knew its range from a previous Halifax visit. Ninety minutes later he approached Second Officer Metcalf:

'I made the remark to him that I thought the ship had run her distance far enough to make Sambro Light, and that she should lay with her head off shore... I had got the latitude and longitude of the ship's position at one o'clock, and also at the same time had got the latitude

Left *Local fishermen begin pluck-ing* Atlantic*'s survivor from their precarious hold on the wet rocks* (Library of Congress).

Right *Third Officer Cornelius Brady and fisherman Thomas Clancey anchor the line as* Atlan-tic*'s passengers desperately pull themselves to safety in a pounding surf* (Library of Congress).

and longitude of Halifax from one of the saloon passengers and had made the calculation myself. I estimated that the ship would go eleven and a half and twelve knots, without allowing anything for set of current. At this time I thought that we had run far enough to see Sambro Light.'

Metcalf's response was brusque: 'I am not captain, you are not mate. I cannot do as I wish and alter course.' About thirty minutes later, Thomas asked Fourth Officer John Brown for permission to go aloft to sight Sambro. Brown replied simply, 'No, it is too soon,' feeling it was not his duty to grant such permission. Sounding leads remained unused; visibility seemed good despite some clouds and Sambro Light surely would be seen soon off to starboard. The common log showed speed down to 9 knots. At 2.40, Captain Williams' servant boy arrived with the promised cocoa and was referred by Brown to Metcalf. Remembering that Williams was to be awakened at 3.00 am, Metcalf said, 'Never mind calling him. I will call him myself in a moment.' After all, *Atlantic* had not yet reached the planned anchoring position.

At 3.12 am Metcalf left the bridge unattended — again contrary to regulations — and called the captain. Quartermaster Thomas, at the wheel just for-

ward of the chartroom, suggested that Metcalf 'go in and shake the man so as to get him up' from his sound sleep.

As Metcalf shook Williams, a voice rang through the darkness 'Breakers ahead!' Thirty feet forward of the bridge, Joseph Carroll on lookout duty had spotted a white line off to starboard. Lookout Patrick Kiely spotted it, too, and repeated, 'Breakers or ice ahead!' Rushing forward, Metcalf immediately pulled the telegraph signal to 'full astern' as quartermaster Thomas put the wheel hard a-starboard. Even as Metcalf's hand grasped the telegraph handle, *Atlantic* struck. Down in the stokehold, Fourth Engineer William Paterson reacted, too:

'I was standing on the stokehold plates when I felt the ship touch the bottom. I supposed almost directly under my feet on the starboard side of the keel, as if she were grazing over something... She appeared to me as if her bottom was going over the shore with a rumbling noise, not as if she struck full against a rock... I immediately ran up to the engine room. When I got there, I saw the telegraph had been thrown round beyond the usual mark for going astern full speed, as if it had been pulled violently... The fifth engineer was in the act of reversing the engines. I went to his assistance... I then went below to shut the service sea cocks... when I shut the last [of them] I saw the water running out of the starboard after bunker... there was a foot of water over the stokehold floor. I then made my way to the deck, being the last person leaving the engine room.'

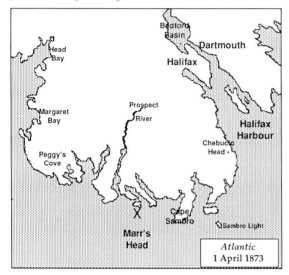

Atlantic
1 April 1873

Atlantic
1 April 1873

As Captain Williams flew out on deck with Metcalf, a horrific sight greeted their eyes: *Atlantic* had impaled herself on a rock known locally Marr's Rock, Meagher's Rock, Maris Head or Golden Rule Rock, some 50 yards off Mosher's (or Meagher's) Island near the village of Lower Prospect, with her stern pointing almost due south. She was some twelve to thirteen miles west of where her officers thought she was.

In seconds, five huge holes were torn in *Atlantic*'s stout iron plating. The grinding, rumbling shock of impact served as the passengers' and crew's only alarm. Throughout the passenger accommodation, chaos reigned. Steerage passenger William Hogan said:

'I heard a fearful crash and the air rushed in, blew out the lights [candles] and upset some of the bunks. Steerage passengers appeared stupefied with the shock. I awakened several of them; they did not seem to understand that they were in extreme danger... I told them we were on a rock.

'Me and my companion made our way to the second deck. I do not know how we got up. I think the stairs were broken down by the concussion. I made for the companionway, and there I found a large crowd trying to get out. Some of the passengers on deck below cried out that the doors were closed, but I think, myself, that they had made such a rush for the deck that they wedged one another there...

'I came up through the companionway. I went to the side of the vessel nearest to the land; this was about four minutes after she struck. By this time the steam commenced to blow off, which made... everything invisible for some time.'

Hundreds of Hogan's steerage companions struggled in darkness as water poured into their accommodation. Where modesty imposed a need to dress, death triumphed: where compassion called for assisting others, drowning was the reward. Hundreds struggled simultaneously to reach exits to upper decks. Corridors were jammed with pushing, desperate people often overwhelmed by torrents of water flooding in. Some steerage passengers managed to escape only through the oversized portholes.

Seven distress rockets were fired before one exploded in Quartermaster John Speakman's hand, halting further firings. Heavy waves struck the ship's stern, and it pivoted eastward. *Atlantic*'s entire port side was exposed, and one by one waves battered portside lifeboats into splinters or washed them away. Officers and crew scrambled to lower the remaining starboard boats, using axes to cut falls. Fully-laden boat 3 was sent off without her plugs being fitted. Boat 7 was swept away and lost.

Above By dawn, only a few remain clinging to Atlantic*'s rigging* (Library of Congress).

Below Brave fishermen navigate their frail craft to save Atlantic*'s survivors, while others, in fear of being dashed to pieces on rocks or hull, wait for survivors to come to them* (Library of Congress).

Waves were now breaking clear over the stern.

Eight minutes after collision, the hundreds on deck — and those still struggling below — felt a trembling as *Atlantic* began canting over to starboard. As the list increased, all were thrown off their feet and slid toward the starboard rail, now underwater. The merciless waves swept dozens away at a time. Lifeboat 5, with thirty to forty people aboard including Second Officer Metcalf, was crushed under the hull.

With a 50° list, water now flooded down every entranceway, drowning those still below, their screams audible above the surf's roar. 'Take to the rigging, it's your only chance!' Williams and his crew cried to passengers. Higher and higher they climbed. The waves swept those lacking agility from lower rigging, while others clung fearfully to deck houses and fittings. With a roar the boilers suddenly exploded.

Third Officer Cornelius Brady found himself

Far left *Third Officer Brady, unable to communicate orally, writes a message of hope for those still aboard the wreck* (Library of Congress).

Below left *The townsfolk of Lower Prospect, Nova Scotia offer succour to the* Atlantic's *shivering, exhausted survivors* (Library of Congress).

Right *In broad daylight, only* Atlantic's *bow remains above water as salvage crews swarm aboard* (Russ Lownds collection).

trapped in his cabin when the collision occurred, and eventually liberated himself by smashing a hole in the door. When *Atlantic* began to capsize, he climbed into the mizzen mast's rigging, then clambered down and moved forward:

'When I got forward I made out a rock in front of the ship. I unrove the signal halyards forward, and also had the forward fore-trysail vang [a heavier rope] unrove; it was a new rope. I took them down on the side of the ship and sent Quartermaster Owens with the signal halyards to the rock. He failed, and I had to haul him back to the ship. I then sent Quartermaster Speakman; he succeeded in getting to the rock and I immediately followed him. We then hauled the vang from the ship to the rock, about 25 yards from the ship.'

Using this tenuous link and three other ropes, some 250 men made the perilous 40-yard journey to the rock, while others remained on board clinging desperately to rigging or the port rail, still above water. As night wore on, several in the rigging tried to make their way hand-over-hand to the rock, but failed as waves tore ropes from the grip of their frozen hands.

Convinced they could do nothing further on board, quartermaster Robert Thomas and an unidentified passenger swam through 600 ft of surging water to Mosher's Island. Once there, they alternately raced and tripped through darkness to the home of fisherman Thomas Clancey and implored him to summon townspeople to help.

Third Officer Brady now persuaded Quartermaster Speakman to swim from the rock to Mosher's Island with another rope. *Atlantic* was now linked to shore via the rock, but only fifty made the second journey to safety; the others simply were too exhausted. Among those to cross was Brady. Learning that rescue boats were being launched, Brady fashioned a signboard and wrote 'Cheer up. The boats are coming!', then held it up for Captain Williams to see.

As night's darkness softened at 5.00 am, the tide began to ebb, increasing the stresses on *Atlantic*'s punctured hull. The structure could stand no more, and with a thunderous crack the hull broke near the foremast. The stern portion, abandoned by all but the dead, sank. Only the bow and masts remained above water. Clinging to rigging, steerage passenger Patrick Leahy saw a terrible sight:

'It was just gleaming day; a large mass of something drifted past the ship on the top of the waves and then

Left *A contemporary sketch by newspaper artist Joseph Becker depicts efforts to locate bodies* (Library of Congress).

Below right *Of 200 children on board, twelve-year-old John Hindley is* Atlantic's *only surviving child* (Russ Lownds collection).

was lost to view in the rough of the sea. As it passed by, a moan — it must have been a shriek, but the tempest dulled the sound — seemed to surge up from the mass, which extended over fifty yards of water: it was the women. The sea swept them out of the steerage, and with their children, to the number of 200 or 300, they drifted thus to eternity.'

Not a single woman survived. At 6.30 am the first boats arrived and they began to remove survivors from the rock. Captain Williams, believing those on board and in the rigging faced more imminent danger, persuaded fishermen to come alongside despite the risk, promising $500 for each boat load they took away. Brady commandeered a boat and returned to the wreck. Eventually he persuaded Captain Williams to abandon ship. Although the master was suffering from frozen hands and legs, he was later severely criticized for leaving while some eighty people remained in the rigging. Overnight, his hair had begun to turn white.

Boat after boat rescued survivors but further problems quickly developed ashore as the tiny village of Lower Prospect struggled to provide food, shelter and clothing to several hundred unexpected guests. Recognizing their imposition, more than a dozen survivors elected to walk through

foot-deep snow to Halifax, some 22 miles away.

In subsequent testimony, Captain Williams said all survivors had been rescued by 8.45 am. He was not correct. First Officer John Firth and twelve year-old steerage passenger John Hindley were very much alive, but weakening fast as they clung to the mizzen mast's rigging. Young Hindley had been travelling with his father, mother and brother. When *Atlantic* struck, he immediately rushed on deck to see what had happened. His parents and brother drowned in their bunks. Firth had remained both to comfort the lad and because he could not swim. The worsening sea now made it impossible for rescue craft to approach *Atlantic*'s wreckage; Firth and Hindley were marooned. Upon learning of this, Prospect's Anglican minister, Rev William J. Ancient, a 36-year old Royal Navy veteran, decided to take personal action.

With a volunteer crew at the oars, Ancient made his way to *Atlantic* but could not board. As the minister pleaded with boatmen to go closer, John Hindley lost his grip and plunged into the surf. Immediately the boat crew pulled him in. He was the only child saved of 200 on board. Firth remained, displaying remarkable strength after ten hours in the rigging.

'[Reverend Ancient] got into the main rigging and procured a line, then advanced as far as he could towards me and threw it to me. I caught it, made it fast around my body and then jumped clear. A sea swept me off the wreck, but Mr Ancient held fast to the line, pulled me back and got me safely in the boat. I was then so exhausted and benumbed that I was hardly able to do anything for myself, and but for the clergyman's gallant conduct I must have perished soon.'

News of *Atlantic*'s loss had not gone further than Lower Prospect. With hundreds of survivors requiring food, clothing and shelter, and with profound salvage and legal considerations ahead, at 1.00 pm Captain Williams ordered Third Officer Brady to walk to Halifax for help.

Brady did not arrive at the door of S. Cunard & Co, then White Star's Halifax agent, until about 5.30 pm, and his astounding story was greeted with incredulity — it was, after all, April Fool's Day.

But a closer look at the shaken, exhausted, bruised Brady galvanized agents and government authorities into action. As Halifax telegraphed the news to J.H. Sparks, White Star's New York agent, the government steamer *Lady Head*, the Cunard liner *Delta* and the steam tug *Goliath* raced to the scene, and brought all 400 survivors to Halifax.

At 7.30 am on 2 April, a coded telegram brought news of their first catastrophe to White Star's Liverpool offices:

'Brady Third Officer arrived Halifax *Atlantic* illegitimate [is a total wreck] Cape Prospect about cheshire [700] chain [passengers lost] boulogne [250] people including Captain saved intended imprecation [putting in short of coals]; have dispatched Pennell naval [awaiting further particulars].'

The consternation in White Star's offices can only be imagined. Ismay's reaction is reflected in George Fletcher's diary: 'My poor friend is no Waterloo veteran, that's clear, for his heart bleeds too freely at the thought of so much precious human life sacrificed... [I] must go to him... he trembles under the recent calamity'. Captain Williams' 3 April telegram to Liverpool contained further numbing details:

'Ship totally lost. Broken abaft foremast. Cargo washing out. Wreckers at work until New York Wrecking Company [White Star's designated salvors] come. Thirteen saloon passengers and 429 others saved. Purser, chief steward, second officer and fifth engineer lost: rest of officers saved. Shall leave third officer and four men at wreck to attend to bodies. Will forward passengers to New York and Portland; 200 go tomorrow, balance next day... Wind rising from south, wreck exposed to sea. Passengers supplied with all necessities.'

Captain Williams returned to oversee the salvage of the cargo and the recovery of bodies. He defended his course, his actions and the coal supply to a Halifax reporter, who concluded his story, 'Such are Captain Williams' responses to direct questions. He may have been criminally negligent, but he seems to have been a man in the supreme moment. Through the *Herald* the world can read and judge.'

Left *During the days following the wreck, sightseers from the Halifax area thronged the rocks overlooking the wreck site....*(Russ Lownds collection).

Below left *...as salvage efforts continue* (Russ Lownds collection).

Final figures were to show that 565 had perished in the world's worst merchant shipwreck. It demanded impartial answers to many troubling questions. Within 24 hours Collector of Customs E.M. Macdonald was ordered to convene at Halifax a formal inquiry seeking the facts. In four days of testimony commencing 5 April, Macdonald and two nautical assessors heard testimony from 22 witnesses. *Atlantic*'s officers were unaware of extra-strong westward currents off Nova Scotia in early spring. They were unaware that visibility, while reasonable at sea, was severely limited around the coast's lighthouses, restricting the distance from which they could be seen. They were unaware that speed had been increasing prior to collision. While they had Admiralty charts of the area, they were unaware of its rugged coastline and the myriad of rocks along its shore.

At 3.00 pm on 18 April Macdonald issued his report. It said Williams' decision to go to Halifax was 'prudent and justifiable.' It commended his post-accident conduct and that of his crew, finding it 'was marked by intrepidity and coolness and a desire to do everything in their power to save the lives' of passengers. But Macdonald left no doubt as to the accident's cause:

'• It seems impossible to account for the error in estimating the ship's speed except on the ground of incompetency or carelessness in calculating on the part of those attending to the log.

• It seems to have been culpable rashness for [Captain

Below *Not far from the wreck site, at nearby Terence Bay, the Rev William J. Ancient — himself a hero in the rescue of* Atlantic*'s passengers — intones the burial service for 277 victims of the disaster's horror* (Russ Lownds collection).

A granite shaft erected in 1915 marks the mass grave of Atlantic's *victims. Half of the monument's cost was contributed after the wreck by Thomas H. Ismay, then White Star's owner* (Authors' collection).

Less than a mile from the better-known Atlantic *monument, a modest white marble shaft marks the resting place of* Atlantic's *many Catholic victims* (Authors' collection).

Williams] to order the ship to be run towards the land for three hours at her then-full speed, without taking precautions to guard against any possible error in his estimate of his position.

• The greatest... and fatal error is... that the lead was never used although the ship was within soundings for eight hours before she struck; this is a neglect of duty for which there can be positively no excuse.'

White Star had insufficiently provisioned the ship with coal. Macdonald said revocation of Williams' master's certificate was justified, but, in the light of his subsequent rescue actions, would be suspended for two years.

Fourth Officer Brown and the late Second Officer Metcalf had 'improperly' prevented the steward from waking Williams at 2.40. In addition, Brown should have seen Sambro Light but didn't. His certificate was suspended for three months. The public wanted more. As one editorial writer said, 'Though the penalties do not come up to public expectations we should be thankful that the Court of Inquiry has found anybody guilty of anything in this age of whitewashing investigations.'

White Star, however, was shocked by the finding of insufficient coal. While Halifax's inquiry carried the full weight of a Board of Trade proceeding, they successfully petitioned for another hearing which opened 28 May. Using ship's plans, coal suppliers' testimony and builders' evidence, White Star fought vigorously to clear its name, for the verdict would destroy the fledgling company's reputation. A key fact was that *Atlantic* had sailed with at least 963 tons of coal aboard; during her worst-ever passage she had used no more than 896 tons.

On 11 June assessors again found *Atlantic* had sailed short of coal. 'No passenger ship of her class should be short of coal on the eleventh day of her voyage to New York as the *Atlantic* in our opinion undoubtedly was,' they said. White Star appealed again, to the Board of Trade's chief surveyor. At last came an exoneration of coal supply, if not seamanship:

'The *Atlantic* was lost while performing this voyage to Halifax; for that voyage, she had an ample supply of fuel. Her loss was not through being driven on a lee shore, helpless, her fuel spent and the engines without power. She was run at full speed, engines and boilers all in perfect order, upon well known rocks, in fine weather. So efficiently were the engines and boilers working that the vessel had actually overrun the distance intended at the time she struck. The question of fuel supply cannot, therefore, have had anything whatever to do with the loss of the *Atlantic* on her voyage to Halifax.'

Additionally, Chief Engineer John Foxley had greatly underestimated and understated remaining coal to Williams. Indeed, '...At the time the vessel's course was altered for Halifax there still remained sufficient coal on board to have taken her to New York and to leave seventy tons in the bunkers, even if the weather had not improved,' the surveyors found.

In Halifax, salvage crews had done their work well despite dangerous conditions. Much cargo was washed ashore; tons more was removed by divers entering the hull through dynamited holes. As they did so, police investigated rumours that victims' remains had been pilfered. In New York, survivors and cargo consignees filed suit against White Star for loss of life and property. Their claims were settled two years later for pittances based on prevailing maritime law.

Some 428 victims' bodies were recovered, several up to fifty miles from the disaster site. Lurid details of their recovery filled Halifax newspapers for weeks. On a clear, warm day 277 were interred in a mass grave on a rocky hill overlooking Sandy Cove, near *Atlantic*'s resting place. Reverend Ancient quietly intoned the burial service. Simultaneously, less than a mile away, Reverend Father James Quish conducted a similar service for Catholic victims.

Captain Williams remained steadfastly by his ship, supervising operations. In late May he left for New York, and from there to Liverpool where he was reunited with his wife and three children. In June, *Atlantic*'s final victim, saloon passenger Henry Wellington, was recovered. The remains of her hull were sold to salvors for $4,000.

Although White Star immediately expunged *Atlantic*'s name from all publicity, it did not forget. With Thomas Ismay contributing personally, it established a fund to maintain victims' graves, and in December 1915 contributed half the cost of a monument to them. Today the marker stands alone, often cloaked in the mists that haunt Nova Scotia's coast. The crash of breakers against the nearby shore and the seagulls' shrill cries echo the sounds of White Star Line's first night of tragedy.

Accidents and incidents

15 January 1874   After leaving Liverpool, *Celtic* struck floating wreckage and lost all propeller blades. *Gaelic* towed her to Queenstown, and passengers disembarked before *Celtic* was towed to Birkenhead's Alfred Dock for repairs. Her passengers left for New York on 23 January aboard *Baltic*.

CHAPTER 3

Adriatic, 1872 and *Britannic*, 1874

UNLUCKY PAIR

Important aspects of White Star's destiny appear to have been fashioned during social occasions. Tradition has it that *Titanic* was first discussed over after-dinner coffee. Tradition also holds that the line itself was conceived during a game of billiards.

After his purchase of the White Star Line, Thomas Ismay wished to expand his company's fleet and routes, but required capital to do so. He approached Gustav Schwabe, a prominent Liverpool businessman and financier, for advice. Schwabe's nephew was Gustav Wolff, junior partner of Harland and Wolff, the famous Belfast shipbuilders. Schwabe promised White Star the necessary financial backing at very favourable terms if Ismay would order all the company's ships from Harland and Wolff. It was a proposal that Ismay eagerly accepted. With the assistance of his friend George H. Fletcher, he organized the company and negotiated with Harland and Wolff the first steamships' contracts.

Oceanic's successful maiden voyage in March 1871 appeared to assure the new company's future. But Atlantic travellers, loyal to ships of the established lines — Cunard, Guion, National — did not at first desert their carriers. Nevertheless, Ismay, locked in to his agreement with Schwabe and Harland and Wolff, kept adding liners to the White Star fleet. Quickly they came: *Atlantic*, whose maiden voyage was in June 1871; *Baltic** in September 1871; *Republic*, February 1872; *Adriatic*, April 1872; *Celtic** in October 1872...

*Baltic and *Celtic* were new names given to vessels launched as *Pacific* and *Arctic*, respectively, after it was recollected that Collins Line vessels bearing these names had been lost in disasters: *Pacific* disappeared in 1856; *Arctic* sank in collision in 1854.

It was not until May 1872, when *Adriatic* set a westbound crossing record of 14.52 knots, soon followed by *Baltic*'s 15 + knot eastbound crossing in January 1873 that the public began to notice and patronize the new White Star liners. In the mid-nineteenth century, speed seemed to be all that mattered. A day, even a half day shaved from an

Thomas H. Ismay, White Star Line's founder, forged a strong link with the Harland and Wolff shipyards with his initial order for five steamships (Authors' collection).

Atlantic crossing attracted public notice. The line lucky enough to own the fastest ship found not only it, but other vessels of its line heavily booked. To establish and maintain this speed — and regularity of departure and arrival — captains were driven to demonstrate their efficiency: a corner cut here, a regulation stretched there, a safety rule interpreted at its broadest...

In rain and fog, ships departed punctually; through wave and wind they crossed with certainty; in storm and snow they arrived on schedule. There was no apparent danger. Passengers, unaware of the strain to which ships and crews were being subjected, knew only that they left port and arrived several hours before passengers on other lines' ships. And they rewarded the company with continued patronage.

Now waiting to happen were the predictable accidents — some petty, some major, some

Launched in April 1872, Adriatic *was White Star's first record breaker, making a westbound Atlantic crossing at 14.5 knots* (White Star Magazine).

disastrous — which befell ships of *all* companies engaged in competitive Atlantic operations. Until it adopted a 'comfort instead of speed' policy later in the century, numerous accidents plagued White Star's own operations. Perhaps nowhere is this more evident than in the histories of two of the White Star's early liners, *Adriatic* (1872) and *Britannic* (1874). At one time each had held the record for westbound Atlantic crossings; each had a 28-year lifespan. But each seems to have been born under an unlucky star, plagued by numerous accidents typifying the operational pressures under which almost all ships of the period operated.

Launched on 17 October 1871 the 3,888 ton, 452 ft *Adriatic* carried 150 cabin and 1,000 steerage passengers. Running water was provided in each first class cabin. At first the ship was illuminated with gas manufactured aboard from a non-explosive oil. But the scheme failed when numerous piping leaks developed as it was subjected to the ship's motions at sea.

Adriatic had a promising start when, three months after her 11 March 1872 maiden voyage

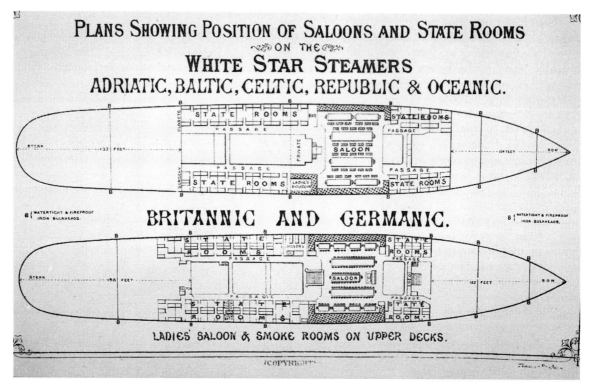

An outstanding feature of White Star's early steamers was the saloon's location amidships, as these deck plans show (Authors' collection).

between Liverpool and New York, she captured the westbound record from Cunard's *Scotia*. But on a December 1872 westbound crossing, her New York arrival was delayed by loss of two of her single propeller's four blades in a severe storm. (The propeller, with its 22 ft 6 in diameter, was then the largest in merchant service.) Though partially crippled, *Adriatic*, under Captain Hamilton Perry's able command, managed to save twenty seamen from the sailing vessel *Allan*, which heavy seas had damaged to a sinking state. *Adriatic* arrived off Sandy Hook 22 December after a fifteen-day voyage, her 47 cabin and 141 steerage passengers safe.

Less than two years later, on 24 October 1874, *Adriatic* was in collision, outbound near Sandy Hook. Details are recounted in a statement signed by Captain Perry, his officers and the New York harbour pilot then in charge:

'*Oct. 24, 4.20 p.m.* — About one mile below buoy of the mud flats, steamship *Parthia* steaming down the bay on our port side. We ported considerably to pass her at a good distance, as we were overhauling her.

'*4.35 p.m.* — Passed steamship *Parthia* distant about one cable's length on our port side, both vessels then steering the same course. After we had overhauled her half our ship's length she immediately ported her helm and bore down toward us, we porting also to keep out of her way.

'*4.43 p.m.* — Steamship *Parthia* collided with us, her starboard bow striking us on our port quarter, forward of jigger rigging, doing considerable damage, we at the same time starboarding our helm to prevent our propeller [from] striking her bows.

'*4.48 p.m.* — Stopped to examine damage. Finding we could not proceed until after repairs, steamed toward Quarantine to anchor.'

After 'a force of mechanics worked on *Adriatic*'s repairs night and day,' the liner departed New York on the morning of 28 October, passing Sandy

Hook at 9.40 am. *Parthia*'s captain and pilot testified that *Adriatic* starboarded her helm in passing and that, in trying to swing away, *Parthia* had struck the other vessel a 'swinging' blow to her port quarter. As it appeared both vessels were manoeuvring to give room to the incoming Dutch steamer *Rotterdam*, no blame was fixed, both masters apparently sharing in culpability.

Several months later, on 8 March 1875, with Captain Perry still in command, *Adriatic* rammed and sank the small schooner *Columbus* while inbound at Liverpool. With the Mersey pilot on board, *Adriatic* had passed the Crosby light ship steaming dead slow in the clear night. Suddenly the foc's'le head's lookout warned of a sail. *Adriatic*'s helm was immediately put hard-a-starboard and her engine stopped. The liner responded well, but struck the smaller vessel a glancing blow on its starboard quarter.

Captain Perry burned rockets and blue lights, and when two nearby steamers came within hailing range, Perry asked them to see whether assistance was needed on the smaller vessel. He then docked his ship, reporting the accident to authorities soon after landing. *Columbus*'s captain, his wife and crew were plucked from her topgallant yard by the steamer *Enterprise*. The captain's child was the sole fatality. *Adriatic* suffered no damage.

Nor was she damaged during an incident in the early morning hours of 31 December 1875, having left Liverpool on 30 December. At about 2.30 am off Mine Head, County Waterford, Ireland, the lookout sighted off the starboard bow a green light which soon shut in and changed to red. The light again changed to green, and, seeing the ship so undecided as to how she would pass, *Adriatic*'s first officer ordered her engine slowed, stopped, then reversed. He called Captain Jennings to the bridge. The approaching vessel's light again changed to red and remained so as it attempted to cross *Adriatic*'s bows.

Adriatic's engine was now full astern, but the stranger continued bearing down, finally and suddenly succeeding — according to Captain Jennings — in hooking its port jib guy on *Adriatic*'s port anchor stock, carrying it away and snapping its own hook. Sail sheets, blocks and other rigging from the

vessel rained down on *Adriatic*'s foredeck. Jennings later stated positively that the vessels' hulls had never come together. The stranger had shown no lights other than the observed navigating signals, nor did she display any signals before, during or after the encounter. As she passed on into the black night, Jennings ordered two *Adriatic* lifeboats lowered but after cruising about for 45 minutes and finding nothing the boats returned and were hauled aboard before *Adriatic* proceeded on her voyage.

A ship had indeed been in the vicinity of *Adriatic*'s course that night, at the very time, according to its

Britannic of 1874 quickly set her own Atlantic records. The company's pride in her achievements is reflected in this contemporary advertisement (Authors' collection).

White Star Mail Steamers.

(EXTRACT FROM THE "LIVERPOOL MERCURY," October 17th, 1876.)

EXTRAORDINARY TRANS-ATLANTIC STEAMING !

Our readers are so familiar with the rapidity and regularity of the White Star Steamers, that it seems almost invidious now to call their attention to any particular voyages, yet the subjoined abstract of the *Britannic's* passages calls for special mention. Under the command of Captain Thompson, she has, for four voyages in succession, steamed from Queenstown to New York, and *vice versa*, under eight days, maintaining a remarkable uniformity of speed. The following is the abstract in question :—

OUTWARDS.				HOMEWARDS.			
Voyage 1876	D.	H.	M.	Voyage 1876.	D.	H.	M.
10—JUNE....	7	16	36	10—JUNE ..	7	19	48
11—JULY....	7	19	57	11—JULY ..	7	22	31
12—AUG.	7	20	46	12—SEPT	7	22	55
13—SEPT....	7	17	37	13—OCT. .	7	16	23
Average ..	**7 18 44**			Average..	**7 20 25**		

On the four outward trips the *Britannic* ran a distance of **11,216** nautical miles, being an average of **2804** per trip, which gives a speed of a little over **15** knots per hour, or **360** knots per diem. Homewards, she steamed **11,549** nautical miles, or **2887** per trip, equal to **15·32** knots per hour, or **367·68** per diem. These consecutive performances are worthy of record, as they stand unrivalled in the annals of ocean steam navigation sailing plan, that the encounter had occurred. The *Harvest Queen*, a sail vessel owned by C.H. Marshall & Co, inbound for Liverpool from San Francisco, had stopped at Queenstown. Departing for Liverpool during the evening of 30 December, her course and speed would have placed her in *Adriatic*'s vicinity.

Though Captain Jennings vehemently denied colliding with *Harvest Queen* or any other vessel, the *Queen* was not seen again. Wreckage on a Wexford beach was positively identified by a representative of her agents as coming from the lost packet. A former mate identified two jibsheet blocks that had fallen on *Adriatic*'s deck during the collision as being among those whose onboard construction he had supervised. Members of *Adriatic*'s crew were certain that collision and death had occurred. They later reported hearing cries of drowning men after the liner had stopped to search the area; they also charged an inadequate search by *Adriatic*'s boats.

Harvest Queen's owners brought a $175,000 (£35,000) suit against White Star, and upon the liner's 13 February 1876 arrival in New York the writ was served. A bond double the amount sought had to be posted by White Star before their vessel was permitted to depart.

The ship's misfortunes continued. Departing Liverpool for Queenstown and New York late on 18 July 1878 *Adriatic* was engulfed in dense fog that reduced speed to dead slow. At 4.30 am, the next day, about eighteen miles west of Holyhead, Wales, *Adriatic* collided with the vessel *Hengist*, under a tug's tow to Liverpool. *Hengist*'s starboard quarter was damaged and her main brace carried away, but she completed her trip. *Adriatic*'s captain thought it wise to anchor in St. George's Channel and await the fog's lifting. Throughout the morning, with lookouts posted, the liner lay stopped. Suddenly out of the fog loomed the London brigantine *G.A. Pike*, speeding for Dublin. There was no time to change course. The *Pike* struck *Adriatic* and sank almost immediately. Although *Adriatic*'s boats were quickly lowered, they could save just one of the *Pike*'s six-man crew.

Even at her western terminus *Adriatic* was not immune from accident. While outbound on 23 November 1879 she collided with the Sandy Hook Pilot Boat No. 5 and had to return for repairs to her port side.

During the mid-1880s, many Atlantic shipping companies had suffered severe pressure from increased competition and other economic factors. Almost all experienced a trade depression: but from these problems White Star seemed immune. Even with all her unpredictable, service-incurred incidents, *Adriatic* was selected by a group of about seventy White Star shareholders as site for an expression of their gratitude to the company's two partners, Thomas Ismay and William Imrie.

On Wednesday 16 September 1885 a gala dinner attended by 100 guests was held aboard *Adriatic*, anchored in the Mersey. Dinner was served at 5.00 pm, and afterwards Ismay was presented with a handsome silver gilt dinner service — three years in the making and valued at more than £4,000 — and an oil portrait of himself painted by Sir J.E. Millais. Imrie was presented with two oil paintings of his own choosing. It would seem *Adriatic*'s ill luck had finally run its course. Following the 1879 accident there are no reports for almost ten years of peril or injury to herself or other ships. But on 4 October 1889 *Adriatic* suffered considerable damage when she smashed into her New York pier. And several years later, westbound under Captain E.W. McKinstry's command, she encountered an immense mid-Atlantic storm. She arrived at New York 1 April 1895 after a ten-day crossing, reporting no serious injuries among her 834 passengers, but with number 11 lifeboat gone and three others stove in.

Following *Britannic* and *Germanic* of 1874, White Star added no new North Atlantic liner for fifteen years, though its Australian, New Zealand and transpacific fleets were supplemented. But the 1889 arrival of *Teutonic* and *Majestic*, a pair of elegant record setters quickly captured the public's imagination and recaptured much of the company's lost trade. The aging *Adriatic* was rendered redundant, though she lived ten more years.

As 1899 began, *Britannic* and *Germanic* were still working, and the ten-year-old *Teutonic* and *Majestic* were reaching the zenith of their respective careers. On 12 January the magnificent *Oceanic* was

Britannic's *luxurious interiors equalled and frequently exceeded most everything else afloat* (Authors' collection).

The grand saloon, frequented by both men and women.

The men enjoyed the comforts of their own smoking room.

Britannic's splendour is reflected by her grand staircase.

Even her steerage accommodation was clean and spacious.

launched. With White Star's plans to enter the twentieth century with great new liners, *Adriatic* was unnecessary. When her end came, it came quickly. There was to be no lay-up in semi-retirement; no service on secondary routes; no sale to a less affluent company. On 12 February 1899, one month short of her 1872 maiden voyage's date, *Adriatic* departed Liverpool for scrapping at Preston, Lancashire.

Though her days, too, were numbered, *Britannic* also was still afloat at century's end. Designed by Sir Edward J. Harland himself, the 5,004-ton, 455-ft vessel was laid down as *Hellenic* but underwent a name change prior to her 3 February 1874 launch. Following her June 1874 New York-Liverpool maiden voyage, the new vessel quickly settled in on her intended route. Originally equipped with an adjustable propeller shaft that could be lowered or raised to increase her engine's thrust, *Britannic* had to return to Harland and Wolff after nine crossings when the arrangement proved unsatisfactory. Once a new shaft was installed, *Britannic* responded by capturing both west- and eastbound records with passage times under $7\frac{1}{2}$ days. She remained accident free for almost seven years. But in early 1881 her luck changed. On 31 March, outbound for New York after an evening Liverpool departure, she collided with and sank the Dublin schooner *Julia*. The schooner's crew were saved, and *Britannic*, undamaged, proceeded on her voyage.

Later that year a more serious incident occurred. Under Captain Hamilton Perry's command, *Britannic* departed New York 25 June for Liverpool. After a late-evening stop at Queenstown, *Britannic* encountered heavy fog on the final leg of her voyage. On 4 July, at about 7.30 am off Kilmore, County Wexford, Captain Perry heard fog signals which he believed to be coming from Tuskar Light. Accordingly he set his course for Holyhead. The gun signals, however, actually were those of Hoots, which were fired every ten minutes (while Tuskar's were fired every five minutes.) Shallow water was sounded at 7.35 and immediately Perry ordered the engine reversed. But *Britannic*'s forward speed was too great, and a minute later the ship grounded.

There were no injuries and it seemed there was no damage to the ship. Later that morning, passengers and mail were landed by the ship's boats and taken to Wexford, thence to Dublin and Liverpool. To lighten the ship and enable her to float off with the tide, Perry ordered cargo jettisoned. Later that afternoon, *Britannic* sprang a leak in number two hold and rapidly developed a 12 degree port list, fortunately while in shallow water. The Liverpool Salvage Association's divers and pumps soon set to work saving the ship. During the next several days additional cargo was removed — this time more carefully — and 1,500 tons were taken to Waterford. On 6 July, sufficiently lightened, *Britannic* righted herself and two days later, at 12.30 pm, was floated, but her ordeal was not yet over.

Slowly proceeding under tow to Liverpool on 9 July, *Britannic* sprang a fresh leak at 8.30 am, when off the Barrels. Her engine room was flooded in an hour, and it was quickly decided to tow her to South Bay where she could be beached on a smooth, sandy bottom. Though flooded up to her saloon deck, *Britannic* was in a good position for pumping. Additional pumps were sent from Liverpool and by 12 July she was again afloat. With her hull tight she left the County Wexford coast at 2 pm, proceeding to Liverpool for repairs and a general drying-out. She arrived 14 July, and upon examination, her injuries were found to be local, with an absence of straining. *Britannic* was able to depart for New York on 18 July, her scheduled sailing day.

In January 1883 *Celtic*, outbound from Liverpool for New York, was disabled by a broken propeller shaft. *Britannic*, inbound from New York, took *Celtic* in tow and assisted in her safe return to Liverpool for repairs. Later, the two ships would meet again... *Britannic* herself was no stranger to broken machinery. On 27 May 1883 and 1 April 1886 she aborted westbound crossings for repairs at Liverpool to broken crankshafts.

A curious incident in May 1883 occurred while *Britannic* completed the final portions of an eastbound voyage. The liner had stopped at Queenstown on Sunday 13 May and put off passengers and mail by tender before proceeding to

Despite her many accidents, Britannic *served as flagship for the company's Liverpool-based service for fifteen years* (White Star Magazine).

Liverpool. During the ensuing twenty-hour voyage, a rumour somehow began and spread at New York that *Britannic* had been destroyed by dynamite, the explosives having been placed aboard at Queenstown. The presence aboard of American multi-millionaire railway magnate William H. Vanderbilt may have inspired the rumour. Vanderbilt dispatched a cable from Queenstown advising his family of his safe arrival. The cable may have been misread or misinterpreted, or it may simply have been wishful thinking by some of his business antagonists. The rumour was strong enough to be reported in several New York newspapers but it was quickly disproven.

The year 1887 began inauspiciously for *Britannic* when, on 14 January, while in the Mersey bound for New York, she sideswiped the British steamship *St Fillans*, arriving from Baltimore. *St Fillans* had several plates smashed and required docking for

repairs. *Britannic* sustained damage to davits and a small boat, but continued on her voyage. On 7 March, inbound from the same round voyage, *Britannic* collided with a barque off Holyhead but sustained no damage and completed her trip. Her next encounter was to be far less inconsequential.

On Wednesday 18 May 1887, under Captain Perry, *Britannic* departed New York for Liverpool with 176 cabin and 300 steerage passengers. On 11 May *Celtic* had departed Liverpool for New York. Commanded by Captain P.J. Irvine, she had aboard 104 cabin and 765 steerage passengers. At 5.25 pm Thursday, 19 May the two vessels collided in fog about 350 miles east of Sandy Hook. Four of *Britannic*'s steerage passengers were killed and nine severely injured.

According to Perry, during the afternoon *Britannic* was sailing through fog, sometimes thick, sometimes lifting. From 4.00 pm on, it was dense, with no wind. *Britannic* was steaming at $14\frac{1}{2}$ knots, a speed her captain thought reasonable. At 5.15 the lookout reported a whistle one point off the port bow, about three miles away. *Britannic*'s course was altered two points to starboard, and her whistle ordered sounded at one-minute intervals.

Celtic, meanwhile, had been steaming on her own course at 13½ knots, a speed her commander deemed prudent. On the bridge, Irvine heard a whistle three points off his starboard bow. Upon hearing it a second time, about five minutes later, Irvine ordered course changed a point-and-a-half to starboard and engines slowed. During the course change he ordered *Celtic*'s whistle sounded two short blasts ('going to starboard') and two minutes later, engines reduced to dead slow. The scene is described by the *New York Herald*:

'A white fog had snowed down upon the ocean and both vessels kept up the monotonous chant of the steam whistles. The officers of the *Britannic* heard the whistles of the *Celtic*, and soon the two big steamships were engaged in an awful game of blindman's buff. Crowds of *Britannic*'s passengers ran from side to side as the sound of the

Celtic's hoarse warning came weirdly, now from one direction and now from another through the damp, thick vapour. Both vessels slackened speed as they approached nearer and nearer.

'Suddenly a huge shadow loomed up. There was a general cry of delight as the majestic *Celtic* swept grandly into sight. It was followed by shrieks of terror. The sharp, giant prow of the oncoming steamship was headed straight for the *Britannic*. The *Celtic* reversed her engines. It was too late.

'As the two vessels struck there was a terrific roar, and the sea was churned into foam by the shock. The prow of the *Celtic* struck the port side of the *Britannic* abaft the mizzenmast, tearing a gap four feet wide in her side at the water line.

'It was a glancing blow. Plunging ahead with her helm hard a port, the torn prow of the *Celtic* swept back along her ponderous rival groaning and tearing away the massive iron bulwarks of the main deck like so much brown paper.'

On 19 May 1887 Britannic *and* Celtic *collided 350 miles east of Sandy Hook.* Celtic's *Captain Peter J. Irvine was censured for failing to reduce speed while steaming through fog* (Authors' collection).

Long Britannic's *master, Hamilton Perry was 'very severely censured' for failure to sound his whistle before the collision with* Celtic (Authors' collection).

Requisitioned by the British government in August 1899, Britannic *carried troops to South Africa's Boer War* (Private collection).

Britannic's number 4 hold, filled with 17,000 bushels of grain and some light merchandise, quickly flooded. On deck, three of her boats had been stove in, and considerable damage had been done to her hurricane deck houses and after turtleback. Had the blow struck 16 inches further forward, the compartment containing her engines would have been breached and flooded, and, unquestionably, she would have sunk. *Celtic*'s bow was snapped off entirely below deck. Above that it hung over like a clumsy bowsprit. Temporary bulkheads rigged by her carpenters kept her from flooding.

After an acutely graphic description of damage done to *Britannic*'s steerage passengers by the collision, the *Herald* continued in a welter of late nineteenth century prose:

'There arose a wild, mad rush for the boats. Three of them had been smashed by the prow of the *Celtic*. Cap-

tain Perry ordered the sailors to lower away all the remaining boats and to take the women and children off first. But the masculine brutes fought their way to the front, trampling on the weak and helpless as they went. The fog grew thicker and thicker as the savage scene became more and more tumultuous. The women were pale, silent and heroic. Three noble sisters of St. John the Baptist stole around in their black robes exhorting their sister passengers not to fear death if they had to go down with the ship, but to pray for courage.

'Many of the cowardly men sprang over the sides of the *Britannic* into lifeboats. One sailor or fireman forced himself into a boat.

'Then the trumpet voice of Captain Perry rang out. "You coward," he cried. "Come back on this ship! Look at me. Isn't my life as precious as yours?" '

'There was a flash of cold steel in the air as the brave commander drew his revolver and loaded it in the presence of the multitude. "The next man that goes over the side of the ship will be shot dead." '

Transfer of *Britannic*'s passengers to the less seriously damaged *Celtic* quickly began, and six boatloads were soon safe. By midnight *Britannic*'s carpenters had stopped the inrushing water with temporary repairs to the gash, which extended four feet below the water line. Shortly after repairs were completed, the two vessels, lights blazing and minute guns firing to assure one another of continuing safety, slowly steamed for New York.

During the night, the bodies of the four passengers killed in the collision were sewn in canvas sacks and reverently consigned to the deep. As the sun rose brilliantly over a calm sea the Wilson Line steamer *Marengo* arrived and escorted the two stricken vessels. Later, toward nightfall, Inman's *British Queen* altered course to assist.

Arriving at New York at 1.00 am on Sunday 24

In 1900, Britannic *was dispatched to the Australian Commonwealth's inauguration, bearing an honour guard. Despite grounding in the Suez Canal, she arrived safely* (State Library of New South Wales, Australia).

May, the vessels remained outside the harbour, detained by fog. *Britannic* was met $2\frac{1}{2}$ miles out by the Merritt Wrecking Company's steamer *J. G. Merritt*, which pumped out water. Normally drawing about 25 ft, *Britannic* had sunk to a 30 ft draft and was listing well to starboard. The tug *Fletcher* removed mails from both *Britannic* and the *Celtic*, anchored $1\frac{1}{2}$ miles away. *Celtic* was then towed to the White Star pier at the foot of West Tenth Street, while *Britannic* was towed to a Brooklyn drydock for repairs. *Britannic* resumed her interrupted voyage with a 15 June New York departure.

On 7 June 1887, at the British Consul's New York office, Vice Consul William R. Hoare convened an inquiry, assisted by three Atlantic steamship captains. After a full day's testimony by both vessels' masters and officers, the court on 9 June declared both Captain Perry and Captain Irvine guilty of not observing official regulations for

prevention of collisions at sea. Perry was 'very severely censured' for failure to comply with the requirement that 'a steamship under way [in fog] shall make with her steam whistle... at intervals of not more than two minutes a prolonged blast.' Irvine was 'severely censured' for not reducing speed. A copy of Hoare's decision was filed with the Board of Trade in London.

A small fire in *Britannic*'s cotton cargo was discovered while at Queenstown, eastbound, on 5 September 1889. Several bales were jettisoned and the fire quelled, only to break out again on 6 September. It was not until she docked at Liverpool and her cargo was unloaded that the fire was extinguished.

Inbound from New York on 2 January 1890, *Britannic* collided off the Mersey with the brigantine *Czarawitz*, out of Fowey and bound for Runcorn. *Czarawitz* filled quickly and sank; *Britannic* was undamaged.

On 16 August 1899 *Britannic* departed Liverpool on her last transatlantic trip. Declared surplus, she was requisitioned almost at once by the British government as a transport. The Boer War had begun during the second week of October, 1899, and ships were needed to carry troops, supplies and animals to South Africa. Designated *Transport No 62, Britannic* departed Queenstown on her first transport voyage 26 October. Ten subsequent round voyages were completed from Southampton.

Painted white for the occasion, *Britannic* was dispatched 12 November 1900 to Australia, bearing the Guard of Honour representing Great Britain at the Australian Commonwealth's inauguration. All went well until the ship attempted to navigate the Suez Canal. She grounded somewhat ignominiously, but was quickly refloated and completed the ceremonial voyage without further incident.

Released from government service several months after war's end, *Britannic* arrived at Southampton 28 October 1902, completing her final trooping voyage. She was sent to Harland and Wolff in Belfast for new engines and boilers and refitting for Atlantic passenger service. But a builder's survey revealed that such an expenditure would not be cost-effective in so aged a vessel, particularly since the first two members of the projected 'Big Four', *Celtic* (II) and *Cedric*, were already afloat. In July 1903 *Britannic* was sold for scrapping; on 11 August she departed Belfast in tow for Hamburg, where she was demolished.

A proud name, a proud ship — *Britannic* served her owners and those who sailed in her well. Though beset by moments of adversity, she plied her assigned route for long periods without incident; the final period of her eventful life was in her country's service, for which her owners were duly praised. She had proven as steadfast and as durable as her name ... *Britannic*.

Accidents and incidents

9 June 1874	In dense fog, the coastal steamer *Matteawan* collided with the anchored *Celtic* off New York's Quarantine. *Matteawan*'s bow was stove in, her railing was smashed, and a shower of wood splinters was thrown over her upper deck, crowded with passengers. No one was injured, but her damage was estimated at $2,000. *Celtic* sustained very little injury. As Captain Kiddle put it, '£100, at most, will do the business'.
23 November 1874	Fire broke out on board *Baltic*, lying at Granton, caused by the upsetting of a paraffin lamp; the blaze was extinguished without serious damage.

24 November 1874	In leaving London's Victoria Dock, *Belgic* collided with and sank two barges, one laden with the rudder of an ironclad ship, the other empty. She proceeded on her voyage.
20 November 1875	While at sea bound for San Francisco from Hong Kong, *Gaelic* was overtaken by a furious gale which blew away her main trysail and smashed in the after part of her wheelhouse.
3 February 1876	*Baltic* collided with the steamer *Prince Llewelyn* from Buenos Ayres while docking at Princes Dock, Liverpool. *Prince Llewelyn* lost her jib boom, while *Baltic* sustained no damage.
29 August 1876	*Germanic*, bound for New York, fouled the British steamer *Circassian*, inbound from Quebec while both ships were in the Mersey. *Germanic*'s rigging was damaged.
25 July 1877	*Oceanic* lost her propeller on a trip from Yokohama to Hong Kong, completing the voyage using her sails.
19 September 1877	As she was about to depart from San Francisco with American mails for Japan and China, *Oceanic* was detained ten days in port by an accident to her machinery.
1 November 1878	While changing docks at Liverpool, *Britannic* struck the Morpeth pierhead and sustained damage.
31 January 1879	At latitude 48°N, longitude 34°W, *Celtic* reported a loose propeller. Five days later, at latitude 51°N, longitude 19°W, she reported the blades of her propeller broken. On 7 February, several tugs were dispatched from Queenstown to escort her into port.
17 February 1879	The schooner *Ocean Queen* collided with *Republic* at anchor in the River Mersey. The schooner had to be towed clear and beached near Newferry.
22 December 1879	*Republic* encountered five days of furious gales and high seas as she steamed westward from Liverpool and Queenstown. A huge wave struck her port quarter, stove in her funnel, smashed a lifeboat (later thrown overboard) and did considerable damage to deck work. Engineers worked feverishly to re-rig the funnel, 'using oars for splints and sheets of canvas for bandages.' When weather moderated, they replaced the fire-prone arrangement with thin iron sheets.
17 August 1880	The River Mersey was the site of a collision between *Baltic*, bound for New York, and the steamer *Longford* from Dublin. *Longford* was towed ashore and filled with water. *Baltic*, badly damaged, was taken into dock for repairs that required discharge of much of her cargo.

20 September 1880	*Baltic* arrived at Sandy Hook where she was detained four hours by fog. As she steamed for her New York pier, she ran into the schooner *Sarah Burns*, puncturing a hole in the latter's side.
7 November 1880	Leaving New York one day late due to a persistent fog, *Germanic* struck the 1,076-ton full-rigged Dutch cargo vessel *Samarang*, tearing a large hole in the latter's port side amidships. *Samarang* quickly sank so that only her spars and her deck remained above water. Her crew was rescued by *Germanic*.
10 December 1880	The German steamer *Mosel* passed *Republic* drifting with a machinery problem at latitude 41.86 N, 63.40 W. *Republic*'s captain asked to be towed to New York, but changed his mind as *Mosel* had insufficient coal to do so. *Republic* reached New York alone on 14 December.
23 November 1881	On a voyage to Liverpool with merchandise and passengers aboard, *Coptic* encountered a hurricane that lasted twelve hours. The storm stove in several lifeboats and the after turtleback. Two seamen were washed overboard and drowned.
2 December 1881	*Arabic* collided in the Mersey with the steamer *Plove*. Damage was 'unknown.'
6 December 1881	*Celtic* arrived in New York with 302 passengers, reporting a continuation of hurricanes for six days which swept her decks and smashed her boats.
20 February 1882	The inbound *Republic* collided in the Mersey with the American ship *Palestine* while the latter was at anchor. *Palestine* had her bowsprit broken and was 'otherwise damaged,' while *Republic* damaged a lifeboat.
17 November 1882	As she headed for her dock at the foot of New York's West 10th Street, *Baltic* ran into and sank the barge *Peter Reuter* which was heavily laden with iron and under tow. As the *Baltic* backed away, the barge keeled over, throwing her four crew into the water. One man was severely injured by the falling iron which pinioned him under water. He was hospitalized. Captain Parsell called the collision 'unavoidable.'
11 May 1883	*Gaelic* was reported at Hankow, China with a broken propeller shaft following a trip from San Francisco *en route* to Hong Kong.
2 June 1884	*Arabic* arrived at Hong Kong from San Francisco via Yokohama with damage to her propeller that necessitated drydocking.
5 April 1885	After leaving Queenstown for New York with 850 passengers on board, *Germanic* encountered a terrific storm and a 'tidal wave' when about 500 miles west of Fastnet. Her pilot house was destroyed, all boats were swept away and the skylights were smashed. Then a tidal wave 'of enormous force and volume' burst into the reading room, smashed through the bulkhead and poured a great flood into the saloon and staterooms. So severe was damage that it was deemed advisable to return to Liverpool for repairs, the first time a vessel of the line had been required to return to port because of the weather.

20 September 1885	*Republic*, under charter to the Inman Line, collided with the Cunarder *Aurania* while leaving New York Harbor amid pilots' confusion over both vessels' intended courses. The *Republic* heeled over 'until the port portholes were at the water's edge' before she regained equilibrium. Her bow was spread open by a hole 4 ft wide at the top and a foot at the bottom, ranging from the knighthead to the water line. She had to be drydocked for repairs. *Aurania* sustained a large, V-shaped dent in her port quarter but continued her voyage.
28 January 1886	*Belgic* broke her piston rod on a voyage from Hong Kong to Yokohama. Repairs at the latter port delayed her eight days before she proceeded for San Francisco.
20 November 1886	Boxes of cheese were damaged, 53 bales of cotton and several other pieces of cargo were ruined by fire or water when *Germanic* caught fire at Liverpool.
16 December 1886	With 20 cabin and 349 steerage passengers and a large cargo on board, *Britannic* encountered a terrible gale with squalls of hurricane force, hail and rain. At 2.00 am she shipped a heavy sea, smashing two boats. Two days earlier, an emigrant passenger had 'died of apoplexy' and was buried at sea.
10 December 1887	At 3.00 am, the Italian barque *Rosa Madre*, lying at New York's Quarantine with a cargo of liquorice root, was run into by the *Republic*, inbound from Liverpool. The barque was struck on her starboard quarter, breaking everything above deck, the wreckage jamming the steering gear and rendering it inoperative. *Republic* lowered a boat, but with *Rosa Madre*'s hull undamaged, it was not required.
7 May 1888	*Baltic* was forced to return to Queenstown when her low pressure valve spindle broke. It took ten hours to repair.
22 August 1888	*Oceanic*, inbound from Hong Kong and Yokohama, collided with the coastal steamer *City of Chester* near San Francisco's Golden Gate. The coaster was struck amidships, cutting her almost in half near the gangway, causing her to reel from the blow and sink within five minutes. Some 34 lives were lost.
27 January 1889	Upon arrival off Sandy Hook, *Republic* grounded for almost five hours before finally refloating. Soon after her passengers were landed on the pier in New York, a furnace flue in the lower forward boiler fractured, killing three men and seriously injuring seven others. Captain Edward J. Smith said only that damage to the ship was slight, and could be repaired in a few hours. He added that the injured were able to walk from the ship to the ambulance.
13 May 1889	*Ionic* returned to Lyttelton, New Zealand with a broken crankshaft, her voyage to London being cancelled.
1 July 1889	While being towed to a Belfast anchorage before departing for Liverpool and her maiden voyage to New York, *Teutonic* grounded in Belfast Lough but was refloated six hours later.

4 October 1889	As *Adriatic* entered her slip alongside the new covered pier at New York, the flood tide caught her stern and caused the bow to strike the pier with great force. Her starboard anchor caught the new dock house, and carried it away for some 50 ft before its stock fractured and sent the anchor through the roof while hundreds of wellwishers on the pier ran for cover.
31 January 1890	Fire broke out in several mattresses between decks on *Teutonic* at Liverpool. Flames were extinguished after causing 'trifling' damage.
18 April 1890	The freighter *Runic* returned to Holyhead with her machinery out of order. Repairs delayed her voyage to New York one day.
December 1890	As she departed Rio de Janeiro for Plymouth, *Coptic* ran aground on Main Island. Edward J. Smith was in command.
28 May 1890	Fire broke out aboard *Runic* at Liverpool a day before she was to sail for New York. Her inflammable cargo of 2,000 bags of sulphur, a quantity of drums of caustic soda and several bales of jute and rags added to the blaze. Eventually, the hold had to be flooded to extinguish the flames.
19 July 1890	The forward spindle on *Germanic*'s engine fractured, and the vessel stopped in mid-ocean for four hours while engineers repaired the break. The ship arrived safely at Queenstown on 24 July.
14 February 1891	*Teutonic* shipped several seas while she was heavily buffeted by a strong gale during a 48 hour period. Her foresail was blown into ribbons, and water poured into passengers' staterooms. Upon arrival at Liverpool, she was detained by heavy fog outside the Mersey Bar for some thirty hours.
10 July 1891	The freighter *Nomadic* damaged her stem by striking a pier head at Liverpool.
1 November 1891	*Germanic* was struck by a terrible storm while bound for Queenstown. One lifeboat was smashed and washed overboard. No one was hurt.
14 November 1891	*Tauric* ran hard aground in the Romer Shoals, two and a half miles east of Sandy Hook, while inbound from Liverpool. Refloating was accomplished only after more than half of the 800 head of cattle on board were transferred to the cattle boat *General McCullum*, while many tons of general cargo were offloaded onto a lighter. After 25 hours and with five tugs' assistance, *Tauric* was finally dragged off.
28 November 1891	The livestock carrier *Tauric* collided with the steamer *Baltimore* in the Mersey. *Baltimore*'s bows were damaged, and *Tauric* also sustained slight injury.
24 December 1891	*Germanic* broke her crankshaft while anchoring at Queenstown. She was towed back to Liverpool, where 900 sacks of mail and her saloon passengers were transferred to the Cunarder *Bothnia*, while steerage and cargo were transferred to *Adriatic*.

26 March 1892	The steamer *Indiana*, while docking at Liverpool, collided with *Teutonic*, indenting three of the White Star ship's plates. The *Indiana* then proceeded to damage seriously a nearby collier.
27 March 1892	A minor fire aboard *Runic* at Liverpool was quickly extinguished.
13 October 1892	*Nomadic* had one engine disabled, but reached Liverpool safely.
11 November 1892	*Tauric* collided in the Mersey with the Allan liner *Buenos Ayrean*, staving in her own bow and twisting the latter's stem.
27 November 1892	The livestock carrier *Naronic* arrived at Liverpool from New York having lost 34 head of cattle on the voyage.

White Star livestock carriers

Ship's Name	Reg. Tonnage	Dimensions (ft)	Launch Date	Disposition
Cufic	4,639	430.7 × 45.2 × 30	10 Oct 1888	Foundered in North Atlantic 18 Dec 1919 (c.40 lost)
Runic	4,833	430.7 × 45.2 × 30	1 Jan 1889	Ran ashore in fog, Port Stanley, Falkland Islands, total loss, 30 Nov 1921
Nomadic	5,749	460.8 × 49.1 × 30.9	11 Feb 1891	Scrapped 1926
Tauric	5,728	460.8 × 49.1 × 30.9	12 Mar 1891	Sold Dec 1929, scrapped
Naronic	6,594	470 × 53 × 31.6	26 May 1892	Departed Liverpool for New York 11 Feb 1893, vanished at sea
Bovic	6,583	470 × 53 × 31.6	28 Jun 1892	Scrapped 1928
Cevic	8,315	500 × 60 × 38	25 Sep 1893	Scrapped 1933
Georgic	10,077	558.7 × 60.3 × 36	22 Jun 1895	Captured and sunk by German raider *Moewe*, 10 Dec 1916

CHAPTER 4

Naronic, 1893

THIRTEENTH VOYAGE

In the thousands of years man has sailed the seas, it has only been since 1902 that merchant vessels at sea could maintain wireless contact with land and other ships. In October 1902 transmission experiments were conducted between the powerful British station at Poldhu, Cornwall, and the American liner *Philadelphia en route* between New York and Southampton. Readable signals were received from up to 1,550 miles away. But the experiment and subsequent universal acceptance of wireless did nothing to aid in the rescue of more than 2,200 seamen lost between 1840 and 1899 in transatlantic freighters and liners which left port and simply vanished. Fire, storm, collision with ice or half-submerged derelicts — these were the reasons usually offered for such losses.

There is, however, one intriguing loss near the end of the nineteenth century involving a ship whose enigmatic disappearance is still reason for speculation and conjecture. Her loss might be ascribed to a North Atlantic storm raging during her final voyage. But, severe as the storm was, no other ships — including some considerably smaller — were reported lost in it. Her loss might have been ascribed to age or to faulty construction. But she had been built by Harland and Wolff; she had been at sea less than a year, and this was only her seventh westbound crossing — her thirteenth voyage...

The live cattle trade across the Atlantic commenced in July 1874. The first steamer to bring cattle from North America to Liverpool was the *Europe*, owned by H.N. Hughes and nephew. Three of the 373 head of cattle transported were lost during the crossing. A year later the *San Marcos* arrived at Liverpool with 276 head for the firm of George Roddick.

By 1877 importation of American live beef had become an appreciable factor in British trade. Annual totals increased rapidly until 1889 when some 451,799 animals were landed. Though numbers then decreased slightly (probably due to improvements in refrigeration, permitting carriage of carcasses), by 1893 eight shipping lines with nearly fifty transatlantic cattle vessels ran to Liverpool alone.

While phasing out its sailing vessels, White Star began to seek a type of carrier which could suit current company requirements. Wishing to capitalize on the evolving, lucrative cattle trade, the company ordered designs for a pair of ships, *Cufic* (1888) and *Runic* (1889). These vessels for the Liverpool trade were for general cargo transport, but were the first vessels to contain special facilities for stabling live cattle aboard. They were White Star's last single-screw ships and their first with triple-expansion engines.

The success of *Cufic* and *Runic* encouraged White Star to introduce an enlarged, improved series of cattle steamers, beginning with the 5,749-ton twin-screw *Nomadic* (1891), followed by *Tauric* (1891), *Naronic* and *Bovic* (1892) and *Cevic* (1893). The series culminated in 1895 with the 10,077 ton *Georgic*, more than twice the tonnage and 120 ft longer than the group's first ship, *Cufic*.

Aboard many cattle ships livestock was crowded into all areas of the vessels. Far too frequently, unspeakable cruelties accompanied the livestock's loading, transporting and unloading. Inadequate ventilation, overcrowding, insufficient water and feed, the handlers' brutal natures caused many deaths and cripplings of shipboard cattle. When vessels encountered storms or rough seas, horrors were compounded. American regulations of 1890 and the British *Transatlantic Cattle Order*, 1891, though not totally effective, went far in establishing humane treatment of shipboard cattle.

White Star managers viewed their cargoes' worth in terms of safe arrival, and cattle were no exception. The company established and maintained safety and comfort standards for livestock beyond those of other companies' vessels. Commanders were left in little doubt about management's views, as expressed in White Star's *Ships' Rules and Uniform Regulations* of 1907:

'Carriage of Livestock — The carriage of cattle, sheep and horses being an important part of the Company's business, Commanders are enjoined to give the safe carriage of the animals their particular attention; no suspicion of cruelty is to be tolerated, and every care is to be exercised in carrying out the regulations regarding fittings, ventilation, disinfection, etc.

The cattle trade was a one-way affair from North America to Liverpool. Upon discharging its live

Launched in 1888, Cufic *was White Star's first livestock carrier* (Mariners Museum, Newport News, Va.).

cargo at Birkenhead's special facilities, each ship was cleaned, ventilated and disinfected thoroughly prior to reloading with general cargo for New York. Occasionally westbound ships carried small numbers of live animals — race horses, breeding cattle, circus animals, and the like — but general cargo predominated and was carried in holds separate from the cattle pens. Although White Star ships had facilities for a small number of passengers, cabins usually were occupied by cattle drovers. There are a few instances of revenue-paying passengers on westbound voyages, but this was certainly not a common occurrence.

When launched on 26 May 1892 the 470 ft 6,594 ton *Naronic* was the largest cargo steamer afloat. The four-masted schooner-rigged vessel was constructed of steel and had three decks, nine bulkheads and sixteen water ballast tanks capable of holding 1,193 tons. In describing her the magazine *Marine Engineer* stated:

'...The spacious accommodation provided for the 1,050 cattle, which she will be able to carry on her upper and main decks, will comprise every improvement that the most careful consideration and experience can suggest. The stalls, fresh water supply, and ventilation will be unsurpassed...'

Naronic's two triple-expansion engines provided the twin-screw vessel with a 13-knot speed. Normal

crew complement was sixty. Although certified to carry twelve passengers, she had cabin facilities for fifteen. (Her sister ship *Bovic*, of the same dimensions but eleven registered tons smaller, was launched 33 days after *Naronic*. *Bovic* had a long, uneventful life, ending her days as Leyland's freighter *Colonian* before being scrapped at Rotterdam in 1928.)

On 11 July 1892 *Naronic* left Harland and Wolff's Abercorn Basin finishing jetty and proceeded down Belfast Lough on her trial trip. After compass adjustments, a run of several hours showed the ship and her machinery to be 'most satisfactory'. Later that day *Naronic* steamed across the Irish Sea to Liverpool.

The new ship quickly took on 1,295 tons of general cargo and on 15 July 1892 departed for New York on her maiden voyage under Captain Thompson's command. Five more round trips followed at approximately 34-day intervals, a total of twelve Atlantic crossings. On the 18 October 1892 Liverpool departure a new commander, Captain William Roberts, came aboard from *Adriatic*. He still was in command in February 1893 as *Naronic* was prepared for her thirteenth voyage.

The vessel was a popular ship; her first and second mate, four of her five engineering officers and all of her greasers had been aboard for all twelve previous voyages; the rest of her crew had been

As the Imo, *White Star's second cattle transporter* Runic *collided in Halifax Harbour in 1917 with the munitions ship* Mont Blanc *(Mariners Museum, Newport News, Va.).*

aboard for up to five trips. While taking aboard her 2,876 ton cargo, 1,017 tons of South Wales coal, and stores for her crew, she was berthed at Liverpool's Alexandra Dock.

Cargo was loaded under chief stevedore Poulson's control, while dockmaster Robert P. Graham supervised: earthenware, steel strips, oil, glass, machinery, fish hooks. Soda ash, bleaching powder, chlorate of potash. Rice, sugar, chillies, potatoes. Tallow, cattle hair, calf skins... 'General cargo': thousands of items for nearly ninety consignees. As customary on westbound trips, no cattle were on board. The capacious pens' sole occupants were two horses consigned to W. Burgess, a former American diplomat residing in Trenton, New Jersey. The only other live animals aboard were contained in fifteen crates: fowls and pigeons *en route* to Baltimore, Maryland and W.J. Robertson, who planned to exhibit them at a show in New York City's Madison Square Garden.

During early February 1893, widespread, violent gales swept the North Atlantic. Ships limped into ports telling of immense waves and severe, almost hurricane-force winds. But weather ashore was merely seasonal — blustery and cold —

and there were no indications that a monstrous storm raged in mid-Atlantic. Monday, 11 February 1893, sailing day in Liverpool. The weather: clear, with strong west-northwest winds, heavy seas and a mist reported off the port. *Naronic*: cargo stowed, crew aboard, ready to sail for New York, scheduled arrival date 22 February.

Among the last persons to board *Naronic* that morning were fourteen cattle drovers returning home. Employees of Eastman's Cattle Yard, located at 59th Street and North River, New York City, they were deadheading back across the Atlantic under their hire's customary terms. As they boarded, one of them may have been carrying that day's Liverpool *Mercury*. On its shipping news page appeared a brief paragraph which later might be deemed somewhat portentous:

'The Alleged Overdue White Star Liner: The telegram from New York published in some of the newspapers this morning to the effect that the White Star steamer *Teutonic* was some five days overdue, and that considerable anxiety was felt, is totally incorrect. So, far from being overdue, she arrived out at New York at her usual time, and left that port on Wednesday last, the 8th inst., on her return voyage. She is due in Liverpool on Wednesday next.

Captain William Roberts resided at Liverpool, as did a majority of *Naronic*'s crew. An experienced officer in White Star service for twenty years, he held an extra master's certificate and had commanded *Naronic* for her three previous voyages. Captain Roberts knew from reports reaching Liverpool that he faced a stormy crossing. But he had confidence in First Mate George Wright, and in his chief engineer, John Duncan, both of whom had been aboard for at least three previous voyages. The ship was thoroughly secured. Ventilators supplying below-deck cattle pens with fresh air had been stowed and their coamings plugged and covered with canvas hoods. Cargo hatches

With the success of their first two livestock carriers, White Star launched Nomadic *in February 1891 (Mariners Museum, Newport News, Va.).*

were battened down and covered in preparation for the open sea.

Naronic's daily coal consumption at sea was about fifty tons. To permit a New York turn-around without refueling, her bunkers were filled to capacity and 200 additional tons were placed on deck. But as bunkers were consumed, this coal would be taken below, and it appeared its presence on deck would not materially affect stability. In fact, Captain Roberts and White Star's marine superintendent H.W. Hewitt agreed that as soon as *Naronic* left port her number 7 ballast tank was to be filled to its 140-ton capacity, providing additional stability.

Cargo manifest and clearance papers in order, the company's winter track chart at hand, Captain Roberts welcomed aboard Captain William Davies, a licensed Liverpool pilot who was to guide *Naronic* through the Mersey's intricate shoals. Davies noted that as *Naronic* left the dock she drew 20 ft 3 in forward and 20 ft 9 in aft, a mean of 20 ft 6 in, normal for her cargo and coal supply.

The down-river passage went without incident, and at Point Lynas Captain Davies descended the swaying ladder to the pilot vessel's pitching deck.

...followed one month later by Tauric (Mariners Museum, Newport News, Va.).

Naronic's screws beat the choppy waters even faster as the ship quickly became enveloped in the off-shore mist. *Naronic* vanished into the reaches of the Irish Sea...

Indeed, *Naronic* vanished.

When she failed to arrive at New York as scheduled on 22 February there was no undue alarm. All westbound vessels were reporting delays, citing the great mid-Atlantic gales. The Red Star liner *Noordland*, which had departed Antwerp on 12 February, reported on arriving at New York 27 February that she had encountered a severe storm one day out, with northwesterly winds exceeding 60 mph. This storm was directly on the track over which *Naronic* should have passed: when four days out, supposing progress of 250 miles per day, *Naronic* would have been somewhere near 48°50' N, 30°W, where the gales were reaching maximum strength.

February became March, and still no word of the ship. On 6 March several steamships arrived in New York, most several days overdue, reporting tremendous seas and rough passages. On 6 March American marine insurance companies began to refuse further risks on *Naronic*. American Lloyd's was quoting the high re-insurance rate of 36½ per cent, while the Atlantic Mutual Company would take no further insurance whatsoever.

Two thousand tons larger than Cufic, *the 470-ft* Naronic *sailed for less than nine months before her mysterious disappearance* (Library of Congress).

The company's hopes rested on the possibility that *Naronic*, her hull and possibly her engines storm-damaged, had sought refuge in the Azores, some 600 miles south of her projected track. Were *Naronic* to reach an Azores port, her presence there would take some time to confirm. As the days passed, other White Star steamers deviated from their regular courses to search for *Naronic*. Arriving at Queenstown on 15 March, *Teutonic*'s captain reported he had taken a long southerly course and had seen nothing of the missing ship. *Tauric* arrived at New York on 14 March and despite a sharp round-the-clock watch using extra lookouts, had seen no trace of *Naronic*.

Some speculation as to *Naronic*'s fate bore what seemed a semi-official stamp. White Star captains Ward and Lindsay suggested that a storm-crippled *Naronic* may have drifted into the gigantic eddy called the Sargasso Sea, where she could be trapped for a long time before being reported. The consensus was that *Naronic* had encountered a heavy ice field or had run into an iceberg and had

sunk before lowering a lifeboat. On 14 March Lloyd's agent at Fayal, the Azores' chief port, reported that *Naronic* had not put in there. Thus it was not until 15 March, when *Naronic* was 34 days out and 22 days overdue, that White Star's New York agent Maitland Kearsey admitted she had been given up as lost. He said,

'We still hope that she may be safe, but it does not look as though she is afloat, for almost every part of the Atlantic has been traversed by steamers or sailing vessels, and she would in all probability have been sighted had she been afloat. The idea that she is in the swirl of the Sargasso Sea is rather far-fetched and not probable, as she would be controlled in her movements entirely by the prevailing winds.'

While it was still remotely possible *Naronic* was afloat but drifting helplessly, Liverpool and London re-insurance rates rose to an unheard-of 75 per cent. One newspaper reflected hopefully that 'her crew and passengers will not have suffered from want, as yet, for she was well provisioned and had a sufficient quantity of canned and fresh food in stores and cargo to last them for three months.'

In near-hysteria rumour spread via the *New York Herald* that *Naronic* had aboard 'several hundred

immigrants' when lost. The company quickly assured the public that *Naronic* could not carry more than fifteen passengers and on this voyage had only the fourteen cattlemen and her sixty-man crew aboard.

On 19 March the British steamer *Coventry* arrived at Bremerhaven from Norfolk, Virginia, at last providing some definite word on *Naronic*'s disappearance. Her Captain Wilson reported that on 4 March at 2.00 am in latitude 44° 02′ N, longitude 47° 37′ W, a ship's white-painted lifeboat had been sighted floating keel up. Twelve hours later, in latitude 34° 44′ N, longitude 45° 25′ W, another drifting boat was spotted. Captain Wilson steamed close alongside it. Although half full of water, the boat was in good condition and not stove in. Its mast floated at the bows, made fast to the painter as if used for a sea anchor. The words on the bows: '*Naronic*. Liverpool.'

(Neither boat was picked up. This caused speculation that every small boat found drifting could have been *Naronic*'s. Captain Lewis of the American liner *Chester* reported sighting one on 25 March, overturned and drifting near 42° 30′ N, 53° 04′ W, some 450 miles west of *Coventry*'s

Strikingly similar to her sister, Bovic *underwent stability tests in an attempt to determine* Naronic*'s fate* (Mariners Museum, Newport News, Va.).

sightings. But *Naronic*'s boats would have drifted eastwards, not westwards.)

Few ships generated more bottle hoaxes than *Naronic*. Four bottles supposedly from her were 'discovered,' two in America, two in the United Kingdom. The first was a champagne bottle washed ashore at Ocean View, Virginia. Allegedly written by John Osborn, a *Naronic* cattleman, the note inside was dated 19 February and said:

'The ship is sinking fast. It is such a storm that we can never live in the small boats. One boat with its human cargo has already sunk. We have been struck by an iceberg in the blinding snow. The ship has floated for two hours. It is now 3.20 in the morning and the deck's level with the sea. Will the finder of this message please forward it to the White Star agent at New York, Mr Maitland Kearsey.'

No one aboard *Naronic* was named 'John Osborn.' And prevailing winds and currents made it highly unlikely the bottle would have washed up on a Virginia beach.

A second 'westbound bottle' was discovered by William Clare almost directly on his door step at Bay Ridge, a New York Bay inlet about seven miles from the city. Discovered on 2 April, the bottle's note said, 'March 1, 1893 — The *Naronic* is sinking with all hands. We are praying to god [*sic*] to have mercy on us. — L. Winsel.' Once again the note bore a name not among *Naronic*'s passengers or crew.

The next bottle appeared 26 April in a place precisely described to the Board of Trade's Marine Department: 'Wexford, found ashore high and dry on Sands ½ mile NNW of Ballygea [*sic*] pier at ½ ebb.' The undated and anonymous note inside the square bottle was written in black lead pencil on grey note paper, and said, 'Sinking fast explosion happened about 3 am good bye sweet world S.S. *Naronic*.' The barely legible writing appears hastily scrawled. But the signature is punctilious with full points after each 'S' and the ship's name clearly underlined. Of the four bottles attributed to *Naronic*, it alone may not be a hoax.

By April's end *Naronic*'s passenger and crew lists had appeared in shipping-related publications and the popular press. It is strange, then, that the final note-in-a-bottle is perfectly legible, dated, and clearly signed with a non-existent name. A deputy receiver of wrecks of Carnarvon described the 'exact spot where found' as 'Floating in Holyhead New Harbour about 50 yards outside the "Mackenzie Pier" on 15th May '93 at 6.00 pm'. It read,

'Feb. the 3rd 1893

The S.S. Naronic is sinking fast in Mid-Ocean and all have perished except 4 of us and we will be perished in an hours time the finder will send it to my parents at 17 Victoria Road West Norwood London.

John Priestman
& the Captain'

The Board of Trade's Mr H. Crowhurst sought John Priestman ('or Kirkman') at West Norwood, where there was no Victoria Road; at 17 Victoria Place and 17 Victoria Villas, West Norwood; and 17 Victoria Road, Upper Norwood. Now thoroughly acquainted with West and Upper Nor-

wood, he was forced at last to state, 'No such name [is] known there or anywhere about the neighbourhood. I believe it to be a false alarm.'

The bottles and the curious urgency apparently motivating the hoaxers add depth to *Naronic*'s mystery. Another mysterious element was a 28 April 1893 *New York Times* interview with John Lucock, a Pittsburgh, Pennsylvania electrician. Lucock's brother Richard had been *Naronic*'s second engineer. After her Liverpool arrival on her last eastbound voyage, Richard apparently had written his brother a letter saying the ship's boilers were in very bad condition and they had a difficult crossing from New York to Liverpool. Richard added that unless repairs were made at Liverpool the return trip likely would be a dangerous one. John Lucock concluded his interview, saying Robert was a very conservative man who would not write anything inaccurate about the boilers. In the same edition, the paper ran a brief article describing other family members of *Naronic*'s crew:

'Liverpool — The wives of Roberts and Wright, Captain and First Mate respectively of the lost White Star Line steamer *Naronic*, now believed lost with all hands, have both gone insane and have had to be placed in an insane asylum.'

Statistics brought the disaster into focus. The ship, valued at £121,685 ($590,000) was uninsured; the £61,855 ($300,000) cargo was insured. All sixty British and fourteen American citizens had been lost.

It was not until June 1893 that an official board of inquiry investigated the probable cause. The inquiry in Liverpool's Sheriff's Court, St George's Hall, heard testimony regarding *Naronic*'s structure and cargo. Refuting John Lucock's interview, investigators said:

'The engines and boilers were described by the Board of Trade surveyor as being of the best, and in every way fitted and finished in the best possible manner... The engines were not only the best of the make and class but they were overhauled every voyage...
'*Naronic*'s fittings were found to have met highest standards. Her watertight integrity was assured by her excellent construction. Officers and crew were proficient.'

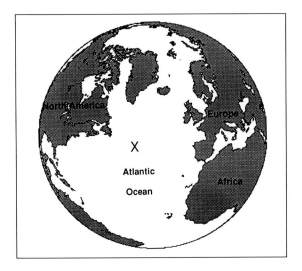

The general cargo's stowage had been supervised by Mr Poulson, 'a master stevedore of Liverpool and London, a man of great experience.' There had been no deck openings except ventilators and hatches, well-protected or firmly battened down before departure. The coal stored on her upper deck would have been moved to regular bunkers before *Naronic* might have encountered truly heavy weather.

The inspectors' conclusions regarding *Naronic*'s state upon departure were,

1. That she was in a good and seaworthy condition as to hull, equipments and machinery.
2. That she was provided with a sufficient number of efficient bulkheads, so that if any two compartments were open to the sea, she would be able to float in moderate weather.
3. That as laden she had sufficient stability.
4. That her cargo was properly stowed.
5. There was nothing in the cargo which was likely to explode or ignite spontaneously.
6. There were proper appliances on board to extinguish fire.
7. She was fully provided with life-saving apparatus.

Bovic's Captain Thompson, *Naronic*'s commander for her first three voyages, reported that he had encountered bad weather in her on several occasions and had never found her tender or requir-

ing stiffening. From knowledge of his westerly voyages in her, Captain Thompson estimated her 20 February position as about 150 miles southwest of where *Coventry* had found the floating lifeboats.

From this position it would seem *Naronic* had not encountered ice. Considering his Liverpool departure date and the drifting boats' 4 March position, she would not have been far enough north. No ice reports had been made by any vessel anywhere near that approximate position around that date. And, as the report stated, 'Her construction and spare buoyancy render it unlikely, though not impossible, that she was lost through striking a floating wreck.'

Engine or boiler defect? Ice? Collision? Sudden loss of stability? No possible cause seemed consistent with facts that seemed to have promised a safe passage. The inspectors' 25 July 1893 report concluded, 'Unless, therefore, any further evidence is hereafter forthcoming, the probable cause of the loss of this vessel remains a mere matter of speculation, and adds one more to the mysteries of the sea.'

The *New York Herald* on 5 March 1893 published *Naronic*'s complete cargo manifest. While they never specifically referred to it, the Board of Trade's inspectors unquestionably used it during their investigation. It contains a clue as to the probable cause of *Naronic*'s loss. Although the inspectors had concluded that 'There was nothing in the cargo which was likely to explode or ignite spontaneously,' the honourable gentlemen appear either unversed in or indifferent to the presence in the cargo of highly hazardous, explosive chemicals. They included chlorate of potash (potassium chlorate); 'acid' (probably sulphuric and/or nitric acid); sodium sulfide; chlorinated lime (bleaching powder). Potassium chlorate and sodium sulfide can explode through rapid heating or percussion. Potassium chlorate explodes on contact with sulphuric acid. Chlorinated lime, upon exposure to air (as might happen if its container were breached) rapidly decomposes and releases oxygen and chlorine gas.

Sulphuric or nitric acid would interact with the ship's metal hull or the bundled iron in the ship's cargo, releasing hydrogen gas. Hydrogen itself is highly explosive, but even more so when mixed with oxygen that the potassium chlorate's decomposition would supply. Should any one of these chemical reactions have occurred, the result ultimately would be a sudden, violent explosion.

Probable cause? The severe storm into which *Naronic* steamed, with its mountainous waves making a mockery of ballast and careful cargo stowage. Its incessant pounding on hull, superstructure and hatch covers might... can... will loosen a rivet here, a seam there, allowing sea water to trickle, then pour into a cargo hold. It causes twisting, turning and rolling sufficient to cause shifting of cargo stored, perhaps, next to glass bottles of acid, which fall to the deck and smash, or are struck by other cargo and burst open. The possibilities exist. The probable happens. The storm's voice is outshouted by the gigantic roar of a ship's bottom being blown out, and another as icy sea water meets hot boilers.

Naronic's fate: a mid-ocean explosion during a fierce Atlantic storm (Michael V. Ralph).

The ship settles instantly. There is scarcely time to unship the lifeboats. Perhaps there is an instant to spot an empty bottle rolling about, to scribble a note, but not enough time to throw the bottle overboard. Writer, bottle and message sink with the ship. But through the roil of steam and air, the bottle surfaces and begins its eastward trip to County Wexford, a half-mile from Ballygeary Pier...

There are two postscripts to *Naronic*'s story. The first tells of largesse in Victorian industry's bountiful corporate world, when group insurance and workman's compensation were far in the future:

'All hope of ever hearing any details of the loss of *Naronic* has now been abandoned. A fund for the widows and orphans of the unfortunate crew has been started in Liverpool, and the White Star Company have found employment for a number of the widows at their works at Bootle, in upholstery work, sewing and sail making, etc. (*Shipping World*, 1 July, 1893)

The second confirms the great haste with which the *Naronic* was abandoned:

'London, 26 October 1893 — Captain Anderson of the Norwegian ship *Emblem* writes under date of 20 September from Buenos Ayres that he found on 21 July in lat. 36° N, long. 33° W one of the boats of the White Star Line steamer *Naronic*, which was lost at sea nearly a year ago.

He adds that the boat was bottom up and contained nothing whatever. It was thickly covered with barnacles.

There was a large hole in the bottom. The lashings of the boat appeared to have been cut in a great hurry, and with much force, as the rail beneath which the lashings had been fastened was severed. The patent underhooking apparatus had not been used.

'*Sinking fast explosion happened about 3 a.m. goodbye sweet world S.S. Naronic.*' Perhaps...

Accidents and incidents

15 February 1893	*Ionic* returned to Cape Town in tow of the *Hawarden Castle* after breaking her propeller shaft.
17 February 1893	*Belgic* arrived at San Francisco from Hong Kong and Yokohama with several cases of smallpox aboard. She was held at quarantine until fumigated.
26 February 1893	*Majestic*'s starboard engine broke down, forcing the ship to sail for several hours at reduced speed.
27 November 1893	At Liverpool, *Bovic* discharged several bales of hay 'apparently more or less damaged by cattle urine and seawater'.
6 April 1894	*Bovic* collided with the Norwegian barque *Duen* in Carnarvon Bay and sustained slight damage.
26 May 1894	While loading tea in Arnoy Harbour, *Belgic* was run into by the steamer *Ulysses*. Neither was damaged, but a tea-laden barge between them sank.
30 July 1894	*Majestic* ran into and sank the fishing schooner *Antelope* off the Grand Banks. All but one of the schooner's crew were saved.
17 January 1895	Captain Edward J. Smith reported loss of 75 head of cattle as the *Cufic* arrived at Liverpool from New York.
30 January 1895	An electrical wire sparked a fire in *Tauric*'s number four hold at Liverpool. A hole was cut through the deck and steam extinguished the flames. The ship's electrician died from suffocation, and *Tauric*'s cargo was heavily damaged.
1 April 1895	Number 11 lifeboat was washed overboard and three others were stove in as *Adriatic* encountered severe storms on a westbound crossing.
8 August 1895	As she departed Harland and Wolff's yard prior to her maiden voyage, the freighter *Georgic* grounded in the new harbour channel. She was subsequently towed off.

17 August 1895	The freighter *Runic* collided with the Liverpool landing stage prior to her departure for New York, receiving slight damage.
9 September 1895	While bound for Yokohama from San Francisco, *Belgic* went ashore at King's Point in Sateyama Bay, Japan. After one month she was refloated and entered the Yokosuka drydock for repairs to her bottom.
11 December 1895	Shortly after leaving Liverpool for New York, *Germanic* collided with and sank the inbound 900-ton steamer *Cumbrae* in dense fog, practically cutting the smaller vessel in half. *Germanic*'s bows were stove in. *Cumbrae*'s passengers were rescued. *Germanic*'s voyage was cancelled, her mails and passengers transferred to *Adriatic*.
23 May 1896	Arriving at Liverpool from New York, *Georgic* struck the dock entrance and damaged her stem.
15 August 1896	*Gaelic* went aground at Shimonoseki, Japan and lay on the mudbank with 12 ft of water in the forehold until refloated and drydocked at Nagasaki on 28 August.
4 April 1897	Bound for Liverpool from New York, *Georgic* collided with the British steamship *Queens Channel*, whose bow was damaged slightly.
12 June 1897	Arriving at Liverpool from New York, the freighter *Nomadic* collided with the British vessel *Barnesmore*, which was leaving for Montreal. *Nomadic*'s stem was twisted, but she continued her voyage. *Barnesmore* returned to Liverpool with her port bow damaged.
17 August 1897	While backing out of her New York dock, *Teutonic* ran into and sank an ice barge in tow of the tug *Peter Nevins*.
September 1897	*Coptic* collided in Kobe harbour with the Japanese steamship *Minatogawa Maru*. Several of *Coptic*'s plates were stove in and her stem was twisted.
28 February 1898	After landing her cargo in Liverpool, *Bovic* struck the dock entrance, damaging her bows.
3 March 1898	*Georgic* caught fire at Liverpool, but the blaze was extinguished before much damage could be done.
21 September 1898	*Teutonic* collided at New York with the U.S. transport *Berlin*, outward bound with provisions for American forces at Ponce, Puerto Rico. *Teutonic*'s bows grazed the *Berlin*, which continued her trip later. Damage to *Teutonic* was minimal.
2 January 1899	On a voyage from Liverpool to New York, *Bovic*'s tiller fractured, forcing use of jury-rigged hand gear. Upon her return to Liverpool, cargo was transferred to *Tauric* and *Bovic* entered drydock for a new rudder head.
6 February 1899	*Tauric* arrived in Liverpool from New York with her deck damaged and a large part of her deck cargo lost overboard.

CHAPTER 5

Germanic, 1899

BY ICE UNDAUNTED

White Star owned very few operationally unsuccessful ships. *Afric* (1899) was returned to her builder after her maiden voyage for 'improvements.' *Titanic* (1912) had a fatal design flaw which ultimately caused her loss scarcely 7,670 hours after her launch. *Adriatic* (1872) and *Britannic* (1874) were unpredictable vessels which ran aground or collided with other vessels somewhat indiscriminately.

On the other hand, *Oceanic* (1899) and *Celtic* (1901) were so soundly built that it took a Shetland storm's total fury to destroy the former after being aground almost a month; while the latter, also after running aground, took five years to dismantle where she lay. *Olympic* (1911) was one of the twentieth century's most successful liners. But for sheer longevity, no White Star ship — indeed, scarcely any major liner — could compare with *Germanic* (1874), sister to the less fortunate and shorter-lived *Britannic*. The two vessels were quite similar in design, proportions, propelling machinery and appearance. But *Britannic*, after a career spanning 28 years, was scrapped in 1903. *Germanic* went on, under a variety of owners, names and adventures, for an astonishing life exceeding 75 years.

Like her sister, *Germanic* was designed by Sir Edward Harland himself. She was 455 ft long between perpendiculars, 468 ft overall, and had a beam of 45 ft 2 in, giving an almost exact 10:1 length-to-beam ratio. At launch on 15 July 1874 she had a gross tonnage of 5,008, a measurement that varied by less than 100 tons over her long life, despite several structural modifications.

Her engines, too large to be built then by Harland and Wolff, were constructed by the

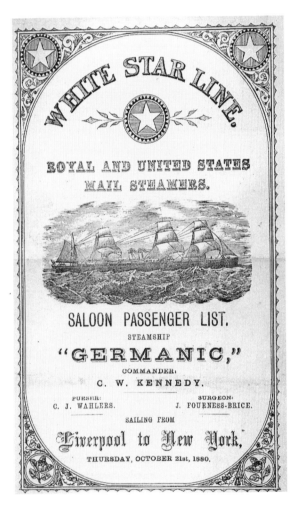

Transatlantic passenger liners proudly distributed beautifully decorated lists of passengers abroad (Authors' collection).

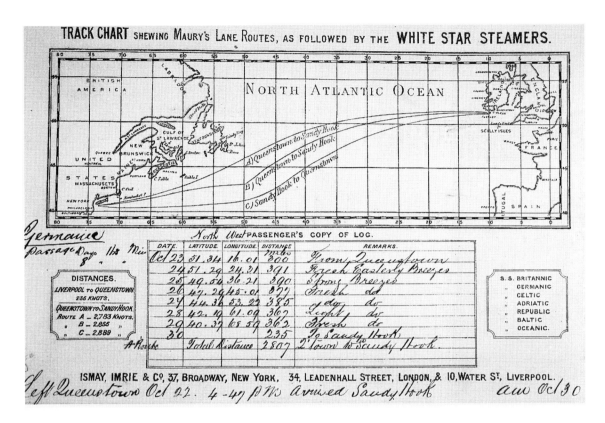

Lambeth firm of Maudslay, Sons and Field, and were shipped from London to Belfast for installation. They provided her with a 15 knot cruising speed, and a top speed of about 16 knots. The £200,000 *Germanic* provided comfortable, even luxurious accommodation for 220 cabin and about 1,500 steerage passengers, with a crew of 135.

Following her 30 May 1875 maiden voyage from Liverpool to New York and return, her performance improved gradually, until in February 1876 she completed an eastbound voyage in the record-breaking time of 7 days, 15 hours and 17 minutes, with an average speed of 15.79 knots; in April 1877 she set the westbound record, crossing in 7 days, 11 hours, 37 minutes, her average speed 15.76 knots.

During the 1880s the yards from her original four-masted barque rigging were removed from mizzen and main masts, and it appears her funnels were heightened somewhat. Beyond these, *Germanic* underwent few modifications during her first twenty years. The engines performed well; the daily coal consumption of 100 tons made her economical to operate, although when more modern machinery appeared in North Atlantic ships, *Germanic*'s average 15-knot speed left her a day or two behind the competition.

Teutonic (1889) and *Majestic* (1890) now became White Star's premier liners, and *Germanic* and her sister were hard-pressed to run with them. But the sixteen-year-old vessels responded admirably. In 1891, original boilers and engines intact, each made 16-knot Atlantic crossings.

In December 1894 *Germanic* was sent to Harland and Wolff for modernization. Harland and Wolff's triple-expansion engines replaced the originals, new high-pressure boilers were installed, a second open deck was added and the funnels were further lengthened. With completely remodelled passenger

accommodation, the liner returned to service in May 1895.

With Captain Edward R. McKinstry in command, *Germanic* departed Liverpool for New York 11 December 1895. There was dense fog, and double lookouts were posted. But soon after leaving the Mersey *Germanic* collided with the inbound Glasgow steamer *Cumbrae*, striking her a slanting blow between forecastle and forehatch that penetrated 14 ft. Captain McKinstry maintained sufficient way to keep *Germanic*'s bow inside the gash, and *Cumbrae*'s 28 passengers and crew were quickly transferred. When the vessels separated, *Cumbrae* immediately lurched over and sank moments later. The impact twisted *Germanic*'s bow, and she was withdrawn for repairs. After missing one round voyage she rejoined the Liverpool rotation early in January 1896. Three years of routine voyages followed. But in February 1899 an accident at New York placed *Germanic* in an unusual plight.

During her early February westbound crossing she encountered a severe storm. Ice — flintlike in its hardness — accumulated in rigging and superstructure. *Germanic* arrived at New York on the morning of Saturday 11 February with a 4° starboard list. Mails were not put off at Quarantine, as customary, because ice accumulation blocked normal egress. At about noon the liner docked at Pier 45 at the foot of Manhattan's West 10th Street with her bow to shore, her port side to the wharf, six feet from pier's edge because of the ice covering her side. Sufficient ice was chipped and axed away from ropes and gangways to permit passenger debarkation and offloading of mails. She then was breasted off 25 to 30 ft from the pier to allow barges to come alongside, coaling commencing at about 2.00 pm and continuing until evening.

It was bitterly cold, and the port was swept by strong northwest-to-westerly winds. Snow began falling about 8.00 pm Saturday and continued through Monday. Coaling, suspended on Sunday 12 February, was completed Monday with an estimated 362 tons loaded. While cargo was being discharged, Captain McKinstry ordered twenty crew members to clear off the ice, to which the storm was adding continually. It is estimated that more than 1,800 tons of it had accumulated in the vessel's rigging, sides and deck structures. Crew were frostbitten as they worked, and had to take frequent breaks.

On Monday 13 February, between 3.00 and 4.00 pm, *Germanic* suddenly took an 8° list to port; an hour or so later, she swung through to take an 8° starboard list. McKinstry ordered crew and workmen to the hold to trim the ship to an even keel, but *Germanic* did not respond, continuing to maintain the starboard list. Holds were almost empty, and McKinstry ordered them finished off and cargo awaiting loading taken aboard. Two after holds were quickly emptied and between 4.30 and 7.00 pm, 250 boxes of outbound bacon were taken on through number four hatch to help stiffen the ship. Its stowage was supervised by dock superintendent Mr Pender and foreman stevedore Joe Donnelly.

Coaling barges now flanked *Germanic* on both sides. On the pier side, one or two ports, each 3 ft 6 in by 2 ft, were open for loading. Despite the cargo's trimming, the ship did not stabilize. Nor was the redistribution of coal, still coming aboard, of any help. *Germanic*'s starboard list increased to 10° as the wind howled and snow continued to fall. At 9.00 pm, the tide reached flood.

Without warning at 9.10 pm, *Germanic* responded to her trim. But because of her ice encumbrance, she did not respond normally. Instead of coming to an even keel, she swung sluggishly through an 18° arc to again take an 8° port list. The ship listed so unexpectedly there was no time

to close the two open coaling ports, and water began pouring through them into the ship.

Collision mats could not be secured because of ice accumulation below the ports' lower edges. McKinstry immediately ordered a quantity of copper ingots, on the pier awaiting loading, to be taken aboard and placed on the upper deck's starboard side to steady the ship. Using already-rigged cargo-handling tackle the men quickly loaded 13 pigs of 500 lb each, but without effect.

Water continued to pour through the ports and the flood rose steadily in the holds. McKinstry sought and obtained company permission to order divers, and soon men from the Merritt-Chapman Wrecking Company were on hand, but they, too, were unable to secure the ports. With four compartments flooded nearly to the middle deck *Germanic* settled slowly and firmly into the river bottom's mud.

The following morning, Tuesday 14 February, the salvage boat *Manhattan*, owned by Culver Wrecking Company and chartered by Merritt-Chapman, came alongside about 10.30. But her pump was not connected and working until 3.00

Above left *Shown at Liverpool's Princess Landing Stage,* Germanic *plied the North Atlantic route for many years without mishap* (Private collection).

Right Germanic's *ten-to-one length-to-beam ratio, which may have contributed to her New York sinking, is apparent in this dramatic, high-seas photograph* (National Maritime Museum, Greenwich).

Above *Top-heavy with ice,* Germanic *listed. As water poured through open coaling ports, she sank at her pier the night of 13 February. Morning found her submerged but upright* (Marine Engineering).

Right *On her 11 February 1899 New York arrival, ice had to be chipped from rigging and gangways to allow* Germanic's *passengers to leave the ship* (Authors' collection).

pm due to continuing low temperatures and ice in the slip, which made work difficult.

Tuesday afternoon, temperatures rose slightly enabling stevedores to remove ice from *Germanic*'s hull and decks. By that night, ice had been broken away and thrown overboard. At 6.00 pm Merritt-Chapman's own salvage vessel *Hustler* arrived alongside. The pump she placed down number four hatch at 10.00 pm broke down and did not commence work until 8.00 am Wednesday.

Germanic came up at 2.30 Sunday 19 February. After pumping was completed, her hull was sounded and secured, and on Tuesday 21 February she was towed to Erie Basin in Brooklyn, where she

was drydocked for four days. Water drained and the hull's integrity assured, *Germanic* took aboard a grain cargo and departed for Belfast. Crew were paid off on 17 March and the ship taken to Harland and Wolff's Queens Island yard for repairs.

The owners exonerated all of her officers, including Captain McKinstry. Salvage, repair and refurbishing costs totalled £40,000 and *Germanic* soon returned to service. Her first post-accident arrival at New York was 18 June 1899.

Though repaired and refurbished, *Germanic* was now more than 25 years old and aging rapidly. On 23 September 1903 she made her last White

Star voyage before being placed in reserve. Transferred without name change to IMM's American Line, she made her first Southampton-Cherbourg-New York crossing in April 1904 and her last six months later.

Sold in late 1904 to the Dominion Line, *Germanic* was converted at Belfast to an emigrants-only ship and renamed *Ottawa*. Placed on Dominion's Liverpool-Quebec-Montreal service, her first voyage in this role was 27 April 1905, her last 2 September 1909; she then was laid up. The Turkish government purchased *Ottawa* (ex *Germanic*) in 1911, and on 15 March she sailed from Liverpool to Constantinople, where she was renamed *Gul Djemal* and put to work transporting Turkish troops. After several years she was turned over to commercial service, sailing between Constantinople and Black Sea ports.

With the First World War's outbreak she

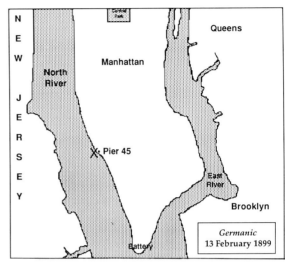

Below *Salvage operations quickly began and lasted several days* (Authors' collection).

Left *As water was pumped out and ice was chipped away, the ship slowly lifted off the harbour floor* (Author's collection).

Below *Surrounded by salvage equipment, her rigging cleared of ice,* Germanic *neared refloating* (Marine Engineering).

Right *One of the North Atlantic's longest-lived liners,* Germanic *of 1874 ended her days in 1950 as the Turkish emigrant ship* Gulcemal, *shown here in a 1930s' photograph* (Authors' collection).

returned to transport duty. On 3 May 1915, while carrying troops, she was torpedoed and sunk by British submarine *E.14* in the Sea of Marmora. With German help she was raised, repaired, and again put into service as a naval auxiliary in the Black Sea. At war's end she was used to repatriate German troops.

Again in commercial service, for the Ottoman-America Line, the 45-year-old liner carried 1,000 refugees — Christians fleeing religious persecution — from Constantinople to New York. The voyage which began 6 October 1920 almost ended in disaster, with United States immigration officers refusing to permit the refugees' entry. Permission eventually was obtained, and the trip proved so rewarding that the Turks undertook four further emigrant voyages to New York via Black Sea and Mediterranean ports, the last being in October 1921.

In 1921–22 the ship was again refurbished and deployed in Black Sea service. Sold to Denizbank Denizyollari Idaresi, in 1928 her name became *Gulcemal*, and she continued in Black Sea passenger and cargo service. Still afloat at Istanbul in 1949, *Gulcemal* served as a stores ship with superstructure cut down but engines still intact. Still later she became a floating hotel-barracks. It was not until late 1950 that this remarkable, durable vessel was disposed of. On 29 October *Gulcemal* (ex *Gul Djemal*, ex *Ottawa*, ex *Germanic*) departed Istanbul in tow for scrapping at Messina.

Twice sunk, twice raised and refitted, this amazing Atlantic record-holder's 75-year career is exceeded only by the 86 years of Cunard's *Parthia*. And *Parthia*, while truly a gallant vessel, was never sunk, and never held an Atlantic speed record. *Germanic*... truly by ice — by age — undaunted.

Accidents and incidents

25 October 1899

As she left her Liverpool dock at 3.00 am to take up anchorage before boarding passengers, *Germanic* was struck on the port quarter by a steam hopper barge, tearing a 12-ft square hole in her hull. *Germanic*'s voyage was cancelled and she returned to her dock for repairs; *Canada* took *Germanic*'s mails and passengers.

11 June 1900	*Teutonic*'s starboard engine broke down, forcing Captain E.R. McKinstry to steam at half speed for 24 hours while repairs were made. Passenger J. Pierpont Morgan 'preserved a calm demeanour and conversed with his usual urbanity in the cabin,' reassuring people, while his daughter 'organized games to keep the more nervous passengers amused and divert their minds from the suspicion that something was wrong with the ship.'
4 August 1900	Fire caused by spontaneous combustion was discovered in *Bovic*'s hold at New York's Pier 49. Captain Thomas J. Jones at once mustered his fire fighting crew and called the city fire department. Lest spreading flames threaten *Oceanic*, moored at the next pier, Jones ordered cargo hold number three emptied of its highly combustible cotton, which was thrown into a nearby street. Damage totalled $1,000.
5 August 1900	Nineteen hours out of Queenstown, fire was discovered aboard *Cymric en route* to New York. It raged for 36 hours before being extinguished. While the ship herself was not damaged, $10,000 worth of cargo in number one hold was destroyed or damaged.
12 September 1900	On her voyage from Hong Kong to San Francisco, *Coptic* grounded at Shimonoseki, Japan, but later got off, apparently without serious damage.
16 December 1900	The freighter *Cufic* lost her propeller at position 51° 34′N, 21° 24′W. The crippled liner was spotted by the Bristol City Line's *Kansas City*, but the latter could not get a line aboard for three days in the heavy weather. Attempting to get a line aboard, *Cufic*'s chief officer, Mr Crosby, drowned. Later, the steamer *Throstlegarth* completed *Cufic*'s tow into Queenstown and thence to Liverpool for repairs. *Kansas City* was awarded £6,800 salvage.
21 December 1900	*Germanic* damaged her port bow colliding with the pier head at Liverpool.
19 January 1901	*Cymric* collided with the British steamer *Caribu Prince* in the Mersey, having several plates stove in and her deck damaged. She left on schedule for New York.
24 February 1901	A huge wave appeared out of nowhere as *Teutonic* sailed in a moderate sea westbound to New York. The wave submerged a deck house, flooding officers' cabins and twisting railings and ladders. Two passengers caught on deck by the flood were seriously injured.
7 April 1901	A bolt fractured in *Majestic*'s starboard engine, forcing the ship to proceed on the port engine alone as repairs were made. *Majestic* arrived in New York nearly a day late.
5 August 1901	The freighter *Georgic* was slightly damaged in a collision with the dock at Liverpool.

7 August 1901	Fire broke out at 5.00 am in a linen closet aboard *Majestic* just before she reached New York. A hole was cut in the decking and water poured in on the fire, apparently extinguishing it. Five hours later, however, smoke again poured from the closet, filling adjacent staterooms with malodourous smoke. Steam was injected into the space. Captain Edward J. Smith said no report of a fire reached him. Others said electrical wires started the blaze.

On the same day, *Oceanic* collided with and sank the coastal steamer *Kincora* in the Irish Channel. Seven crew aboard *Kincora* — half her complement — drowned. *Oceanic*'s bows were damaged. |
24 February 1902	*Doric* arrived in Honolulu a day late after encountering 'fearful storms' *en route* from San Francisco to the Orient.
10 March 1902	*Georgic* collided with the British barque *Oakhurst* at Liverpool; the barque was badly damaged.
25 September 1902	*Teutonic* collided with the Dublin packet *Mayo* at Liverpool. The latter was damaged.
16 October 1902	While at New York, the freighter *Cevic* was run into by a steam dredge and had several plates damaged.
3 January 1903	Cargo was damaged in starboard hold number three when a water tank burst aboard *Coptic* at San Francisco. She proceeded without making repairs.
18 January 1903	Off Fleming Cap, the British steamer *Saxon King* collided with *Georgic*, striking her starboard side at the foremast. *Saxon King*'s davit rails and bulwarks were carried away and her stem was twisted, allowing the forepeak to flood. *Georgic* had several dented plates.
14 March 1903	Fire broke out on the upper cattle deck and the forward part of number five hatch aboard *Nomadic* at Portland, Maine, causing slight damage and jettisoning of 73 bales of scorched or water-damaged cotton bales.
15 April 1903	*Celtic* collided with the British steamer *Heathmore* in the River Mersey. Slightly damaged, *Celtic* put into dock for temporary repairs to a small hole in her port side, amidships.
5 October 1903	Some 145 miles east of Sandy Hook, the White Star freighter *Armenian* signalled 'Not Under Command' to the passing *Finland*, but refused the latter's assistance while repairs were made to machinery.
26 October 1903	A quantity of cotton, leather and general merchandise in *Celtic*'s cargo hold number four was destroyed by fire at Liverpool.

26 November 1903	*Cedric* sailed into New York after having been falsely reported sunk in mid-ocean with all on board by Lamport and Holt's *Titian*. White Star told anxious relatives the report was not credible 'because the *Cedric* is so built that she is practically unsinkable.'
13 December 1903	Amid heavy westerly gales and a snow storm, lightning struck *Teutonic*'s mainmast, wrecking the truck and sending wreckage through a skylight into the dining saloon where passengers were about to begin dinner.
21 March 1904	*Georgic* collided with the British steamer *Kalibia* in St George's Channel. Both ships were able to reach port safely.
3 June 1904	The steamer *Halifax* was forced ashore through a collision with the *Republic* at Boston, but was refloated the next day. *Republic* was the subject of a court action in Boston by the Canada Atlantic and Plant Steamship Co, claiming *Republic*'s officers were negligent. Neither ship was seriously damaged.
31 October 1904	White Star's freighter *Victorian* arrived at Liverpool with 254 cotton bales ruined from a fire that broke out at sea.
17 November 1904	*Canopic* narrowly escaped destruction as Pier 5 of Boston's Hoosac Tunnel Docks caught fire. The liner had to be towed out from the pier to escape the conflagration.
18 November 1904	Four days out of New York, in heavy gales, high seas and snow, a portion of *Oceanic*'s bulwarks was carried away and two portholes smashed, allowing considerable water to flood the vessel.
15 March 1905	*Cedric* was struck simultaneously fore and aft by huge seas on the port side, smashing several ports, carrying away the ship's bell, badly damaging number one hatch's cover, buckling the forecastle's side, and splintering much interior woodwork. At the height of the storm, a baby boy was born in steerage. Also on board were 21 measles cases.
14 May 1905	*Baltic* was delayed six hours due to machinery problems.
28 May 1905	*Majestic* suffered a minor fire at Liverpool.
29 June 1905	The freighter *Tropic* suffered severe damage after going ashore 15 miles north of Constitución, Chile. Her second officer and purser reportedly drowned. After being refloated five days later, it was found that decking beneath the engines had buckled, boiler stays had broken, the bottom had been pushed up under the boilers and machinery deranged.
6 July 1905	Four engineers were scalded in a steam explosion in *Majestic*'s engine room.

28 July 1905   Fire broke out in an electrician's room aboard *Teutonic*, apparently caused by 'improper use of sulphur' during fumigation of the ship while at New York. It was extinguished after one hour.

23 August 1905   Fire damaged woodwork in third class compartment number four as *Oceanic* lay at Liverpool. It was extinguished by ship's crew and did not interfere with *Oceanic*'s imminent departure for New York.

25 December 1905   *Celtic* was struck Christmas night by an immense wave. Water burst into second class areas, throwing holiday merrymakers into a panic, cleaning out 15 engineers' cabins, ruining Christmas dinner, snapping stanchions, carrying away a two-ton gate and smashing two heavy plate glass windows of the second class smoking room.

6 January 1906   *Georgic* caught fire at Liverpool. The blaze caused minimal damage.

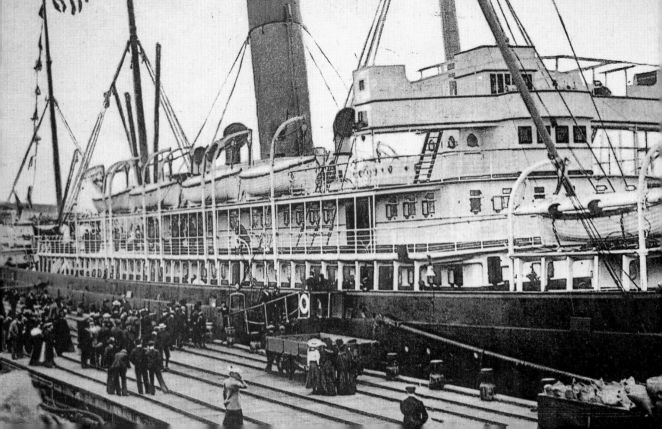

CHAPTER 6

Gothic, 1906

FLAMES AFLOAT

White Star — North Atlantic innovator. Renowned for its comfortable express services between Europe and America. But since its inception, a company with equally strong and innovative ties to Australia and New Zealand. The ships of the red swallowtail pennant with five-pointed white star began their inaugural voyage to Australia on 13 July 1852 when the 1,800-ton *Ellen* departed Liverpool for Messrs John Pilkington and Henry Threlfall Wilson, owners of the original White Star Line.

Within months of his takeover, Thomas H. Ismay decided steam would power the future White Star fleet, and on 27 August 1870, the new company's first vessel *Oceanic* was launched at Harland and Wolff's Belfast yards amid some uncertainty over her intended use; several contemporary sources described her as being 'designed for the White Star Line of Australian packets' which could use the newly-opened Suez Canal to provide fast service to the teeming gold fields in Australia and New Zealand. But *Oceanic*'s twelve-day bunker capacity seemed to restrict her to a far more difficult challenge: the highly competitive North Atlantic run.

As Ismay focused management's attention on building the fledgling steam fleet, sailing ship

Above left Gothic *was owned jointly by the White Star and Shaw Savill lines, and joined their service in 1893* (Alex Shaw Collection, Steamship Historical Society of America).

LeftGothic *offered spacious accommodation for 104 first class and 114 steerage on the 44-day voyage from London to Wellington, New Zealand* (Authors' collection).

passages to the Antipodes continued, under the subsidiary North Western Shipping Company's ownership, but managed by Ismay, Imrie and Company. By the 1880s, White Star's steamship construction programme had more than fulfilled all the company's current needs. With spare tonnage now available, and with White Star vessels successfully crossing the Pacific under an Oriental and Occidental Steamship Company charter, Ismay sought to enter the lucrative New Zealand trade.

The New Zealand Shipping Company and the Shaw, Savill and Albion Company had been locked in a strangling rate war, and Ismay's overtures to the latter firm were warmly received. By 1883, the two companies had agreed to a joint service that would last for more than sixty years. White Star would provide the ships and the crews; Shaw, Savill would provide management on routes they knew well. Later, both companies would build and own the service's vessels jointly.

On 26 May 1884 the 4,300-ton *Coptic* began the first voyage from London to Hobart. *Ionic*, having broken the London-Wellington record in 1883 while under New Zealand Shipping Company charter, was added to the new joint service in December 1884, and in January 1885 her sister ship *Doric* joined the fleet. They were White Star's first steel ships, and their first designed for the Pacific trade.

By 1892 it was clear that additional tonnage was warranted, and Harland and Wolff was instructed to begin work on yard number 267, *Gothic*. The first twin-screw vessel on the New Zealand run, she was the largest and most luxurious as well, with many of the company's North Atlantic innovations

R.M.S. "GOTHIC"

APRIL 3RD 1895

HOT

CONSOMME WITH RICE
CORNED BEEF & VEGETABLES
MACARONI AU GRATIN
BAKED POTATOES
FRUIT PIE

COLD

SALMON
ROAST BEEF
OX TONGUE
CORNED BEEF
BRAWN
ROAST MUTTON
YORK HAM
BOLOGNA SAUSAGE
PASTRY
CHEDDAR   EDAM   GRUYERE

Twin house flags decorated an 1895 Gothic *menu (Auckland Institute and Museum).*

incorporated in her design. Best of all, her huge size permitted significantly increased accommodation and recreation space for her 104 first class and 114 steerage passengers, qualities appreciated on a 44-day voyage.

The 7,755-ton *Gothic* was handed over in November 1893 and began her maiden voyage to Wellington on 30 December 1893, after being visited by thousands. As the largest ship ever to enter the Port of London, she received a rousing send-off.

Gothic returned to London three days faster than planned, making her maiden voyage a resounding success, On her third trip, she broke the ten-year-old record from Plymouth to Wellington, making the passage in 37 days, 10 hours and 16 minutes,

averaging 14.16 knots over the 12,910-mile route. The homeward record soon fell to *Gothic* as well. With a reputation for speed, regularity and comfort, *Gothic* continued on her designed route, a highly popular and successful ship that had set new standards in accommodation, though with some reputation for rolling.

While never formally requisitioned, she carried many New Zealand troops on her regularly-scheduled visits to South Africa during the Boer War. In 1902 she was joined by the first of White Star's new New Zealand vessels, the 12,345-ton *Athenic*, soon followed by *Corinthic* and the second *Ionic*.

On 26 April 1906, *Gothic* left Wellington on a voyage that would test her very fabric and the mettle of passengers and crew. After calling at Montevideo on 16 May and Rio de Janeiro on 20 May, she stopped at Teneriffe in the Canary Islands on 2 June. There large quantities of fruit were added to her already-full cargo which included 22,633 carcasses of mutton, 44,031 lamb carcasses, 1,446 bales of wool, 1,000 sheepskins, 1,364 bales of flax, 576 casks of tallow, 2,258 boxes of potatoes, 543 bales of hemp and 1,000 bags of bran.

The voyage resumed its routine nature as the ship steamed toward London at about 13 knots with a complement of 118 first class and 97 steerage on board. As one passenger later put it, 'We have been on the *Gothic* ever since April 26, and however good company you may have, things begin to go a bit slow after twenty days without seeing land of any kind. When something does happen, there's something to talk about and to think about.'

The 'something' first appeared on the evening of Sunday 3 June when passengers noticed a peculiar greasy odour in the air. Upon leaving the first class dining saloon after dinner, some found the after portion of the ship's upper deck screened off from view. Tight-lipped stewards said only that the cargo was being turned over.

Gothic's Captain Charles A. Bartlett, making his first voyage in his new command, knew better. Late that afternoon, smoke had been observed issuing from number four hold, and ship's officers suspected several wool bales had begun to smoulder. Captain Bartlett ordered steam directed into the hold to quell the outbreak, of still-undetermined magnitude.

Concerned but not alarmed by the persistent odour, passengers spent the night sleeping fitfully. As they came to breakfast the next morning, Bartlett decided to risk opening number four hatch for an inspection. A blast of smoke and heat rose at once. Sailors descended cautiously into the hold. Several smouldering bales soon were hoisted out by the ship's cranes and immediately thrown overboard. Other bales merely scorched by the flames were placed under canvas on the promenade deck. By midnight, clearing damage in number four hold had been completed.

By morning, only a lingering aroma and the presence of several wool bales on decks remained to commemorate what had seemed a close call. But the fire in number four hold was but a prelude.

Wednesday, 6 June. *Gothic* was less than a day's sailing from Plymouth. Once again the pungent smell of burning wool filled the evening air. At first, Bartlett and his officers thought it might be emanating from the scorched bales on deck.

Under section 206 of the company's *Ship's Rules and Uniform Regulations* the *Gothic*'s chief officer was

to conduct his nightly keel-to-bridge inspection at 8.00 pm. As he worked his way forward he passed number four hold where all was quiet. He continued forward, peering in the engineers' mess, walking the corridors through the first class staterooms, through the magnificent domed first class saloon, then descending to the baggage room. The pervasive smell grew stronger, and the room's floor was hot. While there was no smoke, tremendous heat was emanating from cargo hold three directly below, which contained wool, tallow, flax and frozen mutton.

Upon hearing of the situation, Captain Bartlett again put the ship's firefighting procedures into effect, directing several steam jets into the hold to quell this new outbreak. Passengers slept soundly, unaware of the threat below. By morning, smoke began issuing from the mainmast's ventilators high above the boat deck. The steam had little effect.

Now only several hours away from Plymouth, Bartlett decided to keep hatches in place until passengers could be taken ashore and the port's firefighting facilities could be called upon. Steam smothering continued.

The purser's calmly worded notice posted near the dining saloon notified passengers of the new fire: 'Owing to a further outbreak of fire amongst the wool, it is advisable for all passengers to disembark at Plymouth as the steamer may experience considerable delay.' There was no alarm, no panic, no move for the boats. Indeed, when *Gothic* arrived

Homeward bound on 6 June 1906, Gothic's *wool cargo ignited in the hold (1) and subsequently spread to the first class dining saloon (2) (Authors' collection).*

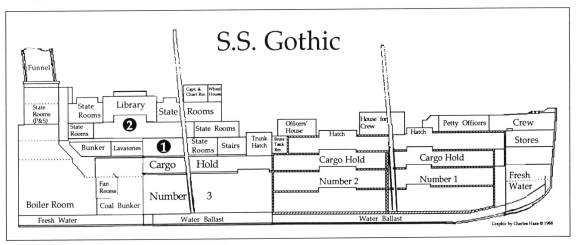

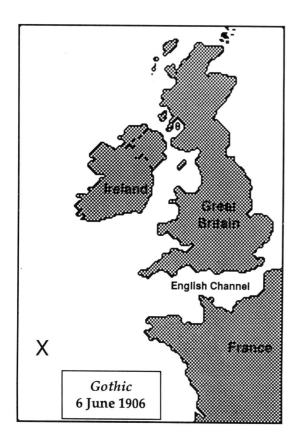

Gothic
6 June 1906

down again. Clearly *Gothic* was no place for spectators. As steam injection resumed, Bartlett hustled the remaining passengers onto a tender by 1.00 pm.

With only crew remaining and with government tugs flanking her, the battle to save *Gothic* assumed new proportions. The tugs began flooding the hold with more than 100 tons of water through eight hoses as the ship's eight steam lines continued their work. Smoke obscured the view for thousands of spectators thronging the Barbican and the Hoe, Plymouth Harbour's promenades.

The first class passengers' baggage was hauled up and piled on deck. The captain, officers, crew and naval personnel struggled to contain the blaze before it ignited the 576 flasks of highly-inflammable tallow beneath the burning wool bales. With men and huge volumes of water shifting her cargo, *Gothic* by 2.00 pm had developed a severe port list which, in her tender condition, could prove fatal should a sudden squall spring up. In consultation with harbourmaster Lockyer, Bartlett agreed that his ship threatened nearby vessels.

Tugs therefore towed the heavily-laden liner into the Cattewater. In her crisis, *Gothic* thus became the largest vessel to enter Plymouth's inner harbour. At about 4.30 pm Bartlett ordered seacocks opened to beach the liner on Clovelly Bay's mudbanks. She touched bottom still listing sharply to port. Captain Lockyer, now directing operations with Bartlett, deployed two large anchors and two tugs to counteract the ship's tendency to fall over on her port side as the tide ebbed.

Ferries crossing the harbour between Phoenix Wharf and Mount Batten found their routes interrupted by the burning liner's presence. Despite the course changes, their business dramatically increased as hundreds sought a closer look at the drama aboard *Gothic*. The heroic struggle continued, but made little headway; the greasy outer coating on the unscoured wool resisted the torrents of water now inundating the hold, while the flax, tallow and frozen carcasses simply fed the flames.

Firefighters often collided with one another or were hit by streams from the hoses in the hold's darkness. They emerged on deck soaked, baked

at Plymouth Sound, more than half the passengers chose to stay on board, watching the crew fight the blaze. At 10.30 am the Great Western Railway tender *Cheshire* brought 101 passengers and the mails ashore under White Star agent Frank Phillips and H.M. Customs officials' supervision.

As the tender moved away, Bartlett ordered the hold's hatches raised. Dense volumes of choking smoke billowed upward, enveloping the ship. Bartlett quickly ordered a flag signal sent to agent Phillips, now ashore, urgently summoning assistance of government tugs from the nearby Devonport naval dockyard.

A glance showed the fire was seated near the bulkheads below and forward of the dining saloon. With 114 passengers still on board, the fire now threatening to engulf the entire forepart of the vessel, and with thick, suffocating yellow smoke everywhere, Bartlett ordered hatches battened

Right *The burning* Gothic *was towed into the Cattewater, Plymouth Harbour, where fire-fighting efforts began in earnest* (Western Daily News).

Right *As tons of water were pumped into her hold,* Gothic *developed a list to port* (Western Morning News).

Below *Enveloped in smoke,* Gothic *provided a thrilling spectacle to thousands gathered along Plymouth Harbour's shores* (Western Daily Mercury).

and blackened. The intense heat and icy water caused plates to buckle on the starboard side, amidships.

Meanwhile deck cargo was being discharged into barges alongside, aft, while frozen meat and other perishables below were shielded from smoke by three or four layers of tarpaulin until they could be removed. After hours of toil, *Gothic*'s men were beginning to show the strain but would not quit while their ship's survival was at stake. Dozens of reinforcements were summoned from the shore.

Spreading upward, the flames soon penetrated the dining saloon, burning a large hole in the forward flooring while carpeting throughout the room smouldered. All hoses that could be spared were diverted to save the room as fire-extinguishing hand grenades were thrown into the fire without effect. As the flames were beaten back temporarily, workers salved as much of the saloon's furniture as they could, bringing it up on deck. Water was directed on the forward bulkhead which flames now had breached.

The fire continued its relentless course, and during the night sailors and stewards worked together to remove everything portable — chairs, tables, curtains, a piano, bedding — from the dining saloon, the music room and the adjacent first class cabins. The purser and several of the crew sent their personal belongings ashore.

By 7.00 pm, the list had increased, but the wind soon changed direction and the tide fell, causing the ship to assume a more upright position as the fight continued through the night. Pumping had ceased by 4.00 am on 8 June: the fire was out. A Plymouth physician boarded the ship to tend to officers and crew who had been severely affected by heat and dense smoke. Several who slept on deck, utterly exhausted from their efforts, cried out in pain when they tried to open eyes sealed shut temporarily by heat and smoke. Amazingly, these were the only casualties.

The salvage steamers *Lady of the Isles* and *Rescue* now joined government tugs in pumping out the tons of water on board. Damage assessment began

Left *As her portside rails draw ominously close to the water,* Gothic *is beached* (Western Morning News).

Right Gothic's *splendid first class dining saloon is shown here before the fire....* (Auckland Public Library photograph collection).

...and after reconstruction **below** *as* Gothland, *transformed into austere emigrant accommodation* (Harland and Wolff collection, Ulster Folk and Transport Museum).

under the leadership of Captain McCurdie, White Star's marine superintendent. Signs of battle presented themselves in abundance. Paint was scorched everywhere. Woodwork was charred and burned. The deck had been torn up and splintered. The beautiful saloon was 'a picture of desolation,' completely gutted and ruined by fire and smoke damage, a huge hole in the floor and another in the forward wall.

Below the saloon, a large open space with pieces of charred wood floating about marked the former location of the first class staterooms. The main deck had been partially destroyed, with planking burned through in many places and its iron supports bent and twisted while red-hot. Cargo hold number three had been gutted, then flooded. Damage to the cargo alone was estimated at £200,000 (nearly $1,000,000).

By 6.00 pm the liner was refloated, and it was decided to return her to Plymouth Sound. Pumping operations continued to correct the persistent heavy port list. By 9 June, operations were completed. In feeble pre-dawn light *Gothic* departed Plymouth at 4.00 am, resuming her interrupted trip to London. Berthed at the Royal Albert Dock on 12 June, she was given another thorough examination by White Star officials and insurance adjusters.

Board of Trade consultant R.J. Friswell came aboard, too, and found the fire had begun at the lower hold's starboard side, just abaft the mainmast. The oxidation of surface grease caused by air and moisture had encouraged the spontaneous combustion of the wool. The tallow beneath had melted, feeding the fire. As a result of *Gothic*'s fire, new recommendations were circulated among shipowners regarding safe stowage of wool and other combustible cargoes.

Damage indeed was extensive, and a lengthy refit would be required before *Gothic* could return to service. Since Shaw Savill was about to add two vessels, *Arawa* and *Tainui*, to the joint service, *Gothic* would not be needed on her old route following the refit. Accordingly, she was transferred to

the Red Star Line — like White Star, now a component of the International Mercantile Marine Company — and renamed *Gothland*. Harland and Wolff transformed her into a third-class-only ship with several changes in external appearance. *Gothland* sailed from Antwerp for New York on 11 July 1907. In the spring of 1911 the liner crossed from Hamburg to Quebec and Montreal, and on 24 June made her last Antwerp-New York crossing.

She then returned to White Star under her original name for two years of service on her old New Zealand route. On her first 'homecoming' voyage *Gothic* carried more than 1,500 settlers to Victoria, Australia. It was then back to Red Star — again as *Gothland* — for further service from Antwerp to New York or from Rotterdam to Montreal.

Disaster befell her yet again on 23 June 1914 when she struck the Gunner Rocks off the Scilly Isles while homeward bound from Canada. Impaled there for three days, *Gothland* finally was towed off after her 281 passengers had been evacuated. The seriously-damaged ship limped into Southampton for repairs lasting months.

She made several voyages between New York, Falmouth and Rotterdam for the Belgian Relief Commission during World War I, and later made several cargo-only voyages on the old Antwerp-New York route before resuming passenger ship status between Antwerp, Southampton and Baltimore in August 1920.

In 1921, now a dowager, *Gothland* made several voyages from Danzig, Hamburg and Corunna. She spent 1922 out of service, but sailed between Antwerp, Vigo, Havana and New York in 1923. In November 1925, the old liner was sold for £16,000 to breakers in Bo'ness, Scotland.

Fate had spared *Gothic* from destruction by fire and later, as *Gothland*, from loss through grounding. But for the captain who had so courageously battled the flames with his crew, Charles A. Bartlett, fate would have yet another challenge in store...

Accidents and incidents

3 November 1906	*Baltic* caught fire in number five hold while at Liverpool. The hold was flooded and the fire put out, but 640 cotton bales were damaged by fire or water.
6 November 1906	Five steerage passengers were injured when a derrick fell onto *Cymric*'s deck during a gale off the Irish coast. Heavy seas shifted some of her cargo, causing a list and forcing her to heave to for four hours.
7 December 1906	A bad fire in *Celtic*'s number four hold caused $6,000 damage to her cargo before flames were extinguished.
16 February 1907	As *Republic* entered Naples harbour, she collided with the Italian steamer *Centro America*. Both ships were damaged.
8 March 1907	Heading for New York, *Baltic* ran aground $1\frac{1}{2}$ miles outside Sandy Hook and remained there for several hours before floating free. As she began her next eastbound voyage, she collided with and sank a loaded coal barge under tow off 6th Street, Jersey City, New Jersey.

CHAPTER 7

Suevic, 1907

SHIP SURGERY

Almost since the original White Star Line's inception, Australia had been considered an important and profitable destination, and company links to 'The Land Down Under' were strong. Some thirty years after *Royal Standard* sailed between Liverpool and Melbourne, Thomas H. Ismay and his management colleagues decided the company should return to the Antipodean route, with steamship service to Australia and New Zealand.

For the Australian run, Harland and Wolff's draughtsmen soon transformed company specifications into plans for five vessels of two similar designs. The first three comprised *Afric*, *Medic* and *Persic*, each of about 12,000 tons. Each offered 12,500 tons of refrigerated cargo capacity, including space for about 100,000 frozen carcasses. Accommodation was provided for 350 third class passengers who enjoyed full use of all on-board facilities including a smoking room, a dining room seating all in one sitting, and reading room. In 1905, the fare was just £19.

The ships had low, lean profiles — one funnel, four tall masts, little superstructure. Each was propelled by twin quadruple-expansion engines developing 5,400 horsepower for a 14 knot cruising speed. Huge bunkers allowed them to make outward or inbound voyages without additional coal.

Launched on 16 November 1898, *Afric* was to make the first modern White Star voyage to Australia. She was handed over 2 February 1899, but surprisingly was sent to New York for her maiden voyage six days later. White Star may have decided upon a 'shakedown voyage' to test the new design; deficiencies noted during the voyage resulted in *Afric* returning to Belfast for seven

months of modifications.

Yard number 323, *Medic*, had the honour of the first Australian voyage, beginning in Liverpool on 3 August 1899. Making his first White Star voyage, her fourth officer, Charles Herbert Lightoller, later of *Titanic* fame, said of *Medic*'s arrival in Sydney, 'She was a show ship, the biggest that had ever been out there, and the people in

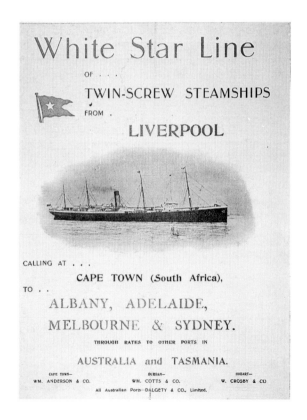

Below left *White Star's Austra-lian service began with* Medic *in 1899, and was subsequently adver-tised in flyers and handbills* (Authors' collection).

Right *Though scarcely luxurious,* Suevic*'s general room provided utility and comfort on the long voyages out and home* (Ulster-Folk and Transport Museum Photographic Archive: Har-land and Wolff Collection).

Right Suevic*'s smoking room was open to all passengers, as was her entire accommodation* (Ulster Folk and Transport Museum Photographic Archive: Har-land and Wolff Collection).

Australia gave us the time of our lives. Everything and everywhere it was *Medic*.'

Persic joined the fleet on 16 November 1899. With low fares, spacious and comfortable facilities, steadiness in almost any weather and no class distinctions, White Star's first three Australian vessels were resounding successes. Modifications made to the final two ships, *Runic* and *Suevic*, increased their capacities. After well decks were filled in and their bridges were sited further forward. Tonnage rose to about 12,500; an additional eighty passengers could be carried. *Runic* was delivered on 22 December 1900; *Suevic* joined the fleet on 9 March 1901, and was at once requisitioned as a Boer War transport.

Indeed, trooping duties greatly hampered the new route's establishment, and it was not until 1902 that the envisioned monthly service could be provided. Outward, ships called at Las Palmas, Cape Town, Albany, Adelaide, Melbourne and Sydney. Homeward, they added Durban. For almost six full years following her release from government service, *Suevic* sailed almost without incident upon her intended route.

The return portion of one such voyage began 2 February 1907, as *Suevic* left Melbourne for London and Liverpool via Cape Town, Teneriffe and Plymouth. On board were 382 passengers including more than eighty children, 141 crew and two stowaways. The latter, both in their twenties, boarded at Sydney. After several days at sea, one sought and received permission to work for his passage; a day later his colleague followed his lead.

A large £400,000 general cargo included several thousand frozen meat carcasses. Commanding *Suevic* was Thomas Johnson Jones, a White Star veteran with 39 years at sea, 35 with White Star and seventeen as a master. This was his final voyage before retirement.

Arriving at Teneriffe on 12 March, *Suevic* departed the following day for Plymouth in clear, fine weather. With a following sea her speed exceeded 13 knots. By Saturday 16 March, winds shifted to the south and west, and a high sea developed. Dinner was a bittersweet affair for Captain Jones. His longed-for retirement was tempered with memories of three decades' service to the

company. Dinner was followed by the final shipboard concert. Jones was touched when his crew presented him with an address; passengers joined in presenting a testimonial in appreciation of his 'good qualities and able seamanship.'

By noon Sunday, *Suevic* was 138 miles from Lizard Light and England's southern coast. Approaching this hazardous area filled with rocks, tricky currents and changeable winds, Captain Jones should have given the headlands a wide berth. But fine weather had deteriorated to a dark, thick night with fog, drizzle and showers, and Jones wished to close in on Lizard Light for a four-point position fix before shaping course for Eddystone Light and Plymouth. The sea became rough.

Lizard Light had already augmented its powerful beam with its fog detonator booming warnings regularly. A 10.00 pm check on the log showed *Suevic* had travelled 122 miles since noon, and should now be within the light's range. Course and speed were maintained despite difficult weather. At 10.15 pm the light's glare was spotted directly ahead and low on the horizon. On the bridge, the chief engineer and officers discussed its appearance. Based on the light's height above the horizon, the latter estimated it to be ten miles away.

They could not know that all afternoon, a flood tide, strong sea swells and freshening southwesterly winds had pushed *Suevic* along. Nor did they know that a low-lying cloud layer may have acted as a reflector, altering the light's apparent height. An order for soundings to be taken was countermanded because of the officers' mistaken assumption.

At 10.00 pm, a lookout shouted, 'All's well.' He could not have been more wrong. One regulation after another from the Company's *Ships' Rules and Uniform Regulations* appeared to be ignored:

'105. In hazy weather, observations are of doubtful value, and fog signals on shore are liable to fail. It should, therefore, be borne prominently in mind that in all cases where the land is approached in thick or hazy weather, the frequent use of the lead is to be regarded as the only really reliable proof of the ship's safe position. When approaching the land in thick or hazy weather, frequent sounds are to be taken, quite regardless of the delay which this may occasion, and in no case is any confidence to be placed in a single cast, but lines of sounding should be taken... with the utmost caution, and any neglect or failure to comply with this will entail the gravest consequences upon anyone who may be found in fault.

'108. A safe berth is to be given to all headlands, islands, rocks, shoals and the coast generally....

'109f. [The officer of the watch] is expected to make himself thoroughly conversant with the usual Channel courses, and to be thoroughly posted in the run of the ship. Any doubt he may have as to the safety of the position of the ship or of the course steered he will immediately express to the Commander in a respectful manner.

402. [The chief engineer's] presence in the Engine Room when the ship is entering or leaving port, docking or undocking, or in any other special circumstances *is imperative.*'

Within moments of spotting Lizard Light, lookouts heard two or three blasts of the lighthouse's fog signal. Still no course change was ordered. At 10.25 pm *Suevic*'s chief engineer, still

on the bridge, spotted the light, and crossing the deck to get a better view of it, saw rocks close to the ship's port side. He ran at once to the engine room.

Lookouts now sang out, 'Breakers ahead!' and the light towered high over the ship. To his horror, Jones realized that his ship was in imminent danger close to shore. Immediately he ordered helm hard-a-port, causing a turn to starboard under indirect helm orders then used.

The ship had turned just two points before she struck rocks at her full 13 knots. The time was 10.27 pm. Captain Jones' farewell voyage ended abruptly with a violent grounding on the sharp pinnacles of Maenheere Rocks, just a quarter-mile from Lizard Point. Up she rose over one boulder, then crashed down upon another before coming to rest with a slight list.

Most passengers had retired, hoping to get a good rest before disembarkation the next day. Others had assembled at small farewell parties in

Suevic lies helplessly after running hard aground off Lizard Point (Mariners Museum, Newport News, Va.).

the ship's public rooms. One lady, it was reported, had been experiencing a dream in which *Suevic* capsized. In another cabin, several gentlemen were discussing a photograph of a shipwreck.

But there were no doubts that something was very wrong. Another passenger, a Mrs Duka, recalled, 'We went on with a terrible crash and I was suddenly thrown from one side of the cabin to the other'.

Meanwhile, Jones and his officers desperately tried to free the ship from the rocks' grasp. Engines were stopped, then reversed at full speed. Despite their best efforts, *Suevic* remained fast. Engines were stopped again.

Immediately upon impact, portholes and watertight doors were closed and all hands were summoned to clear away lifeboats for launching while others called the passengers. Few had to be wakened. Many poured on deck clad only in night clothes, carrying their possessions. They were told, 'Leave everything alone. Come up on deck and be ready.' A Mrs Blair, a patient in the ship's hospital, aft, was almost thrown from her bunk. She was met at the hospital door by Dr J.J. Marsh, who said almost nonchalantly, 'Keep quiet. Nothing has happened — we've only gone aground.' A steward then told her they'd only struck a piece of wreckage, but urged Mrs Blair to dress.

They arrived on deck looking anxious and frightened, but calm. Women and children were taken to the ship's library, men to the dining room, where coffee was offered. Crew constantly reassured everyone there was no immediate danger as they distributed life belts. Captain Jones himself went round telling everyone to be calm and quiet, then superintended preparation of lifeboats. There was no sign of further settling, and with the crew's careful ministrations, calm was maintained.

A survey revealed that fully one-third of the ship was hard aground, pinioned amidships by rocks causing further hull punctures with each wave. Minute guns were fired and distress rockets seared the sky, but soon disappeared in the heavy fog. For at least a half hour, no one ashore saw them. Coastguardmen at Lizard Light at last heard the volleys and initiated rescue procedures. Land-based lifeboats from the Royal National Lifeboat Institution's Falmouth and Lizard bases rushed to the stricken liner, joined later by boats from Cadgwith, Mullion, Porthleven and Coverack. Townspeople from Cadgwith hurried to the beach where lifeboats would land.

As word was received on board that help was on the way, evacuation of *Suevic*'s women and children began. It was decided to lower boats to the water where passengers would board them from ropes and rope ladders down the ship's side.

The large number of young children posed an immediate problem. Able seaman George Andersen and mate Bill Williams took charge of little ones in their strong arms. Said Williams, 'First, we carried a mother and then her babies so as to keep them together as much as we could. I tell you, the way some of those mothers clasped their bairns and God-blessed me made a lump come into my throat. I felt I could have swum ashore with the babies if need be.'

Several children were dropped into boats, amazingly suffering no ill effects. But a young mother who would not be parted from her child slipped and fell into the boat, being rendered unconscious with a deep head wound. One sailor, Mr O'Brien, broke his collarbone when the rope he was using to lower himself into the boat snapped.

At last the first boat was filled and pushed off from *Suevic*'s side with great difficulty, waves threatening to dash it to pieces. Thirty women and children huddled in water up to their knees as crew bailed water frantically.

With its occupants totally drenched, the boat finally arrived on Cadgwith beach, where anxious townspeople waded out in shoulder-deep water to bring the children ashore. When all passengers were safe, a lusty cheer sprang up, reassuring those aboard *Suevic*. Wrapped in blankets, they were taken to nearby private homes and a hotel. Later they were taken by automobile and bus to the nearest railroad station at Helston for departures to Plymouth and London.

The lifeboat returned for more passengers even as the second boat rounded *Suevic*'s lee side to come ashore; only with aid of the shore-based lifeboat men, now arriving, did this boat successfully negotiate rocks and heavy seas. It, too, returned to

Suevic but was smashed to pieces on the rocks as it neared the ship's side. Again, shore-based lifeboats rescued the liner's crew.

Having witnessed several casualties in launching and manoeuvring the two boats, Captain Jones suspended evacuation; it simply was too dangerous. Passengers and crew calmly awaited dawn's arrival, many never leaving the deck. *Suevic*'s crew worked hard to maintain morale. The ever-increasing fleet of shore lifeboats maintained vigil throughout the night.

By 7.00 am, the fog began to lift, and evacuation proceeded more rapidly using both ship- and shore-based lifeboats. When all women and children were gone, it was the men's turn — although already there were allegations, subsequently found to be baseless, that two Salvation Army officers had left with the ladies. In the drive to complete evacuation as quickly as possible, plans to prosecute the two stowaways were dropped.

It took six hours to ferry *Suevic*'s passengers ashore. Jones next sent non-essential crew away. More than 600 people were evacuated successfully under most trying conditions. It had been a difficult night for the Royal National Lifeboat Institute's men — several hundred yards from *Suevic*'s position, and several hours later, Elder Dempster's liner *Jebba* went ashore with seventy passengers aboard. With lifeboat facilities already taxed by *Suevic*'s predicament, rescuers evacuated *Jebba*'s complement via breeches buoy rigged from Lizard Point lighthouse. *Suevic*'s rescue, however, remains among the largest number of lives saved at any one incident by the Royal National Lifeboat Institute. But *Suevic*'s story was only beginning...

Constantly pounded by waves, she now was shifting slightly in her rocky cradle. Though leaking badly in numbers one, two and three compartments, her after compartments were dry; she clearly would not sink soon, nor could she withstand punishment indefinitely. Local observers felt there was no chance of refloating the liner and every possibility she would break in two. Advised of *Suevic*'s plight, White Star's Liverpool office at once contacted the Liverpool and Glasgow Salvage Association, who dispatched two powerful salvage tugs, *Ranger* and *Linnet*, to the scene.

Captain Jones and a skeleton crew of about eighty remained aboard with boilers fired to maintain power. As weather moderated three days later, coasters and barges were sent to receive the ship's discharged cargo and passengers' baggage. A large number of additional passengers — a consignment of parrots and parakeets — somehow escaped and flew ashore, eluding capture.

Discharge of cargo continued round the clock, weather permitting, under large clusters of electric lights. By 22 March, there was 26 ft of water in the forepeak, 28 ft in number two hold, 25 ft in number three hold, 12 ft in the bunker hold. *Suevic* was grinding heavily on rocks, with extensive hull damage and deck fracturing. The foremast was forced upwards 3 inches.

By the following day, aft holds had been almost emptied, though frozen meat carcasses had been ruined by lack of refrigeration. One entrepreneur inquired whether he might purchase the condemned meat to turn it into tallow.

Drama was not confined solely to *Suevic*'s predicament. Roads to Lizard Point were clogged with motor vehicles, bicyclists and pedestrians going to the wreck site. The carnival atmosphere came to an abrupt halt on Saturday 23 March when a young bicyclist dismounted her cycle to fix its dislodged air pump. The driver of a following automobile swerved to avoid her and his car overturned, throwing out its occupants, several of whom were injured. On Sunday, 22-year-old Benjamin Williams was killed after being thrown from a borrowed bicycle and sustaining a broken neck *en route* to the wreck. The crowds — and bicycle accidents — continued into the week. Tuesday 26 March saw 10,000 visitors to the site.

On Tuesday 26 March, nine days after the disaster, an amazing decision was reached: while one-third of *Suevic* was hopelessly aground, the remaining two-thirds contained her most valuable portions, including most of her accommodation, her boilers and machinery, all in perfect condition. After careful assessment, it was proposed to sever the bow to salvage the stern portion.

The concept had precedent: on 16 September 1898 Elder Dempster's liner *Milwaukee* ran aground at Port Errol, near Peterhead, England.

Above *Amputated by 300 dynamite charges, Suevic's bow remains impaled as tugs begin to pull the stern toward Southampton* (Illustrated London News).

Left *Waves begin demolition of Suevic's abandoned bow* (Authors' collection).

Left *Storms have gouged ragged chunks from the bow, which remains miraculously afloat* (Sphere).

The Liverpool Salvage Association used dynamite cartridges to separate bow from stern, the *Milwaukee* was towed stern first to Swan, Hunter & Wigham Richardson, her builders for a new bow, and nine months after her accident she returned to service.

But *Milwaukee* was a ship of only 7,317 tons. Would obstacles raised in salvaging a ship almost twice that size prove insurmountable? On 26 March, the Liverpool Salvage Association received word via telegram from White Star Line's Liverpool office: 'Owners approve salvors severing vessel with view to salving after portion.'

Later that day, to prevent further damage, divers used underwater dynamite charges to blast the twin rock pinnacles that had repeatedly pierced *Suevic*'s hull. Meanwhile, engineers had calculated the best place for separation, at a point 180 ft from the bow, just forward of the second mast but aft of the bridge. The bulkhead immediately aft of the proposed spot was stiffened to withstand heavy water pressure with 12-in pitchpine baulks placed fore and aft up to the orlop deck.

Meanwhile, divers and other workers swarmed over the area placing a series of gelignite charges weighing 2 to 10 lb against the hull. All cutting would have to be done from the outside, as forward holds still were water- and cargo-filled. Each charge was wrapped in canvas and kept in position by sand bags or chain clusters hung over them. Each was detonated electrically. Throughout the charges' placement, heavy swells caused divers to lose their footholds on ladders or the ocean floor. Frequent suspensions of diving operations delayed the work.

The first blast at 8.00 pm Tuesday 26 March exploded with a muffled 'thump,' penetrating *Suevic*'s bottom; one by one further blasts severed starboard side plating. Captain Jones warned of the explosions' danger in the local press:

'As it is intended to sever *Suevic* by dynamite, in addition to a red flag by day and a red light by night, notice is hereby given that as blasting operations are now in progress on the steamship *Suevic*, all boats are warned to keep a safe distance from this ship. There is great danger to all craft in the vicinity of these operations. Visitors

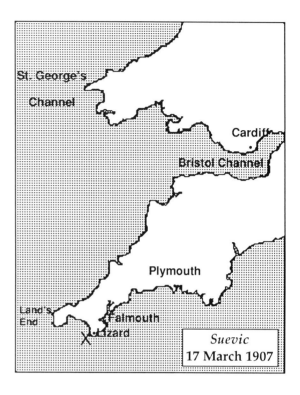

Suevic
17 March 1907

are, therefore, warned not to go afloat. (Signed) T.J. Jones, Commander, ss *Suevic*.'

The warnings indeed were necessary: one explosion had sent an iron shard hurtling a half-mile away. All around *Suevic* the sea was spattered with raining debris. Danger lurked on board, as well; one man was seriously injured by an explosion.

Soon after 1.00 pm on 28 March, the area was buffeted with heavy westerly swells, salvage ships' hawsers snapping repeatedly. All those aboard *Suevic* were ordered to leave, abandoning the ship to the elements. By now, much of the intact holds' cargo had been landed. With weather now suspending operations, the question was whether salvors or the elements would claim the weakened hull.

On 29 March, the Board of Trade's solicitor began preliminary steps for convening an inquiry into *Suevic*'s grounding. By now weather had abated, and blasting operations resumed. Inch by inch, foot by foot, explosive blasts — more than 300 in all — severed *Suevic*'s very fabric, as men inside the liner cut through deck plating.

Saturday 30 March brought a personal tragedy as two teenagers were charged with stealing £1 19s from the Great Western Railroad station's refreshment shop. 'We wanted some money to go to the Lizard to see the wreck,' the older one told the magistrate. He was sentenced to three years in reform school; his accomplice was fined.

Sunday was scarcely a day of rest. In dense fog that evening, a liner proceeding east narrowly avoided running into the wreck, coming within 50 yards. Only the sounding of *Suevic*'s whistles averted a catastrophe.

With each blast the gap between bow and stern widened, increasing workers' risk. In danger of being forced by swell or current into the opening, they clung grimly to any available handhold while placing charges. The ship was grinding heavily, alternately opening and closing the gap. As the after end of the ship began to roll independently of the forward part, jagged plate edges posed a constant threat of amputation. Thousands of thawed and putrified rabbit and sheep carcasses exiting through the gap added to divers' difficulties.

As work neared completion, arrangements were finalized for towing off the severed stern portion. *Suevic*'s engines were kept under steam for a full day before work was completed. Five heavy anchors were laid out in a semi-circle astern, linked to

Suevic by steel wire hawsers kept taut by the ship's winches. These would prevent the after portion from crashing forward on incoming waves. After six days, it was time for the final explosion to sever main deck plating. As the two portions bucked and reared on a heightening sea, men crawled to the edges of the cut to place the final charge.

Aft, the tugs *Ranger, Herculaneum* and *Blazer* strained at their hawsers. The electrical wires were connected. The moment had come. Already the barometer had begun to fall, indicating heavy weather was ahead. If *Suevic* did not come off the rocks now, she never would. It was moments after high tide, 7.00 am on Tuesday 2 April.

With a muffled roar, charges were detonated and *Suevic*'s engines were put full astern. According to a Reuters representative:

'The heavy swell from the Atlantic increased, and it was obvious that the turbulence of the water would assist the parting of the vessel. It was proved to be the case, for with loud sounds of grinding and snapping the after part of the *Suevic* began to rise and fall buoyantly in the swell, showing unmistakably that the disunion of the vessel, which has been laboriously attempted for the last fortnight, had at last been achieved in spite of the heavy seas.'

Said another witness of the moment of separation,

'It seemed as though the liner herself was struggling to be free from the embrace of the rocks which had held her for far too long.

'Suddenly, spectators on the headlands saw the after portion of the *Suevic* rise out of the water to a height of seven or eight feet and then, as it came down on the forward section, there was a snapping and crashing of timber, which was immediately followed by an explosion. The last shot had been fired and the *Suevic* had been severed.'

A quick inspection of the stiffened bulkhead disclosed no leaks, and at 9.00 am some 400 ft of *Suevic* began the final leg of its interrupted voyage, travelling stern-first, propelled by her twin screws the entire way. The 184 ft abandoned bow section lay forlornly on the rocks, visited only by seagulls.

Slowly, patiently, the assemblage moved eastward at five to six knots, with *Ranger, Herculaneum* and *Blazer* towing and *Linnet* serving as *Suevic*'s rudder. Now serving as *Suevic*'s master was Captain Murray, Captain Jones having been relieved.

Threats of heavy weather had set Plymouth as their destination. She would be beached there, temporarily repaired, then dispatched to Belfast for permanent repairs. But the storm veered off, and with White Star concurrence Captain Murray proceeded directly to Southampton.

Past Black Head, Rame Head, past Eddystone Light. Heavy weather returned, but progress continued. On past the Needles and Spithead, where Murray waited for daylight. At noon on 4 April, *Suevic*'s stern reached Southampton and was escorted to the River Test Quay where a large crowd of sightseers struggled vainly for a closer look. White Star officials, including Lord Pirrie, boarded the vessel immediately for inspection and determination of her future.

Two days later, she was berthed in Southampton's number six graving dock, and once water had been pumped out, the full nature of *Suevic*'s state was determined. There was remarkably little damage evident: three starboard plates near the keel were indented two to three inches. There had been no straining of the hull, and the heavy steel keel had been severed as cleanly as with a knife. Above, jagged plates at the separation point required only trimming.

As workers at John I. Thornycroft's Southampton repair yards began clearing wreckage, Harland

Above left *Tugs escort two-thirds of a liner into Southampton Harbour* (Sphere).

Right *As pumps labour, Suevic's stern is manoeuvred toward a Southampton drydock* (Authors' collection).

Above *Workers have cleared damaged decking and plating, and prepared a new rib structure for Suevic's replacement bow (Authors' collection).*

Right *At Harland and Wolff's Belfast yard, a heavy steel bulkhead serves as the new bow's stern (Sphere).*

Above right *Launch flag fluttering, Suevic's new bow goes down the ways at Belfast on 5 October 1907. (Harland and Wolff collection, Ulster Folk and Transport Museum Photographic Archive).*

and Wolff's Belfast yard already was constructing a new, 212-ft bow section, the extra length providing overlap for re-assembling the hull. The bow was to be launched bow-first from normal ship-building ways. So confident was Harland and Wolff about the forthcoming 'bow-launch' that another vessel was begun at the berth's opposite end. So confident were White Star in their builder's competence that the date of *Suevic*'s first post-accident voyage was announced while the bow still was on the stocks.

On 5 October, the launch — a first in maritime annals — provided momentous spectacle for thousands of sightseers gathered along the River Lagan. On-board weights had been carefully calculated to provide proper trim. In seconds, the new bow, complete with deck machinery and a new bridge, was afloat and shepherded to a fitting out basin where final preparations were completed. These included the shipping of two lifeboats and painting her name and port of registry on the after side of the final bulkhead, temporarily her stern.

On 19 October the tugs *Pathfinder* and *Blazer* towed the bow round to Southampton, arriving some six days later after encountering heavy weather in the Irish Sea. Additional preparations to the bow delayed its installation.

On 4 November the drydock containing *Suevic*'s stern was flooded and the bow section gently, carefully was nudged in. Special temporary guide plates — and scrupulous adherence to original blueprints — assured perfect alignment of the two parts. Water again was drained, and work of attaching bow to stern began. Electrical, plumbing, mechanical and ventilating systems, control cables between bridge and engine room — all required reconnection. Mechanical riveting, not yet invented when *Suevic* had been built, actually improved hull strength.

On the afternoon of 8 January, some ten months after her disastrous voyage had ended, *Suevic* left drydock and proceeded to a coaling berth. It had taken two months of hard work, careful planning and skilful ship surgery to reach this day, when *Suevic* lived to sail again. She sailed for Liverpool on 10 January, and again was visited by Lord Pirrie. The workers had done their task well; as adver-

Above left *The tugs* Pathfinder *and* Blazer (*out of picture*) *tow* Suevic*'s replacement bow to Southampton* (Authors' collection).

Far left *Surgery for a ship is performed delicately as heavy horizontal girders precisely align* Suevic*'s two portions* (Authors' collection).

Left *Workers proudly display the final rivets of* Suevic*'s restoration* (Authors' collection).

Above *Returning to Liverpool early in 1908 after successful surgery,* Suevic *continued until 1928 on Australian service* (Authors' collection).

tised, *Suevic* left eight days later on her voyage to Australia via the Cape, Captain Mathias in command. Among her cargo was a collection of live animals so varied that the press called her a 'floating zoo.'

The ghost of *Suevic*'s close call returned to haunt White Star in June 1908, when the County Council of Cornwall filed suit against the company for £50, seeking reimbursement for expenditures incurred under the Diseases of Animals Act in burying and disposing of thousands of rabbit and mutton carcasses. White Star disclaimed liability, saying these were not carcasses in the sense intended by the act, but the county court judge ruled against them. White Star appealed to a divisional court, and again was ordered to pay Cornwall's costs.

Later, the Board of Trade's wreck inquiry issued its own findings. They came down hard on Captain Jones, now retired:

'A good and proper lookout was kept, but insufficient allowance was made for the effect of the weather upon the range of the light when it was first seen... The stranding of the *Suevic* was caused by continuing towards land at high speed in thick, hazy weather, without making any allowances for tide or current, and continuing the same course and speed after the light was seen without taking the usual precaution of using the lead to verify position.

'The ship was not navigated with proper and seamanlike care after 10.00 pm of the 17th March...

'The stranding and consequent damage to the *Suevic* was caused by default of the Master, and while giving full consideration to his previous record and his conduct after the casualty, the Court cannot avoid dealing with his [master's] Certificate, which is hereby suspended for three months.'

Suevic was to have a long and successful 'second life' with White Star. After serving during the First World War under the Liner Requisition Scheme, *Suevic* made her first post-war voyage to Australia on 2 February 1920.

At the end of 1920 she was extensively refitted at Portsmouth, her accommodation being upgraded to provide for 226 second class passengers only. Eight years later she made her final White Star voyage. In October 1928 she was sold to Yngvar Hvistendahl, Finnvhal A/S, of Tönsberg, Norway for £35,000, and converted in Kiel to the whaling factory ship *Skytteren*. This time, the ship with a second bow received a second stern containing a ramp up which whale carcasses could be hauled.

War forced *Skytteren*'s internment at Gothenberg, Sweden in April 1940. Two years later off the Swedish coast, *Skytteren*'s crew made a desperate attempt to escape to Britain but German Navy patrol boats intercepted her. On 1 April 1942, hopelessly outgunned, *Skytteren*'s crew made a difficult, if necessary, decision, and scuttled their ship off Maseskjaer to prevent her capture.

Perhaps words written in *The Engineer* at the time of her miraculous rescue and reincarnation might serve as her epitaph: 'We need not dwell upon the reputation for excellent workmanship rightly enjoyed by Messrs. Harland and Wolff. Even they must have been pleased with the behaviour of this vessel of theirs under most trying circumstances.' And for almost another generation, White Star's patrons enjoyed the comfort of a ship that had returned from the lost.

Accidents and incidents

13 April 1907	*Baltic* collided with and sank a loaded coal barge while leaving New York for Liverpool.
20 May 1907	As substitute labourers replaced striking longshoremen in removing cargo from White Star's freighter *Armenian* at New York's Pier 40, cork and bleaching powder caught fire in her number one hold. The blaze, which was extinguished in a half-hour, was ruled 'suspicious' in origin.
3 June 1907	An arsonist, possibly in league with striking dock workers, set fire to cargo in *Oceanic*'s after hold while she was docked at Pier 48, New York. Among the cargo destroyed was the scenery of noted actor Forbes Robertson. All bedding and fittings of the after steerage women's quarters were ruined. The fire was under control after two hours, having done several thousand dollars worth of damage and delaying *Oceanic*'s voyage several days.
12 July 1907	In dense fog off the Nantucket Shoals lightship, *Romanic* ran down and sank the 66-ton auxiliary fishing schooner *Natalie B. Nickerson*. Three of the latter's crew of 18 fishermen were lost, the remainder being brought to Boston aboard *Romanic*.
12 October 1907	White Star's livestock carrier *Bovic* collided with the schooner *Excelsior* off Tuskar Light. The schooner struck *Bovic* a glancing blow on the port side, but neither vessel was damaged.

25 November 1907	As the freighter *Armenian*, inbound from New York, was docking at Liverpool, the tow rope of the tender *Magnetic* parted, allowing *Armenian* to be carried against the wall of Sandon Dock's half-tide entrance. Several plates on her port quarter and starboard side amidships were dented. She berthed in Canada Dock for survey.
	Cretic put in to Algiers for repairs after her main steam pipe burst. She was *en route* from Naples to New York when the accident occurred.
31 January 1908	A fire on board *Majestic* at Southampton gutted her smoking room and several cabins before it was extinguished.
29 August 1908	*Baltic* suffered a severe fire in her forward holds while at New York. Fire and water damage totalled $10,000.
10 October 1908	Four *Adriatic* crewmen were accused of looting passengers' baggage. Plunder worth $15,000 was discovered in hiding places throughout the ship.
26 November 1908	Four lives were lost when *Georgic* collided with the 2,600-ton American passenger liner *Finance* off Sandy Hook, New Jersey. Proceeding through dense fog at very low speed, *Georgic* rammed *Finance* in the port quarter, and within five minutes, the latter had heeled over 30°, forcing 150 aboard to jump into the sea or run for lifeboats and rafts. When *Finance* sank, she took with her a cargo valued at $300,000.
9 December 1908	A heavy wooden railing was torn from the bridge, and bridge supports were badly twisted when *Celtic* encountered a high wave while bound for New York.

CHAPTER 8

———————————— ————————————

Republic, 1909

WIRELESS WONDER

On 1 December 1902, Margaret Bruce Ismay, widow of White Star's founder Thomas Ismay, recorded in her diary the White Star Line's sale to J. Pierpont Morgan's American combine, the International Mercantile Marine Company:

'Messrs. Morgan have paid all the Shareholders of the Oceanic Steam Navigation Company for their shares. This ends the White Star Line in which so much interest, thought and care was bestowed and which was my dearest one's life's work. Bruce continues with the firm as Manager.'

Far from marking White Star Line's end, the £10,000,000 transaction began a new phase marked by an ambitious building programme and near-monopoly on the North Atlantic. IMM owned White Star, Red Star, Atlantic Transport, Leyland, Dominion, Inman and American Line fleets, and had reached rate agreements with Holland-America, Hamburg-America and North German Lloyd. Indeed, of Britain's major shipping companies, only Cunard evaded purchase, and only with government loan assistance for *Lusitania* and *Mauretania*.

Despite the combine's huge fleet, White Star was considered its prestige component, and deci-

Above left *Launched as* Columbus *for the Dominion Line,* Republic *began White Star Service in 1903 on the Boston-Mediterranean route* (Steamship Historical Society of America).

Left *On White Star's intermediate Boston summer service,* Republic *soon became a popular vessel. She sailed between New York and Mediterranean ports in winter* (Steamship Historical Society of America).

sions during Bruce Ismay's tenure as its new president and managing director continued to favour his father's company. Almost immediately ships began to be shifted from one component company to another to maximize IMM profits and streamline operations. Almost immediately too, White Star assumed Dominion Line's profitable Liverpool–Boston and Boston–Mediterranean routes. The four newest and finest Dominion liners — *New England, Commonwealth, Mayflower,* and *Columbus* — became White Star's *Romanic, Canopic, Cretic,* and *Republic,* respectively. Two Dominion ships on the stocks at IMM's takeover, *Albany* and *Alberta,* were renamed *Laurentic* and *Megantic* prior to launch.

Launched 26 February 1903, the 15,378-ton *Republic* made her first White Star voyage in December after two Dominion trips. She sailed between Liverpool and Boston in summer, New York and the Mediterranean the rest of the year.

'The White Star Line services from New York and Boston to the Mediterranean provide the ideal entry into this vast treasure-house of the art, history and literature of untold ages,' a 1909 brochure proclaimed. The treasure house turned to turmoil on 28 December 1908, as *Republic* lay at Genoa. Five hundred miles to the southeast, citizens of Messina battled for their lives. A catastrophic earthquake had reduced the entire city to ruins, killing 85,000 people and beginning a large migration of survivors — some to Italian points, others, in a more permanent move, to the New World.

Republic departed Genoa on Wednesday 30 December, as scheduled, and left Naples on Saturday, 2 January with several earthquake survivors

Left Republic's *spacious boat deck is depicted in a 1907 White Star publicity brochure* (Authors' collection).

Below *On 10 January 1909 the Lloyd-Italiano liner* Florida *left Naples with 838 passengers and a cargo of macaroni* (Authors' collection).

Below right *After a 22 January New York departure* Republic *sailed for the Mediterranean* (Authors' collection).

on board. Far more heavily booked was the 5,118-ton Lloyd Italiano liner *Florida*, which left Naples for New York eight days later with 824 steerage and fourteen cabin passengers and a general cargo, principally macaroni.

Arriving at New York on 14 January, *Republic* discharged her passengers and cargo, then was readied for her next eastbound crossing. Bookings had been moderately heavy as Americans sought to escape winter's cold.

Captain William Inman Sealby supervised provisioning and cargo stowage. It included 650 tons of supplies worth $61,000 (£12,700) for Rear Admiral Sperry's fleet: large quantities of fresh and smoked meat, turkeys, potatoes, sugar, butter and eggs. The first relief supplies for Italy's earthquake victims came aboard along with, rumour had it, $250,000 in gold for the American fleet at Gibraltar.

Relatives and sightseers cheered as *Republic* sounded whistles warning of her imminent departure 22 January. They scattered when, at the last moment, Mr and Mrs H.A. Hover of Spokane, Washington raced in their car down the pier's length, just managing to board before gangways were hauled up; they were beginning a 100,000-mile round-the-world journey.

Several steerage passengers also arrived with seconds to spare. At 3.00 pm the last hawsers were dropped away and *Republic* began to edge into North River. As she glided slowly backwards, she sideswiped the steamer *Bermudian*, causing several hundred dollars' worth of damage to her.

After a brief delay the voyage resumed. Yet another late passenger, Italian commissioner Dr. Pietro Gilliberti, was ferried out to *Republic* on a tugboat. Out past the Statue of Liberty she sailed. Soon she passed Sandy Hook Lightship, and quickly increased speed to her usual 16 knots. As *Republic* began her voyage, *Florida* entered the final 36 hours of her westbound trip. It had been a quiet passage, and already immigrants were talking excitedly about their New World arrival.

By dinner time, as *Republic* cleared Long Island's eastern end, passengers noticed a thin vapour settling down. By 9.00 pm, it had thickened considerably, but there was little speed reduction. Soon *Republic*'s whistle was sounding every two

Left Republic's *first class dining room reflected a home-like atmosphere* (Authors' collection).

Left *A large skylight formed the first class library's ceiling* (Authors' collection).

Right *At 5.45 am on 23 January 1909 the* Florida's *bow pierced* Republic's *hull abaft the funnel.* Republic's *boiler and engine rooms began flooding immediately* (Robert Fivehouse collection).

minutes as she angled toward the Nantucket lightship marking the transatlantic sea lanes' western terminus. There she would head southeast to her first port of call in the Azores.

By 11.00 pm most passengers were asleep; a few nursed final cigars in the smoking room. Some believed speed had not been reduced despite further thickening of fog; others maintained she was

'poking through it.' Midnight arrived, 23 January began.

Florida, too, had begun to encounter fog, first in wisps, then in dense banks, then continuously. She, too, began sounding her fog whistle at 90-second intervals and slowed down. Thus two ships, with more than 1,500 people aboard, began a tension-filled nautical version of 'Blind Man's

Buff.' Captains and lookouts strained to see and hear through the murk as passengers slept fitfully, awakened frequently by the mournful blast of fog whistles.

As she neared the Massachusetts coast, *Florida* turned southwest, seeking the Nantucket lightship. Lacking wireless and submarine signalling apparatus, Captain Angelo Ruspini hoped for a direct sighting from his doubled lookout. But the dense fog intervened, and Ruspini now resorted to a less precise method of finding the lightship.

'It is customary for in-bound steamers from European ports approaching the coast...in thick weather to hunt for the 30-fathom curve, which sweeps down 40 miles from Nantucket Island, and just outside of which is anchored the Nantucket South Shoal Lightship. Vessels failing to pick up the lightship in the fog keep on sounding until they strike this 30-fathom curve.

'To the westward of the lightship there is a mud bottom, and this also gives a pretty definite position for vessels trying to get their bearings.'

Just thirty miles separated eastbound and westbound 'traffic lanes' at this point. As *Florida* sailed southward, she swept past the lightship and into eastbound lanes in which *Republic* sailed. Perhaps when the sun rose in an hour or so, the fog would lift...

At about 5.42 am both captains heard whistles. On *Republic*, Sealby heard a blast off the port bow, and immediately ordered 'full speed astern' and 'hard a port.' Out of the fog several bright lights, including both port and starboard sidelights, materialized. It was *Florida*, heading directly for *Republic*'s side. In a desperate attempt to avoid collision, Sealby now ordered full speed ahead, hoping to outrace disaster.

On board the Italian ship, Ruspini heard a whistle blast to starboard, and answered with his own. 'In a few seconds there was something like a mountain straight across the path of the *Florida*,' he recalled. With *Republic* crossing from starboard to port, he ordered a starboard turn to swing his vessel behind *Republic*.

There was insufficient time to effect the manoeuvre. With a shuddering but almost silent impact, *Florida*'s bow crashed squarely into *Republic*'s port side just behind the funnel, tearing a vertical cut from promenade deck to well below the waterline.

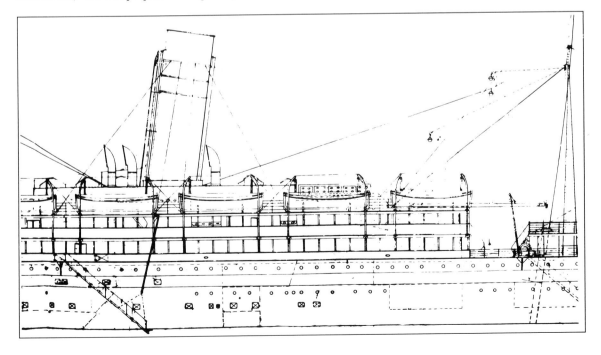

'To many passengers the impression was given that there had been an explosion on board, as the blow...was followed by a dull, roaring sound, and subsequently a noise like the tearing and rending of tinder,' a reporter on board *Republic* wrote.

Wireless operator John Robinson Binns had just turned in after a long day sending 'Good Bye' messages. The sole operator on board, he had fallen asleep immediately:

'The shock of the impact shook me out of my bunk. A crunching, ripping noise followed as the *Florida*'s bows crumpled up on our side. The panels and [port] side of our cabin fell in, one panel being smashed to splinters...My first impression was that we had run ashore, which was strengthened when I peered through the interstices of the wrecked woodwork of my cabin and saw a dark object outside, over which the sea was washing. This I took to be a rock, but later found it was boat number 15 which is always swung out from the ship...[it] had been torn from its davits.'

Soon after sailing, Mrs Herbert L. Griggs had exchanged cabins with Mr and Mrs Michael J. Murphy of Grand Forks, North Dakota. She 'was awake when the crash came. The lights went out, the ceiling dropped in, the electric light wires fell on me, and some of the partition as well. I felt something holding me down, and found that it was a mattress that had been driven in from the next room.'

Mrs Griggs was fortunate. On the saloon deck, *Florida*'s bow had crashed into staterooms 30, 32 and 34, severely wounding Mrs Murphy and fracturing her thigh. Had the cabin exchange not taken place, Mrs Griggs would have been in the destroyed cabin 30. Amazingly Mr Murphy was only cut and bruised.

In cabin 34, Mr and Mrs Eugene Lynch had been enjoying their voyage. Noted Boston philanthropists, they were going to help with Italy's post-earthquake relief efforts. Debating whether to travel by Cunard or Hamburg-America, they had chosen *Republic* on a friend's recommendation. Mrs Lynch was crushed by the collision; her husband sustained multiple right leg fractures, severe internal injuries, contusions and shock.

In adjacent stateroom 32 Mr W.J. Mooney of Langdon, North Dakota was killed instantly. His wife, on the room's opposite side, escaped miraculously: the stateroom's crushed woodwork formed an arch over her, protecting her from injury.

Rev John W. Norris, a New Jersey clergyman, was thrown from his bunk by the impact:

'I had on only my pyjamas when I reached the deck. Soon a steward came up and said that several passengers had been apparently badly injured in their staterooms. I started to go to the staterooms when the lights went out. I had to feel my way and fight against the stream of passengers in the corridor.

'When I got near the point of impact I could hear the water rushing in. I reached Mrs Lynch before she died and ministered to her. She seemed to be conscious. In getting to the adjoining stateroom I had to swing myself across a chasm made in the side of the vessel. The cold water caught me and nearly carried me away, but I was just able to swing myself into what had been Mr Mooney's stateroom.

'I pried out a bunk which had been crushed against the wall. There I found Mr Mooney in a frightful condition, almost dead. Both he and Mrs Lynch were dead before I left them. When I had completed my religious errand it was too late to reach my own stateroom for clothing...'

As *Republic*'s passengers and crew struggled to make sense of sudden chaos, the disaster's other participant, *Florida*, disappeared into the fog. Aboard her, too, there was confusion — and panic. Filomena Cayliafern, a cabin passenger, had been unable to sleep, and was on deck at the moment of collision.

'I walked forward and was peering into the darkness ahead when the hull of the approaching vessel came into view almost ahead of us. There was more and hurried whistling, and then...the bow of the *Florida* went crunching into the side of the *Republic*. There was a shock through the *Florida*, and I gripped hold of the rail. It seemed to me that there were two distinct blows struck. The bow of our steamer seemed to rebound a bit from the *Republic*, and then the two vessels came together again...'

For *Florida*'s steerage, many survivors of Messina's earthquake, the jolt awakened very fresh memories of disaster. Another cabin passenger, Dominic Roberto, saw their fear:

Above far left *After assessing damage, Captain William Sealby ordered* Republic*'s immediate evacuation* (Authors' collection).

Above middle left *Though the wireless room was virtually destroyed in the collision, operator John Robinson Binns remained at his key almost 36 hours, through the entire time of the ship's sinking* (Authors' collection).

Above left *Soon after the collision* Florida*'s Captain Angelo Ruspini faced a near-panic of his steerage passengers, many of whom had recently survived the great Messina earthquake* (Authors' collection).

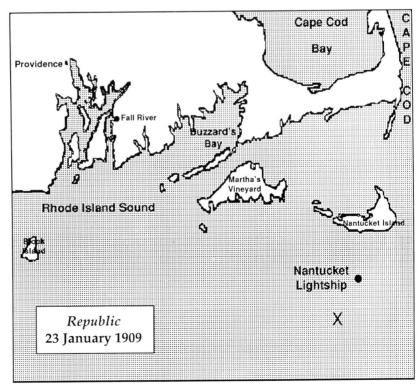

Above *As the dynamos failed, Republic's corridors and staterooms were plunged into darkness. At the base of the grand staircase stewards distributed candles to anxious passengers who thronged the corridors* (Harland and Wolff Collection, Ulster Folk and Transport Museum Photographic Archive).

Left *Summoned by Binns' battery-powered signals, the Cunarder* Lucania *arrives at the collision site, where the sinking* Republic *is photographed by one of her passengers* (Authors' collection).

'Already the steerage passengers awakened from sleep were swarming in terror to the deck. Looking down from the deck we could see them by the light of the ship's lamps running about, some crying, while other huddled under the side of the deckhouse; others were praying.

'All was excitement when the ship's officers went about among the half-crazed, praying crowd and assured them that there was no danger. Some were soon quieted, but others had to be almost driven below before they would cease their wails. In the end a measure of quiet was restored. It was a wildly exciting time and among us all there was a great feeling of unrest and anxiety until we were told that the *Florida* had not been hit in a vital spot and that she would keep afloat. This anxiety was intensified when we saw the crew spring to the boats and get them ready to be dropped into the water.

For some 30 ft, *Florida*'s bow was crushed. Three crew members, asleep in their quarters, were killed instantly. Among them was fourteen-year-old seaman Salvatore D'Amico, who, after losing his entire family and his home in the earthquake, had signed aboard *Florida* to escape the horrible memories. With her first two compartments flooded, *Florida* perceptibly settled by the bow but appeared in no imminent danger.

On *Republic*, meanwhile, Captain Sealby received damage reports: 'Promenade deck railing twisted and broken. Lifeboat 15 torn away. At least two passengers dead in their cabins; injuries everywhere.' Most frightening of all: water was pouring into the engine room and boiler rooms at a rate far beyond the pumps' capacities. Within five minutes, it short-circuited the dynamos, plunging the ship into darkness. The 'black gang' struggled in waist-high water to draw boiler fires. Fourth Engineer J.G. Legg bravely turned on the injector valves, lowering boiler pressure and preventing an explosion. Watertight doors had been closed just before the collision, but could the bulkheads withstand the tons of water now pouring in?

Passenger alleyways were thronged with anxious people who relied on matches, a few flashlights, candles and lanterns lighted by stewards to find their way to upper decks, pausing at the base of the grand staircase to obtain lifebelts. The hubbub of concerned conversation and shouts of crew in swinging out boats failed to mask sounds of water flooding the hull.

Several of *Republic*'s steerage passengers excitedly ran to the lifeboats and tried to climb in until ordered away by a revolver-toting officer. Elsewhere, petty officers circulated among pyjama- and night-gown clad passengers, reassuring the nervous and restoring order. The crew's presence at emergency posts within minutes quickly calmed people. Two distress rockets fired from the bridge called upon the stranger to return to *Republic*'s aid.

Wireless operator Binns, meanwhile, had ascertained that while three walls of his wireless cabin had collapsed, his Marconi transmitter still functioned — though it now was powerless. He struggled toward the bridge to report to the captain but was blocked by wreckage littering the deck. Returning to the wireless cabin he searched for emergency storage batteries: 2,000 lives depended on his success. Diving into a flooded adjacent compartment, he found and connected them.

Within half an hour he transmitted a preliminary message to the Siasconsett, Massachusetts Marconi station: 'The *Republic*. We are shipwrecked. Stand by for Captain's message.' Came the cheery reply: 'All right, old man, where are you?' A messenger then arrived to escort Binns to the bridge for instructions; on the way they passed stewards distributing coffee to passengers.

With Sealby's CQD* authorization, the message faltered outward on battery power — *Republic*'s set now had but a fifty-mile range — but was repeated by Siasconsett's powerful station: '*Republic* rammed by unknown steamship. Twenty-six miles southwest of Nantucket lightship. Badly in need of immediate assisance, but no danger to life. Sealby.'

With his ship noticeably settling by the stern and no hope of stemming the flooding, Sealby faced realities of evacuation: insufficient boats for everyone on board; eighty miles to the nearest land. Providentially, the source of damage became the source of deliverance: as *Florida* drifted into

---

*The distress signal, comprised of 'CQ,' meaning 'all stations, attention,' plus 'D' indicating urgency, took effect 1 February 1904, with the appellation 'Come Quick, Danger' quickly becoming popular misconception. A 1908 international conference ratified SOS but it was not yet in general use when *Republic* needed assistance.

FALLING STAR

view in response to the White Star ship's repeated whistle blasts, *Republic*'s officers arranged via megaphone for transfer of passengers and crew to the less-damaged Italian ship.

At about 7.00 am Sealby addressed passengers on deck from the bridge:

'Passengers of the *Republic*: I want to advise you that the steamer has been injured in collision. We are in no immediate danger, but I want to ask you to stand by me and act with coolness and judgment. There is, I repeat, no immediate danger; but to be on the safe side it is necessary for you to be transferred to the *Florida* as soon as possible. It will take some time, and I expect that you will be cool and not excited. Take your time getting into the lifeboats. Remember, the women and children go first, and the first cabin next, and then the others. The crew will be the last to leave this vessel.'

As crew prepared lifeboats for lowering, *Republic*'s passengers calmly waited, one sitting on deck playing solitaire, another putting up her hair, others sitting on their lifebelts. Several tried to bribe stewards to go below for additional clothing or baggage. Other stewards volunteered the service.

Binns, meanwhile, had limited sending to conserve battery power. In addition, in the dark he had accidently broken his sending key and had to hold the pieces together with one hand while transmitting with the other. He heard Siasconsett rebroadcast the distress message, and welcome promises of help from several ships, including *La Lorraine*, *Furnessia*, *Lucania*, *New York* and White Star's own *Baltic*.

One by one, passengers in bulky lifebelts struggled down pilot and accommodation ladders to the bobbing boats, each taking about twenty aboard, *Florida*'s boats assisting in the evacuation. As they crossed to the *Florida*, passengers could see *Republic*'s damage clearly for the first time. Crew members had rigged a tarpaulin over the hole to slow flooding and prolong the ship's life.

The injured passengers and crew proved difficult to lower over the side, but within two hours, all passengers had been removed without incident — in order of gender, age and class — and the crew began their departure. Sealby and 45 crew, in-

cluding Jack Binns, remained on board, waiting for rescue vessels — especially the *Baltic*. There remained a chance that *Republic* could be towed into shallow water and beached. The bodies of Mr Mooney and Mrs Lynch, placed in coffins, remained behind on the promenade deck.

Those transferred to the *Florida* found conditions less than ideal. As one passenger wrote:

'They covered every deck of the smaller steamship so thickly that there was no room to move about. Here the passengers huddled together for fifteen hours, suffering from cold, hunger and thirst. The *Florida*'s officers did the best they could to give assistance, but they were carrying a large list of immigrants, and as the vessel was in the condition you might expect from that fact, they could do but little for the comfort of the *Republic*'s passengers.'

Meagre food was accompanied by red and white wine and constant mournful sounds from *Florida*'s fog whistle. An attempt to provide the rescued with clothing failed, as *Florida*'s passengers themselves had so little to spare.

Baltic had been near Montauk Point, Long Island, some 64 miles away, when her wireless operator Henry J. Tattersall and assistant G.W. Balfour received news of *Republic*'s danger from Siasconsett at 6.00 am: '*Republic* wrecked and needs assistance; position, latitude 40.17 north, longitude 70 west.' They immediately advised Captain Joseph B. Ranson, who turned round toward *Republic*'s position.

Siasconsett kept Binns — and Captain Sealby — informed. By now, *Republic*'s wireless operator was suffering intensely from the cold and damp which penetrated gaps in the collapsed, unheated wireless cabin. There was no question of leaving for a moment to warm up through exercise, for a vital

Above right *Florida*'s penetration into Republic's hull and her subsequent scraping along Republic's side are clearly visible. In a vain attempt to stop the water's inrush, a canvas tarpaulin patch has been rigged by Republic's crew (Steamship Historical Society of America).

Right Republic's captain and mates, faithful to the end, stand on the sinking liner's after deck house as lifeboats hover nearby (Private collection).

message could be missed. His clothes, still wet from his underwater battery search, clung to his body, and he began to grow numb and stiff. About 2.00 pm his thoughtful steward Douglas brought food and coffee. Eventually, Binns realised exercise was essential if he weren't to freeze, and he decided to take messages to the bridge himself.

'The first time I went to the bridge, I was so chilled I was shaking from head to foot. My teeth rattled and I was scarcely able to talk. Captain Sealby said, "Don't be afraid, Mr Binns, we will see that you get off all right."

'I smiled and told him it was the cold and not fear that made me shake and prevented me from talking audibly.'

With blankets from faithful Douglas, Binns carried on.

Fog persisted throughout the day. As light began to fade late in the January afternoon, it became apparent that *Baltic* could not find *Republic* in the murk. *Republic*'s hours were dwindling, the badly overburdened *Florida* had developed a list and lacked wireless should she require assistance. She could not move, lest forward motion break the bulkhead holding back the sea.

Baltic's Ranson estimated they had covered 200 miles zigzagging through the area. Where was *Republic*? Binns added another clue: 'Have picked up Nantucket submarine bell north-northeast. Soundings 35 fathoms.'

Ranson reversed course whenever he 'lost' the submarine bell or when soundings exceeded 35 fathoms. Since *Baltic* could now read him directly, Binns believed her nearby. Agonizing minutes passed. Binns again:

'The most anxious hour was at about 6 o'clock in the evening, when Captain Sealby heard, only faintly, the explosion of a bomb in the far distance. He at once communicated with me and I [learned] that the *Baltic* had been exploding bombs to apprise us of her whereabouts. We, too, had been exploding bombs, but exhausted our supply, and from now on had nothing but our almost-exhausted and fast-weakening wireless apparatus to which we could pin our hopes of rescue.

'The *Baltic* then informed me that she had but a solitary bomb left, and arranged with us that this would be exploded at a certain moment.'

On *Republic*'s bridge, Sealby ordered his skeleton crew to form an outward-facing circle, each man

Left *After spending the night aboard* Baltic, *some of* Republic*'s crew return to stand by their captain to attempt to save their ship (Sphere).*

Above right *After transferring her passengers to* Baltic, *the battered* Florida, *a canvas patch covering her bow, limps towards New York (Daily Mirror).*

listening intently. At the agreed time, *Baltic*'s crew detonated the final explosive. Five seconds passed. Then Binns reported he thought he heard a faint sound. The third officer next to him thought he heard it too. A bearing was taken, and Binns scurried back to the wireless shack to send it to *Baltic*.

'...A little later we heard the *Baltic*'s fog horn blowing faintly and this increased in volume as she lessened the distance between us. Occasionally we fired rockets but they could not be seen through the fog, although a little later the *Baltic*'s siren was heard so plainly that we knew the ship was close by. Realizing this, Captain Sealby issued orders that the *Baltic* be told to proceed as carefully as possible, as she was now too close on our port side to be safe.

'I had just communicated this message when I heard a cheer, and I at once realized that these sounds of rejoicing could not come from our men, as only Captain Sealby, the officers, myself and the crew were aboard our ship, and they were all busily engaged in standing by the boats.

'Looking aft through my splintered cabin I made out the *Baltic* quite near to the stern of our ship...She was a blaze of light and as I sat there in my little cabin, the thought occurred to me that the most beautiful sight in the world is a ship at sea, especially when that ship is needed to supply a link between life and death.'

Sealby now ordered Binns to send a final message: 'Come to our leeward and take up our boats. Have *Lorraine* and *Lucania* convoy the *Florida*. Wireless now closed.' The exhausted operator then joined officers and crew in the lifeboats. At long last, fog began to lift and rescue ships were spotted. Among them was the Standard Oil whaleback steamer *City of Everett*. Captain Thomas Fenlon said:

'About 3.00 pm we sighted the *Republic* on our port bow close aboard. Headway was taken off the speed...We drifted very slowly close by the *Republic* and offered to assist him. We offered to tow him to shoal water.

'He [Captain Sealby] said he was in communication with his New York office and that they were sending

Merritt and Chapman's wrecking fleet to assist him to make port.

'We then went to the ss *Florida* and offered her captain our assistance. He said he was waiting for the *Baltic* to arrive near him to take off passengers of the *Republic*...

'At about 5.00 pm we were alongside the *Florida* close enough to see the condition of the hull...The only thing keeping her afloat was the tightness of the number one bulkhead...The sea was so smooth that the lifeboats were laying [*sic*] very comfortably alongside [the *Florida*] with no danger of damage whatsoever. At 6.00 pm we launched our number one lifeboat and crew in charge of the first officer and instructed him to make it clear to both captains that our ship was entirely equipped for wrecking and towing.

'Our offer to tow, made the second time, was again refused...All my offers of assistance having been refused, I decided to leave the scene of the collision and continue my voyage...

'In my own mind I feel assured that had the master of the *Republic* engaged the *City of Everett* on arrival at the scene of the collision at 3.00 pm January 23, 1909, we

A Brooklyn drydock receives Florida's *twisted hull* (Steamship Historical Society of America).

would have had the *Republic* anchored in [Martha's] Vineyard by noon January 24th. Of course, this is only one man's opinion.'

Sealby knew the revenue cutters *Gresham* and *Seneca* — equipped with towing equipment — were on the way; perhaps also on his mind was the size of the potential salvage award *City of Everett* might earn. Upon her 7.30 pm arrival — after more than twelve hours of searching and a half-day of fear amongst those aboard *Florida* — *Baltic* passed *Florida* and went at once to *Republic*. 'Why didn't she take us off?' passengers demanded to know. One unsubstantiated rumour had it the $250,000 in gold allegedly on board was being removed.

By 11.30 pm *Baltic* finally completed operations alongside *Republic*. In a conference on *Baltic*'s bridge, Sealby and Ranson confirmed plans for transfer of all aboard *Florida* to *Baltic* and hopes for *Republic*'s salvage.

Under the blinding glare of *Baltic*'s searchlights the second evacuation now began shortly before midnight. *Republic*, *Florida* and *Baltic* lifeboats began ferrying the 1,650 passengers and crew to the latter's safe haven. Again, evacuation was by gender and class, but this time first class men preceded steerage women and children. One American first class passenger demanded to know, 'Will somebody tell me why saloon should be given preference over steerage in a case like this?' The *Republic* officer stationed at the head of the accommodation ladder merely glared.

Transfers were made more difficult by heavy seas and rain. Passengers were forced to climb a pilot's ladder upon arrival. Two women lost their

Right *Florida's accordion-pleated bow is all that remains of her crews' quarters. Three crewmen were killed instantly* (Authors' collection).

Below *Her foredeck thronged with her own passengers and Republic's survivors,* Baltic *triumphantly enters New York Harbor* (Leslie's Weekly).

grasp and plunged into the sea; they were plucked out at once by nearby lifeboats. The injured in their stretchers were hauled up by ropes, the last to come aboard *Baltic*. Eugene Lynch, so severely injured, remained aboard *Florida*. The transfer had taken an exhausting seven hours.

At 10.00 am Sealby and a skeleton crew returned to await the promised tow. Amazingly, Binns was able to reactivate the wireless and Captain Sealby was kept informed of the tugs' slow progress toward his position. Binns said,

'By this time the [Anchor liner] *Furnessia* had arrived and had been standing by; then the *Florida* came alongside the *Republic*, remaining there as a safeguard for those of us left on our ship, and the *Baltic* took up her journey to New York with her tremendous burden of human freight. As she steamed by our stern, every living soul aboard the *Baltic* gave us a hearty cheer.'

Florida, too, now limped off to New York under her own power, under watchful escort. *Baltic*'s Captain Ranson immediately wirelessed word of the successful operation to White Star's New York offices.

Republic drifted, powerless and helpless in the mist. Binns busied himself by repairing the shattered wireless cabin, nailing up several blankets to stop the cold. A volunteer cook brought the crew lunch; spirits began to rise. While *Republic* had a severe port list and was heavily down by the stern, she seemed to be settling quite slowly.

At last the revenue cutter *Gresham* arrived. After a megaphone conference, *Gresham* put two steel lines and a hawser onto *Republic*'s bow, while *Furnessia*, serving as a rudder, attached hawsers aft. An axe was placed near the *Gresham*'s lines; if an immediate separation became necessary, Sealby would burn a blue Coston light. The goal was now simple: beach *Republic*.

Sea conditions, the hawsers' breaking strength, *Republic*'s weakened condition — all dictated a slow procession to *Gresham*'s Captain Perry: at one, perhaps two knots, the trio moved ahead.

By 4.00 pm *Republic* had shipped so much water that Sealby ordered the crew to lifeboats and transferred to *Gresham*. After almost 36 hours at his key, broken only by several hours of rest aboard

Baltic, Binns abandoned his cabin for the last time. Despite his crew's entreaties, Sealby refused to leave his ship, but asked for one volunteer to remain with him. Second officer Richard J. Williams, the senior unmarried man, was selected for the lonely vigil.

At about 5.00 pm the ships were joined by the cutter *Seneca* which had come from the Virginia coast to assist. By 8.00 pm they had travelled six miles toward shore, the half-submerged 15,000 ton liner becoming increasingly unmanageable. The cutters and other ships standing by kept *Republic* in the glare of their searchlights.

By 8.30 *Republic*'s taffrail was submerged, and it was apparent that her final moments had come. On the bridge, Sealby and Williams knew it. Said the captain,

'We could tell it was coming...Suddenly we heard a rumbling and then a cracking sound aft, and the stern of the *Republic* began to go down rapidly.

'I turned to Williams and said, "Well, old man, what do you think about it?"

' "I have an idea it won't be a long race now," Williams answered, "and when you are ready I am."

' "Burn the blue lights," I said, and then, as a signal to the *Gresham* that it was time to cut the hawsers that bound her to the *Republic*, I fired five shots into the air from my revolver. That was the beginning of the last few minutes of the *Republic*. "Take to the fore rigging; get as high as possible," I shouted to Williams.

'From the bridge deck to the saloon deck, both of us carrying blue lights, Williams and I ran. When we got to the saloon deck the water was already coming over that deck aft, and we could see the stern sinking rapidly, the incline of the deck as we ran forward becoming so steep that we began to slip with every step...

'About that time I saw Williams for the last time on the *Republic*. He was hanging on to the port rail, and dim as was the light, I saw he was as game as ever. I took to the fore rigging and climbed up about 100 ft. In my pocket was a blue light, and I took it out, but it would not go off. There was still one more shell in my pistol, however, and I fired that.

'Down, down, down went the *Republic* and soon she was entirely submerged, and a moment later I was in the water. I wore my greatcoat, and the air getting under that made it support me, while the binoculars, the revolver and the cartridges in my pockets acted as a sort of ballast...The water around me by this time was seething and roaring due to the suction caused by *Republic* as she sank, and several times I was carried down, only to be churned back to the surface.'

The great *Republic* disappeared stern first into 30 fathoms of water. After a long wait in frigid water, Williams and Sealby were rescued by a lifeboat from the *Gresham*.

A varied aftermath followed *Republic*'s loss. William Sealby was acclaimed for devotion to his ship and his strong leadership after the collision. Eugene Lynch died from his injuries soon after arrival in New York aboard *Florida*. The remainder of the injured eventually recovered.

White Star immediately took legal action against the *Florida*, seeking damages for the loss of its ship, her cargo, three passengers' lives and all passengers' belongings. Under American law, the maximum they could recover was *Florida*'s value, her freight money and her passengers' fares. Combined, these came to less than ten per cent of the $2,000,000 sought.

Florida was repaired and in 1911 sold to another Italian company. Six weeks before the eighth anniversary of her collision with *Republic*, she collided with the Italian auxiliary cruiser *Caprera* and sank. *Republic*'s name faded from view until 1987 when an American salvage expedition tried, unsuccessfully, to find the gold allegedly on board. Many artefacts, however, were recovered and placed in a Massachusetts museum.

Above left Baltic's *heroic Captain Joseph B. Ranson oversees his vessel's docking* (Authors' collection).

Right *A crush of reporters, relatives and wellwishers throng the White Star pier, welcoming* Republic's *survivors to New York* (Authors' collection).

Wireless was acclaimed as a wonder and a shipboard necessity. The British Board of Trade's lifeboat regulations, last revised in 1894, remained unchanged; the remarkable rescue made possible by wireless showed clearly that revision was unnecessary. Safety in the form of invisible waves had obviated provision of more tangible equipment.

Jack Binns was lionized as a hero by press and public alike for his role in one of history's greatest maritime rescue operations. Overwhelmed by publicity seekers, single women and job offers from every quarter including a vaudeville house, he returned home to his girlfriend amid a tumultuous welcome. The Marconi Company later presented him with a watch and testimonial for courage at the post of duty.

Even before the clamour subsided, Jack Binns signed onto another ship, one of the world's largest liners, *Adriatic*. He served aboard her for two years. Her captain was Edward John Smith. In 1911 he served aboard *Olympic*, again under Smith. And in May 1911 he witnessed the launch of yet another White Star giant, *Titanic*.

But by 1912 Binns decided to leave Marconi's employ and joined the staff of the *New York American*. Anxious to begin his new job, he sailed at once on the *Minnewaska*. He could not wait for *Titanic*'s maiden voyage under Edward John Smith's command…He began work at the *American* within hours of *Titanic*'s own disaster.

Accidents and incidents

27 January 1909	*Majestic*'s Southampton departure was delayed half a day through a derangement of her steering gear.
23 February 1909	With 1,100 passengers aboard, *Cretic* ran aground on Centurian Ledge just inside Boston Harbor while inbound from the Azores. After half an hour she floated free, but her rudder did not respond, and she grounded a second time. After repeated firing of red distress rockets, aid was summoned and with tugs' assistance she was pulled off early the next morning.
26 March 1909	Panic erupted among *Cretic*'s steerage passengers *en route* to New York when a minor fire broke out in straw that had fallen from a mattress. 'A dozen men rushed from the forward deck into the cabin accommodation, shouting and brandishing knives and causing much excitement until they were subdued and sent below.' The fire was extinguished immediately.
11 September 1909	A small fire broke out in *Oceanic*'s after hold while she was at Southampton. It was soon quelled.
4 November 1909	*Adriatic* remained hard aground for five hours at the entrance to Ambrose Channel, inbound to New York.
28 December 1909	Cotton in *Celtic*'s number six hold burned for two full days while at Liverpool.
22 January 1910	Heavy bridge ports were smashed, the bridge telegraphs rendered useless, officers' accommodation flooded and 20 ft of railing carried away as *Laurentic* battled a severe storm on her trip to New York.

12 March 1910	Homeward bound from Brisbane and Melbourne, the freighter *Cevic* docked at Port Said with 7 ft of water in each of two holds. After pumping, repairs were soon effected.
2 May 1910	On a voyage from New York to Genoa via Naples, *Cretic* badly damaged a propeller, requiring drydocking.
27 May 1910	The lake steamer *J.H. Plummer* collided with *Megantic* at Montreal. Damage delayed the latter's departure one day.
30 June 1910	*Baltic* collided with the German-American Petroleum Company's tanker *Standard* 1,089 miles east of the Ambrose lightship. Two holes were torn in *Baltic*'s bows; one caused flooding of her hold. One crewman aboard the tanker broke three ribs and sustained internal injuries, necessitating his transfer via lifeboat to *Baltic* for surgery.
	Upon arrival at Copenhagen, the *Standard* caught fire and, with 1,000,000 gallons of petrol aboard, was destroyed.
8 August 1910	Firemen aboard *Adriatic* mutinied while aboard her at Southampton.
30 August 1910	A 'slight' fire broke out aboard *Cedric* while at Liverpool. Damage was negligible.
23 November 1910	One day after leaving Palermo, a fire broke out in the hold directly beneath *Canopic*'s steerage quarters. Officers and crew battled the blaze for four hours, as more than 1,000 steerage passengers slept, unaware of the danger below them. Eventually the fire was extinguished. 'Then the hatches were hammered down, the decks washed, and there was no sign of the firefighting on the next day when the passengers awoke...'
23 November 1910	*Oceanic* collided with and sank the coal barge *Red Star No. 19* while leaving New York. The barge's aged captain and his wife were thrown into the harbour's waters but were soon rescued by a passing tugboat.

CHAPTER 9

Olympic, 1911–1934

'OLD RELIABLE'

Even with completion of the 'Big Four' — *Celtic* (1901), *Cedric* (1903), *Baltic* (1904) and *Adriatic* (1907) — each larger and more luxurious than the last, White Star's North Atlantic passenger fleet appeared in danger of obsolescence.

Traditionally, the company's Atlantic liners were known for comfort rather than speed. But Cunard's 1907 introduction of the turbine-powered *Lusitania* and *Mauretania* caused White Star's managing director J. Bruce Ismay to realize that

any new tonnage must approach speed standards set by his rivals.

So, to replace the aging *Teutonic* (1889), *Majestic* (1890) and *Oceanic* (1899) and modernize his company's fleet, Ismay met with Lord William J. Pirrie, Harland and Wolff's chairman. Some time during 1907 they discussed construction of two (later three) immense liners, half-again larger than any afloat, which would provide fortnightly round trip Atlantic service from White Star's newly established Southampton terminal. *Teutonic* and *Majestic* would be relegated to the company's secondary Liverpool service, while *Oceanic* would fill in

Following her keel's laying 16 December 1908 Olympic's hull took shape at number two slip in Harland and Wolff's Queens Island yard, Belfast. Titanic's ribs fill slip number three in the foreground. (Daily Sphere).

whenever one of the new giants was laid up for maintenance.

Originally the three sisters were to be about 850 ft long and from 40,000 to 45,000 gross tons. Their combined tonnage would more than double the approximately 127,600 gross tons of the seven White Star liners then in the first class New York mail service. A pair of reciprocating engines would turn each ship's two wing propellers and exhaust into a low pressure steam turbine driving a centre screw.

In the press the new vessels were rumoured to be 1,000 ft long and — probably because of their turbines — to have a speed exceeding 30 knots. Harland and Wolff's first official public announcement on 11 September 1907 described the ships as 'bigger than the *Lusitania*,' of 40,000 tons register and with a speed of only 22 knots, '... the cost of

The Olympic class

	Olympic	Titanic	Britannic
Laid down	16 December 1908	31 March 1909	30 November 1911
Yard number	400	401	433
Launched	20 October 1910	31 May 1911	26 February 1914
End of service	12 April 1935	15 April 1912	21 November 1916
Tonnages: gross	45,324 (46,359*)	46,329	48,158
net	20,847	21,831	24,800
Length (overall)	882 ft 5 in	882 ft 9 in	887 ft 9 in
Beam	92 ft 6 in	92 ft 6 in	94 ft
Moulded depth	59 ft 6 in	59 ft 6 in	64 ft 3 in
Capacity (as planned)			
First class	1054 (750*)	735	790
Second class	510	674	830
Third class	1020	1026	1000

* After 1912–13 alteration

every extra knot after twenty knots being so excessive that the steamship companies are averse to such high speeds.'

An even more conservative speed estimate of '20 knots' coincided with the 16 April 1908 announcement of the first liner's name, *Olympic**, which *The Times* of London managed to record as '*Olympia*.' About a week later, on 22 April, the second vessel's name was announced publicly: *Titanic*.

Construction began well ahead of the originally projected June 1909. With little fanfare *Olympic*'s keel was laid 16 December 1908 in the number two slip at Harland and Wolff's Queen's Island yard, to be followed fourteen weeks later on 31 March 1909 by the keel for *Titanic* in number three slip.

*The name *Olympic* had been selected for a planned sister ship of *Oceanic* (1899) but the project was withdrawn following Thomas H. Ismay's 1899 death.

On 20 October 1910, its passage smoothed by 23 tons of tallow and soft soap, *Olympic*'s gleaming white-painted hull moved down the 750-ft-long sliding ways into the River Lagan. Machinery installation and fitting out were completed in just over seven months from launch. On 29 May 1911 she passed down Belfast Lough for compass adjustments and two days of sea trials. Upon their completion, *Olympic* was handed over to her owners on 31 May 1911, the same day that *Titanic* was launched.

At about 4.30 pm that day *Olympic* left Belfast for Liverpool where she was opened to public inspection. After a day-long stay she departed in the evening for Southampton and maiden voyage preparations.

Olympic's lavish interior, her powerful machinery, her safety: all were topics of widespread,

Right Olympic's side plating shows some of the many rivets used to join sections of the shell (Daily Sphere).

Below Immediately after the 20 October 1910 launch, Olympic's hull is towed toward the fitting out basin (Authors' collection).

avid discussion. But while much interest was shown in *Olympic* before her maiden voyage, her departure received considerably less press coverage than *Titanic*'s did ten months later.

Under command of White Star's senior captain, Captain Edward John Smith, *Olympic* departed Southampton 14 June 1911, made a brief stop at Cherbourg, and completed her crossing between Daunt's Rock and the Ambrose Channel Lightship in five days, sixteen hours and 42 minutes, at an average speed of 21.17 knots. Leaving New York's Quarantine at 7.45 am 21 June under pilot Julius Adler's guidance, *Olympic* moved slowly up the bay and into the North River, threading her way through the flotilla of harbour craft greeting the world's largest ship.

Reaching her own pier, number 59, at the foot of West 19th Street, *Olympic* was safely moored by 10.00 am with twelve tugs' assistance. While safely concluded, the docking was not perfect. During its final moments *Olympic* was involved in the first of several incidents which were to plague her otherwise-successful career.

As the straining tugs aligned *Olympic* with the pier's entrance, the order was given from the bridge, 'Ahead, dead slow,' followed almost immediately by 'Stop!' This manoeuvre was intended to assist the tugs by nudging the vessel ahead and into the docking space. But one tug was too close to *Olympic*'s stern.

Left *In early spring 1911* Olympic *nears completion* (Harland and Wolff Collection, Ulster Folk and Transport Museum Photographic Archive).

Right *The luxury of* Olympic's *first class reading and writing room…*

…a la carte restaurant,…

…and Turkish bath are the talk of the North Atlantic passenger trade (All courtesy Liverpool Central Libraries).

Caught in the starboard propeller's swirling backwash, the 103-ft, 198-ton tug *O.L. Halenbeck* was twisted about and became trapped under the liner's stern overhang. Before the tug could get clear her ensign's mast was snapped off and she was driven into an underwater cable. The impact with the cable and the churning force of water from *Olympic*'s propeller drove the *O.L. Halenbeck* downward. Her decks were awash and she seemed in danger of sinking. Her stern frame was smashed, her rudder and wheel shaft disabled.

As hundreds of spectators watched anxiously, the tug managed to right herself. As *Olympic* moved to her mooring, the *O.L. Halenbeck* limped to a nearby pier and tied up.

(Perhaps 'hitting a man when he's down,' the *O.L. Halenbeck*'s owner, Peter Cahill, waited until 29 April 1912, exactly two weeks after *Titanic*'s loss, before entering a $10,000 (£2,060) damage claim. It was met with a White Star countersuit

After departing Southampton 14 June 1911 on her maiden voyage, Olympic *arrived at New York 21 June where she passed the outbound rival Cunarder* Lusitania *(Authors' collection).*

which claimed negligence in the *O.L. Halenbeck*'s navigation. For lack of conclusive evidence both suits were eventually dismissed.)

Olympic emerged almost undamaged: some scraped paint, a slightly dented plate, but no sprung or loosened rivets. Her construction's integrity was demonstrated for the first time.

Olympic proved a very popular ship and a very profitable one, earning $75,000 (£15,500) on her first round voyage. She amply vindicated her owner's 'comfort *vs.* speed' gamble against the rival *Lusitania, Mauretania* and the German express liners. During July and August 1911 her first and second class facilities were booked almost to capacity. Westbound, her comfortable third class cabins and public rooms attracted many British and continental emigrants.

Olympic quickly established a regularity of passage which was to earn her the title 'Old Reliable.' The new liner's performance during early voyages was satisfactory as she shared regular Southampton departures with *Majestic* and *Oceanic*. It appears likely that in the summer of 1911 a third huge ship — previously discussed but not settled — was

ordered. It was hoped that this ship, provisionally named *Gigantic*, would join her sisters in 1914.

Meanwhile at Belfast, *Titanic* neared completion, with work on her interior arrangements about to begin. Early in September 1911 White Star announced a sailing date for *Titanic*'s first Southampton departure: 20 March 1912. But because of an accident to *Olympic*, this date would be altered.

Olympic's fifth westbound voyage began on 20 September 1911. As it did so, the twin screw light cruiser HMS *Hawke* returned to Portsmouth after day-long power trials in the nearby Solent. Again *Olympic* was under 61-year-old Edward J. Smith's command. Also, as on her four previous Southampton departures, the liner was under compulsory command of veteran Trinity House pilot George William Bowyer while in harbour waters.

The master of HMS *Hawke*, assigned to the Fourth Division, Home Fleet, was Commander William Frederick Blunt*, 41, a 23-year navy

*During World War 1 Blunt served with distinction at the Heligoland Bight, Cuxhaven and the Battle of Jutland. Awarded the DSO in 1914 and made a CBE in 1919, he retired in 1921 and became Rear Admiral, Ret. in 1922. He died 5 July 1928 at his home in Kenya Colony.

Based at Portsmouth the 360-ft cruiser HMS Hawke *was, in 1911, part of the Home Fleet's Fourth Division* (Authors' collection).

veteran. HMS *Hawke* was 360 ft long with a 7,530-ton displacement. Her normal complement was approximately 530.

At 882 ft 5 in the 45,324 ton *Olympic* was the world's largest vessel. On this voyage she carried 1,313 passengers and 885 crew.

After departing the White Star Dock at 11.20 am, *Olympic* proceeded down Southampton Water's 24-mile length. At the seaward end of Southampton Water lay the Isle of Wight and two routes to the English Channel: a starboard turn led down the Solent, while a port turn led through Spithead. Captain Smith regularly selected the Spithead route, whose entrance required a somewhat intricate manoeuvre around a large shoal called the Bramble.

By 12.30 pm *Olympic* was abreast of Black Jack buoy marking Southampton Water's end and the approach to the course round the Bramble. In preparation for the turn, pilot Bowyer ordered the liner's speed reduced from 17 knots. At 12.34 pm, as *Olympic* passed Calshot Spit buoy, the speed

Left *On 20 September 1911 while attempting to manoeuvre around* Olympic's *stern,* Hawke *collided with* Olympic's *starboard side, abaft the fourth funnel* (Popular Mechanics).

Below left *As the* Hawke's *bow pulled free from* Olympic's *side, it scraped paint from the area behind the penetration* (David Hutchings collection).

reduction was felt, and when North Thorn buoy was passed three minutes later, *Olympic*'s speed was 12 knots.

The next buoy, Thorn Knoll, marked the manoeuvre's most intricate part. At 12.40 came the order, 'Port engine full astern, then slow ahead. Cut out the turbine.' Then at a spot about two-thirds of the distance between Thorn Knoll and West Bramble buoys, several actions occurred almost simultaneously: the helm was put hard a-starboard; the port engine was stopped, then reversed; and two deep-toned whistle blasts announced a port turn. *Olympic*'s speed now was 11 knots.

By 12.43 the turn was completed, the vessel steadied on course. The port engine was stopped, then, together with the starboard, ordered full ahead. Speed quickly increased when the centre turbine-driven propeller was activated at 12.44. Two minutes later *Olympic*'s speed had reached 16 knots. At this moment, an event occurred which was to change world history.

High in the crow's nest on *Olympic*'s foremast second officer Robert Hune was keeping careful lookout. Around 12.34 pm, just after Calshot Spit buoy passed, Hune looked to starboard and saw a vessel 3½ to 4 miles distant, rounding Egypt Point on the Isle of Wight and closing rapidly on *Olympic*'s course.

Olympic's other officers, in various locations around the ship, also observed the approaching vessel. Their sightings indicated that the vessel, now identified as HMS *Hawke*, was approximately two miles off when *Olympic*'s twice-sounded whistle had indicated her port turn.* As the turn around West Bramble buoy was completed, *Hawke* was between one and two miles distant.

At subsequent Admiralty Court hearings, Captain Smith described what followed. Upon completing the port turn *Olympic* began to pick up

In addition to the apparent damage to Olympic's *hull,* Hawke *also caused damage below the waterline* (Marine Engineer).

speed. *Hawke* was about one-half mile away, about 15° off the liner's starboard quarter. The cruiser began drawing up, now between 600 and 1200 ft away and going faster than *Olympic*. *Hawke* continued to overhaul on a parallel course (according to Captain Smith) until her stem was almost abreast of *Olympic*'s bridge. *Olympic* now began to move away as she gathered speed. It was at this moment that *Hawke* dropped back and, when about 600 ft off and with her stem at a point approximately between *Olympic*'s second and third funnels, suddenly made a quick turn to port.

*In 1911 an order to 'port the vessel' meant that the tiller or wheel was turned to port, thus altering the vessel's bow and direction to starboard. This so-called 'helm order' was confusing and likely the cause of many collisions. The custom was modified by international agreement in 1928. Current practice is simply to use 'left turn' or 'right turn.' Movements described here are those actually made, as, 'to port' and 'to starboard,' unless otherwise specified.

Aboard *Hawke*, according to Commander Blunt, *Olympic* was regarded as the overtaking vessel and his own as the leading ship. His intent, Blunt testified, was to take the *Hawke* behind *Olympic*'s stern. At *Hawke*'s forward speed and her estimated 600 ft distance from *Olympic* the manoeuvre not only would have succeeded, it would not even have been dangerous, according to Blunt.

On *Olympic*'s bridge, pilot Bowyer observed the approaching *Hawke* when *Olympic* was abreast of North Thorn buoy. Although he noted *Hawke* was moving more quickly than *Olympic*, Bowyer was certain that once *Olympic*'s manoeuvre was completed and speed was resumed, *Hawke* would be outdistanced.

But as *Hawke* drew nearer and then made her own sudden turn to port, Bowyer's composure was shattered. He described the following verbal exchange with Captain Smith:

Smith: 'I don't believe he will get under our stern, Bowyer.'

Bowyer: 'If she is going to strike, sir, let me know in time so I can put the helm hard over to port.' [Shouting]: 'Is she going to strike, sir?'

Smith [calling back]: 'Yes, she is going to strike us in the stern.'

Bowyer ordered the helm hard a port. With *Olympic*'s engines surging full ahead, the helm responded readily. The liner's bow had swung about 7 degrees to starboard when the collision's impact was felt. Bowyer immediately ordered *Olympic*'s engines stopped. But the mischief had been done. Drawn by an invisible force not yet fully appreciated or understood by mariners, *Hawke*'s ram and stem had struck *Olympic*'s starboard quarter below the mainmast.

Testifying at Admiralty Court, George Baker of the National Physical Laboratory described the force:

'Any ship's movement through the water is accompanied by a change of pressure. In the centre there is a field of reduced pressure, and when in shallow water that increases. If anyone is put in within that field they will feel the reduction of pressure. When they get further aft they are partly in the reduced pressure and partly in the field of increased pressure. When one vessel overtakes another and is so placed that the bows feel the power of the reduced pressure and the stern is in the field of increased pressure, the bow will turn in and the stern will move out.

A large triangular hole had been punched through *Olympic*'s plating above the waterline. It penetrated between 6 ft 8 in and 8 ft into the hull, extending from D deck to about 15 ft below the deck flooring. A crack extended 8 ft inward where *Hawke*'s upper stem had penetrated. *Olympic*'s E deck also was punctured in the same way, and the damage extended below the waterline. *Hawke*'s ram later was found to have bits of bronze on it, showing it had nicked *Olympic*'s starboard propeller.

The liner's watertight doors were immediately ordered closed. While there was considerable water in *Olympic*'s two compartments furthest aft, there appeared no danger of her sinking. Fortunately, passengers were in the dining room and the second class cabins in the collision area were empty at the time.

Unable to return to Southampton until high tide, *Olympic* anchored for the night in Osborne Bay off Cowes, Isle of Wight. Standing by was the Red Funnel Line tug *Vulcan* which soon would play a prominent role in the Southampton departure of *Olympic*'s sister-ship *Titanic*. Even a cursory damage inspection showed that *Olympic*'s voyage had to be cancelled. Passengers were offloaded by tender and forced to find other passage.

Thursday morning, 21 September, *Olympic* was towed slowly back to Southampton. She was berthed, and cargo discharge began. Divers, ship's carpenters and company officials appraised damage and quickly determined that the necessary extensive repairs required drydocking. The only facility in the world that could receive *Olympic* was at Belfast. The punctures required patching before *Olympic* could make the 570-mile voyage.

Above right *Down at the bows,* Hawke *returned to Portsmouth for repairs* (Authors' collection).

Right *The damage to* Hawke's *bow is clearly seen at Portsmouth* (David Hutchings collection).

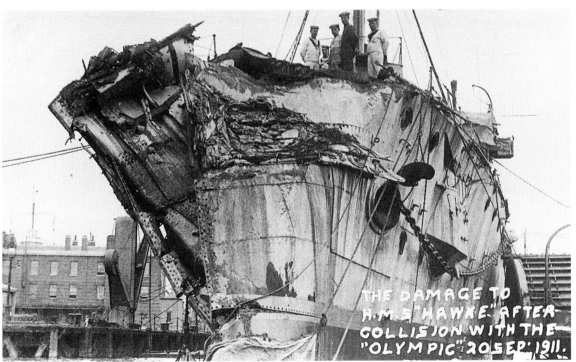

THE DAMAGE TO
H.M.S "HAWKE" AFTER
COLLISION WITH THE
"OLYMPIC" 20 SEP 1911.

On the morning of 21 September, one day after the collision, Olympic *was towed slowly back to Southampton for discharging passengers and cargo* (David Hutchings collection).

At Portsmouth, down by the head, her bow crumpled and her plates torn, *Hawke* was kept afloat by constant pumping. Repairs were to take several months and necessitated replacement of more than 20 ft of her bow.

It took more than ten days to repair *Olympic*'s hull, using wood above the waterline and steel plates below. Finally, with cargo and much of her coal removed, she departed Southampton on Wednesday 4 October for Belfast, manned by a minimal crew. Steaming under her own power at less than ten knots, she arrived at Belfast Lough on 6 October, anchoring in Carrick Roads at 11.00 am.

But before she could cross the sill and enter the Belfast Harbour Commission's new drydock, her water-filled stern had to be lightened further. The starboard propeller shaft, bent in the collision, was removed. (It was replaced later by a duplicate awaiting installation in *Titanic*, then fitting out.*)

*The time needed to prepare another shaft for *Titanic* and the manpower diverted from *Titanic*'s completion to repair *Olympic* delayed *Titanic*'s already-announced maiden voyage sailing date of 20 March 1912 to 10 April.

Repairs to *Olympic* cost more than $500,000 (£103,000). The liner did not return to service until 30 November, losing more than $750,000 (£154,000) that three cancelled round-trips might have provided.

The White Star Line sued the British Admiralty and Commander Blunt for damages, and prolonged litigation ensued. The Admiralty brought a cross-action for *Hawke*'s damage. Nine days of hearings commenced 16 November at Portsmouth aboard the guard ship *Duke of Wellington*. On 19 December the Admiralty Division's president, Sir Samuel Adams, decided *Olympic* alone was to blame, but held that her negligent navigation was solely that of pilot Bowyer, compulsorily in charge. Sir Samuel dismissed White Star's suit with costs, judgement being entered for Commander Blunt. The cross-action judgement was entered for *Olympic*'s owners, but without costs, as they had succeeded only in the defence of compulsory pilotage. White Star appealed the decision, believing their vessel blameless.

On 5 April 1913, after fifteen days of hearing, the Court of Appeal dismissed with costs the owners' appeal in the action against Commander Blunt; the Admiralty's appeal in the cross-action was not continued, and that also was dismissed with costs. Again White Star appealed the decision. Finally on 9 November 1914 the House of Lords unanimously affirmed the Court of Appeal's decision. The Lord Chancellor, Lord Haldane, concluded that *Hawke* was a crossing ship and not an overtaking ship; it therefore was *Olympic*'s duty to keep out of the way, while it was *Hawke*'s duty to keep her own course and speed.

The decision is arguable, especially in light of Blunt's stated intention to steer a parallel course while carrying only 5° of starboard rudder; an alteration of 15° starboard rudder at the last moment was insufficient to prevent the collision (which itself was almost unquestionably a result of the 'interaction resembling suction' between two vessels.)

Those theoretically responsible were seemingly vindicated: the Admiralty promoted Commander Blunt to captain late in 1911, long before litigation ended. White Star appointed Captain Smith to command the company's newest liner on its maiden voyage less than seven months after the *Hawke* incident. And pilot George Bowyer continued to guide White Star ships in and out of Southampton Harbour.

Olympic's crew sued White Star for one month's wages they felt they should have received for a completed round trip voyage. But Admiralty Court ruled *Olympic*'s incident was a wreck under the Merchant Shipping Act; the crew received two days' wages due them from time of hire to the 'wreck,' plus a bonus of one day's pay volunteered by the company.

On 19 October, while *Olympic* was undergoing

A temporary wood patch above the waterline and metal plates below enabled Olympic *to return to her Belfast builders for repairs* (Harland and Wolff collection, Ulster Folk and Transport Museum Photographic Archive).

At Belfast, workers examined the pierced hull plating before repairs commenced (Authors' collection).

repairs at Belfast, White Star announced she would sail from Southampton on Wednesday 29 November. On 20 November, following a day of machinery trials and compass adjustments, *Olympic* departed Belfast at 4.00 pm and arrived at Southampton on the morning of 22 November. On sailing day a heavy fog descended and delayed *Olympic*'s departure a full day. The fifth westbound journey begun more than two months earlier was uneventful, as were subsequent trips during December. But during her first westbound voyage of 1912, the liner encountered a mid-Atlantic gale which Captain E.J. Smith described as the most severe he could recall.

At about 1.30 pm on Sunday 14 January, amid blinding snow and gale-force winds, *Olympic* encountered tremendous seas. An immense wave lifted the liner's bow high in the air, then broke over it. As the ship began to settle in the trough, a huge sea again broke over the bow, inundating it with tons of water which slopped aft. The sea got under one of the forward hatch covers, a five-ton metal sheet, wrenched it loose and sent it hurtling to a corner of the forward shelter deck. The steam winch and anchor windlass on the forecastle deck were torn from their mountings and the forward portside rail washed away. The damaged fittings were repaired, and neither *Olympic*'s westbound arrival nor eastbound departure were delayed.

But on the voyage which departed New York 21 February 1912 *Olympic* suffered further damage. On Saturday 24 February, while about 750 miles east of Newfoundland, *Olympic* struck what appeared to be a submerged wreck and in doing so dropped a blade from her port propeller. The shock was felt throughout the ship, but there was no passenger panic, nor any other damage.

After completing the crossing and dropping passengers at the customary eastbound ports of Plymouth and Cherbourg, *Olympic* arrived at Southampton on 28 February. After discharging cargo and her remaining passengers, she departed a day later for Belfast, again because there was no other drydock large enough. The plan was to replace the propeller blade during a single day. But *Olympic* missed a tide upon her 1 March arrival, and further delays resulted from prolonged stormy

weather. Repairs were not completed for several days, and it was not until Thursday 7 March that *Olympic* could depart Belfast for Southampton, arriving the next day.

There is no record of *Olympic*'s scheduled 6 March voyage being handled by any other White Star vessel. The trip was simply cancelled, until *Olympic*'s own delayed departure on 13 March.

Wednesday 10 April 1912 — a proud day for her builder, her owner, the port of Southampton, and all those who sailed in her: White Star's newest and greatest liner, *Titanic*, departed Southampton at 12.10 pm on her maiden voyage. *Titanic*'s voyage 1 westbound was abruptly and tragically concluded a mere 6,610 minutes later when at 2.20 am Monday, 15 April, the black, ice-strewn waters of the North Atlantic closed over her stern plates. A pathetically few 705 survivors out of 2,228 aboard were left bobbing about the silent sea in twenty small boats.

During the two hours and forty minutes it took *Titanic* to sink after striking the berg, the night air was filled with wireless traffic. One of many to hear *Titanic*'s calls was her sister ship. *Olympic* had departed New York at 3.00 pm Saturday 13 April for Plymouth, Cherbourg and Southampton and was on the southerly, eastbound Atlantic track. At 1.00 am 15 April when she intercepted the distress signal, she was some 505 miles south of *Titanic*'s position.

Within ten minutes of receiving *Titanic*'s distress call, *Olympic*'s master, Captain Herbert J. Haddock, had altered course and ordered full power to try to reach the stricken ship. After exchanging wireless messages with *Carpathia* and other nearby vessels during the early hours of 15 April, Haddock discontinued his rescue attempt — particularly when advised by Rostron of Bruce Ismay's personal wish that *Titanic*'s survivors be permitted not even a glimpse of the nearly-identical sister.

For the remainder of Monday and well into Tuesday, *Olympic*'s strong wireless set transmitted *Titanic* survivors' names to the powerful Cape Race land station. By 2.30 am Tuesday the list had been completed, and *Olympic*'s next duties were the transmission of service messages via Cape Race to White Star's New York headquarters, where vice

Following Titanic's *disastrous loss, the public immediately demanded boats for all. At Southampton, workmen hastily installed additional collapsible boats and rafts before* Olympic's *24 April departure* (Authors' collection).

president P.A.S. Franklin breathlessly awaited confirmation of the fate of *Titanic*, her passengers and crew.*

But soon eastward-bound *Olympic* was beyond range of North American wireless stations. Such news as she received of *Titanic* was now relayed from other ships. *Olympic*, her master and her crew had fulfilled their only direct role in *Titanic's* tragic loss.

Sorrow and shock spread quickly among *Olym-*

pic's passengers. All concerts and shipboard activities were cancelled for the remainder of the voyage. A collection for *Titanic's* crew and their families yielded $7,000 (£1,500). After discharging passengers and mails at Plymouth, *Olympic* arrived at Southampton shortly after midnight 21 April.

For *Olympic's* scheduled Wednesday departure, White Star hastily assembled extra lifeboats providing seats for every soul on board. Captain Benjamin Steele, White Star's marine superintendent at Southampton, received instructions to install sixteen more lifeboats on *Olympic*. That number was soon changed to forty, but when he had placed 35 on board instructions were again altered to provide boats to accommodate 2,500 people. That meant removing eleven of the 'new' boats.

The boats and tackle — blocks and wire roping — were obtained from His Majesty's transports berthed at Southampton. Some boats were almost new, not yet a year old. But ten from HMS *Soudan*

*Franklin had already announced the disaster to reporters shortly after 6.30 pm 15 April (although as-yet unsubstantiated evidence suggests he may have known earlier of the loss.) As *Carpathia* steamed toward New York, however, details were as yet unknown to the world.

After several Atlantic crossings, Olympic returned to Belfast in October 1912 for extensive reconstruction. In the spring of 1913 she emerged in a blaze of company publicity extolling her new safety features, as 'The New Olympic' (White Star Line).

Lifeboats and collapsibles now filled the entire length of Olympic's topmost deck (Authors' collection).

were ten years old, and, while sound, looked their age. Workers were busily engaged Monday in installing the boats on Olympic's boat deck. On Wednesday, however, after examining the collapsibles and finding them unseaworthy to their own satisfaction, 276 firemen, trimmers and greasers walked off the ship moments before sailing time.

Southampton and Liverpool, Cherbourg and Queenstown: bookings already snarled because of Titanic's loss were heavily taxed. Passengers at Cherbourg — all of whom had waited more than two days for Olympic — were offered refunds; many of them booked passage elsewhere.

After their arrest, the striking seamen were put on trial. At a three-day hearing held at Ports-

mouth's magistrates' court, they were found guilty of mutiny. But circumstances (especially those regarding Titanic's recent loss) were such that the Court found it inexpedient to imprison or fine the defendants. They were set free. Olympic's men, in the public action they had taken, achieved a maritime milestone: henceforth, no ship would sail without lifeboat provisions for each person on board.*

When Olympic arrived at New York on 22 May on her first completed post-Titanic crossing she car-

*An amendment to the Merchant Shipping Act of 1894, already under consideration before Titanic's loss, went into effect 1 January 1913. It based lifeboat provisions upon a vessel's length rather than on the previous ratio of cubic footage to tonnage. The new law further demanded sufficient lifeboats for all on board.

ried 43 lifeboats and collapsibles, more than double her original complement.**

According to a story told 75 years after its occurrence, the lifesaving equipment was almost put into use during *Olympic*'s return voyage. The son of Captain Benjamin Steele related how his father described *Olympic*'s near-grounding, several miles off course, as she rounded Land's End on her way to a morning arrival at Plymouth 1 June. The officer of the watch sighted broken water washing over rocks below a promontory and quickly signalled 'Stop! Reverse engines!'

Fortunately the danger was seen in time to avert embarrassment, if not disaster. Given the public's current interest in White Star's safety practices, the company thought it inappropriate to discipline Captain Haddock publicly, and the incident passed unnoticed.

Nor was *Olympic*'s next eastbound voyage uneventful. During her 6 July departure from New York the liner grounded on a sand bank east of Ellis Island to avoid collision with the yacht *Viking*. Aided by the rising tide, six tugs pulled her clear. *Olympic* anchored off Tompkinsville, Staten Island to repair slight steering gear damage. After a ninety-minute delay she proceeded.

On 11 August 1912 White Star announced that *Olympic* would be temporarily withdrawn from service in November and returned to Harland and Wolff for a thorough overhaul. Almost as though in anticipation, *Olympic* suffered yet another small but significant hurt. On 15 September during an eastbound crossing, she dropped another propeller blade. A trip to Belfast now had added urgency.

No repairs were attempted prior to *Olympic*'s 18 September departure from Southampton for New York where she arrived a day late; the damaged propeller had forced slower speeds. On 20 September, while *Olympic* was still steaming westward, the company announced that upon her return the liner would be sent to Belfast for renovation, earlier than planned. Her cancelled voyages from Southampton would be handled by *Oceanic* and *Majestic*, with American Line ships helping to maintain the schedule. *Olympic* arrived at Belfast late in the afternoon of 10 October and by 10.00 am next day was berthed at Alexandra Wharf.

Repairs and renovations cost more than $1,200,000 (£250,000), and when completed in five months, had increased *Olympic*'s tonnage from 45,324 to 46,359, while reducing first class capacity from 1,054 to 750. Bulkheads were extended upwards and an inner skin fitted. Lifeboats were increased from 20 to 68. There were now seats for 3,700 — indeed, 'boats for all.'

Olympic departed Belfast on 22 March 1913 and left Southampton for New York on 2 April. The nagging incidents that had marred her first two years were absent in the eighteen months after refitting. She easily maintained steady three-week round trip schedules between Southampton and New York. Though soon surpassed in size and luxury by HAPAG's *Imperator* (1913) and Cunard's *Aquitania*, *Olympic* gained popularity.

She departed Southampton 29 July 1914 on what seemed a routine crossing. But three days later war between England and Germany began. *Olympic*'s first taste of new conditions came quickly. Upon receipt of war's declaration, Captain Haddock had suspended wireless transmissions and ordered all portholes and windows covered. At about 9.00 am, on 4 August, as the liner approached New York, the British cruiser HMS *Essex* contacted her. *Essex* was to escort *Olympic* to New York Harbor's entrance, protecting her from German warships thought to be lying in wait. *Essex* stayed out of sight, and it was not until *Olympic* berthed that passengers learned they had been under escort. The crossing, half in peace, half in war, was completed safely.

On Saturday 8 August, without mail, cargo or passengers aboard, *Olympic* suddenly departed New York, escorted by *Essex* as far as Sable Island. During the trip's first, most hazardous stage, *Olympic*'s seven reserve boilers were fired, giving her a 23-knot cruising speed, enough to outrun any lurking German war vessels. Approaching the Irish coast, she picked up the cruiser HMS *Drake* which

**The company planned to have *Olympic* pick up *Titanic*'s thirteen recovered lifeboats while at New York and return them to England. The lifeboats, however, had been impounded as the wreck's only tangible assets. They were later evaluated by a court-appointed appraiser and their value applied to settlement of claims against *Titanic*'s owner.

On 27 October 1914 as Olympic neared the end of a New York-Greenock voyage, she answered a distress call from HMS Audacious, sinking after striking a mine off Tory Island. Arriving at the scene, Olympic quickly lowered her lifeboats, manned by volunteer crew (Imperial War Museum).

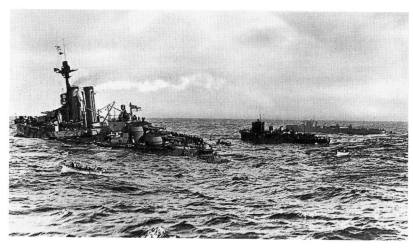

Olympic's Captain H.J. Haddock manoeuvred the liner to form a lee in which Olympic's lifeboats could ferry Audacious's crew to safety, with the loss of but a single life (Imperial War Museum).

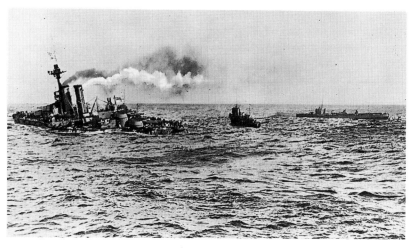

Despite the placement of tow lines from Olympic to Audacious, the battleship could not be saved (Imperial War Museum).

A contemporary German postcard commemorated the loss of Audacious *(Authors' collection).*

escorted her to Liverpool, as the Admiralty had reserved almost all of Southampton's berthage.

For her next two Atlantic round trips, *Olympic* diverted to Liverpool instead of Southampton. An even greater diversion occurred after her 26 September New York departure: *Olympic* headed north for Greenock, Scotland, in the hope that the route and destination would protect her from German minefields and patrol vessels.

An eastbound voyage with 1,600 passengers departing 21 October from New York for Greenock was uneventful until 27 October, when the great *Olympic* proved herself a gallant ship. Alerted by wireless that morning of recently-laid mines around Ireland's northwest coast, Captain Haddock altered course, bringing *Olympic* near Tory Island, where, about 10.00 am, she received a vessel's distress signals. Lifeboats were prepared immediately, and through high seas churned by strong westerly gales, *Olympic* ran at full speed to the scene. Some twenty miles northeast of Tory Island lay HMS *Audacious*, wallowing helplessly, her stern awash.

The year-old, 23,000-ton battleship had struck a mine at about 8.00 am. Badly breached aft on the port side, she had tried to steam for Lough Swilly, but the sea's roughness soon made her unmanageable. It was then that *Olympic* arrived.

Several British naval vessels were standing by. But even as her lifeboats were being lowered by all-volunteer crews into towering waves, it was *Olympic*

that threw out a 6-in wire rope, hoping to tow *Audacious* to safety. But the cable snapped. A 9-in replacement was put over, but the battleship's crew could not secure it.

Amid the most difficult conditions, *Audacious'* entire crew were removed with just a single loss. Some *Olympic* boats made as many as three trips rescuing 250 of the 900 men saved, the rest being removed by boats from other naval vessels. Waves and wind prevented *Olympic*'s recovering fourteen of her lifeboats; they were left adrift when the liner was ordered away at about 7.00 pm. Two hours later *Audacious* exploded and sank.*

Olympic anchored in Lough Swilly from 27 September to 2 October. Her passengers (except one, American millionaire Charles Schwab) were not permitted to disembark until 2 October when *Olympic* steamed round to Belfast. There she was taken out of service and requisitioned as a troopship; her fittings were removed and stored. A 12-pounder gun was mounted forward, with a 4.7 in gun aft. Conversion took ten months; *Olympic* was not ready for war service until September 1915.

---

*The Admiralty desired *Audacious*'s loss to be kept secret. *Olympic*'s passengers had to promise they would not reveal what they had witnessed, and no word appeared in the British press. It was announced that *Audacious* had been raised and taken to Belfast for repairs. To convince the enemy, the Canadian Pacific liner *Montcalm* was mocked up as *Audacious*.

A month later she departed England for the eastern Mediterranean with 6,000 troops aboard. During this first trooping voyage, a drifting lifeboat was sighted soon after passing Malta. It carried sailors from the torpedoed French steamship *Provincia*. Captain Bertram Hayes, now *Olympic*'s commander, stopped to rescue the sailors. For his merciful act he was censured by the commander-in-chief, eastern Mediterranean, for 'indiscretion shown by the master of a transport' in stopping in enemy waters. The French, however, felt differently and awarded Hayes the Gold Life Saving Medal.

On 31 October 1915 *Olympic* completed her first troopship voyage at Liverpool. She was to make four more; three were marked by threatening incidents. In November 1915 a submarine chased her off Cape Matapan, Greece, but she outran the danger. Late in January 1916 near Mudros Island, *Olympic* actually was attacked by a submarine but dodged the two torpedoes fired at her. And on her

last Mediterranean trip in February 1916 she was attacked by a plane from Bulgaria; again luck was with *Olympic* and she sustained no damage.

On 23 March 1916 *Olympic* departed on the first of ten round trips to Halifax to transport Canadian troops. All twenty crossings seem to have been without incident. *Olympic* returned to Belfast on 12 January 1917 for maintenance and installation of six 6-in guns as added protection.

In late summer 1917 she again was laid up briefly for painting. The recently approved dazzle painting scheme, unique to each vessel and designed to confuse U-boat commanders, was applied to her dignified lines. *Olympic*'s pattern, a striking arrangement of greys, blues and browns, was designed by Lieutenant Norman Wilkinson, RNR. Wartime photographs indicate the design was modified at least twice.

Olympic arrived in New York on 25 December 1917 for her first voyage carrying American soldiers. She departed on 11 January 1918. The

Above left *After conversion lasting ten months, Olympic entered war service in September 1915, protected by a twelve-pound gun forward, a 4.7-in gun aft. She spent the next three years as a troop transport* (Imperial War Museum).

Above *In late summer 1917 she received her first 'dazzle' camouflage, designed by artist Norman Wilkinson* (Imperial War Museum).

Right *Later, the design appears to have been modified* (Authors' collection).

Left *On 12 May 1918 while approaching Southampton loaded with American troops,* Olympic *rammed and sank German submarine U.103. Subsequent drydock examination revealed the liner's bow was only slightly twisted by the encounter* (Authors' collection).

Below left *During her war service* Olympic *steamed more than 184,000 miles.* (Authors' collection).

Right *One of* Olympic's *happiest functions was the repatriation of American and Canadian troops following war's end. On this April 1919 voyage, she entered Halifax Harbour with 6,000 Canadian soldiers returning home from Europe's battlefields* (Ray Beck collection, courtesy of Russ Lownds).

22nd trooping voyage was *Olympic's* most adventurous. After a night departure from Southampton on 24 April, warnings of nearby submarines had proven unfounded. Returning to Southampton fully loaded with American troops, she picked up an American destroyer escort to the English Channel.

The liner steamed on, awaiting the daybreak arrival of British destroyers to accompany her to Southampton. Shortly before 4.00 am on 12 May, against the dawn's earliest light, Captain Hayes and the lookouts simultaneously sighted a German submarine surfacing off *Olympic's* starboard bow. Hayes immediately decided to ram the intruder and he quickly altered *Olympic's* course.

The submarine put on full speed and tried to escape by turning inside *Olympic's* turning circle. But the manoeuvre failed and at about 3.55 am, her helm hard a-port, *Olympic's* bow struck the submarine a swinging blow. The submarine sank almost immediately. An American torpedo boat later picked up several survivors, confirming that *Olympic* had indeed sunk German submarine *U.103.* A diver later discovered *Olympic's* stem was twisted eight feet to port and several plates were dented but drydock repairs allowed a quick return to service.

Following war's end *Olympic* made several voyages from England and France to Halifax and New York repatriating thousands of Canadian and American troops. During her distinguished wartime career, not once had her machinery balked. She had steamed more than 184,000 miles, burning 347,000 tons of coal, and carrying nearly 150,000 British, Canadian and American troops and 40,000 westbound passengers, all without loss of a single soul.

Finally on 21 July 1919 *Olympic* return to Liverpool from Halifax on her last trip as a troop carrier. After offloading military equipment and stores, she steamed to Belfast, arriving at Harland and Wolff's for refurbishing and conversion to oil fuel on 11 August. Maintenance, reinstallation of original furnishings and introduction of oil-fired boilers cost almost $2,500,000 (£500,000) and took ten months. Conversion to oil cut engine room staff from 350 to 60, and assured more rapid turnarounds in port.

Olympic's first post-conversion departure from Southampton 25 June 1920 began her golden age as a passenger liner. Though only ten years old, her furnishings recalled a gentler, more gracious age and attracted a faithful, often well-known clientele.

Between June 1920 and the end of 1923 *Olympic* made 49 Atlantic round trips with only routine-maintenance layups. In her maturity, she seemed to have shaken the jinx of petty accidents which blemished her early years. The jinx returned on her second 1924 departure.

Shortly before 11.00 am on 22 March, the Bermuda-bound liner *Fort St George* left her 55th Street dock. A few minutes later *Arcadian*, a rival on the Bermuda run, departed her own dock. As *Fort St George* moved down the Manhattan side of the North River, *Arcadian* crossed her competitor's wake and sailed down the New Jersey side. Witnesses said it appeared the two were racing one another down river toward the Narrows.

Promptly at 11 o'clock *Olympic*'s gangways were hauled up – so promptly that twenty visitors were marooned on board. With a prolonged whistle blast she backed away from Pier 59 into the North River. Whistle still sounding, she began her turn, bow swinging downstream toward the Narrows, stern angling up river.

At this moment the rapidly approaching *Fort St*

Above *After her 1920 conversion to oil,* Olympic *brought to her North Atlantic passenger service the same reliability she had shown in wartime* (Everett E. Viez collection, Steamship Historical Society of America).

Left *Each New York arrival and departure was an exciting event* (Authors' collection).

George swung sharply to starboard toward the New Jersey shore to pass *Olympic*'s stern. *Olympic* continued her turn, momentum carrying her slowly backward. With all the impact of 46,439 tons behind her, *Olympic*'s stern struck *Fort St George*'s port quarter just aft of amidships.

Cracking, grinding and breaking sounds reverberated as *Olympic*'s stern scraped along *Fort St George*'s stern quarter. The Furness liner's mainmast was snapped at its base, as were the hydraulic derrick's twin metal posts; the radio antenna hung loosely from the masts; 150 ft of decking caved in, and ventilators, railing and lifeboat davits were broken and twisted. Damage was estimated at £35,000 (about $150,000).

Reeling from the impact, momentum carrying her further down river, *Fort St George* finally halted,

Her second 1924 New York departure was almost disastrous, as Olympic *backed into the outbound Bermuda liner* Fort St George. *The White Star liner proceeded on her voyage undamaged;* Fort St George*'s voyage was cancelled* (Everett E. Viez collection, Steamship Historical Society of America).

turned and limped slowly back to Pier 95 where she arrived after 1.00 pm. Alerted by wireless, *Arcadian* returned and took aboard some of the stricken liner's passengers.

Olympic proceeding to Quarantine where she stopped and called for divers. But before they arrived her own engineering staff determined damage was insignificant. After testing steering gear, *Olympic* resumed her voyage, having put the twenty marooned visitors off on a tug.

Except for the *Fort St George* collision, *Olympic* remained free from major incident through the 1920s. In the seasonal fogs often blanketing her termini and her route, she was, however, involved in many near misses. Two months after the *Fort St George* incident, while anchored in fog off New York's Quarantine, *Olympic* was almost struck by

the United States Line's 13,700-ton *President Harding* (an occurrence US Lines strenuously denied.) *Olympic* herself on several occasions almost ran down small, unlighted rum-running boats, common along America's coasts during Prohibition. Many small fishing vessels plying the Grand Banks must have bobbed precariously in her wake.

From 1924 through to 1928 *Olympic* averaged fifteen round trips annually between Southampton and New York. Running with *Majestic* and *Homeric* — the former German liners *Bismarck* (1914) and *Columbus* (1913), respectively — *Olympic* was an integral part of the fortnightly Southampton-New York service originally envisioned with *Titanic* and *Britannic*.

As *Olympic* grew older, her venerable facilities were modified during maintenance layups. In 1928 the number of baths was increased, 75 cabins being sacrificed to provide space for them. Simultaneously a new 'tourist' class was created from most of second class and best parts of third.

Despite aging engines, 'period' decor and barely adequate sanitation facilities, *Olympic* continued to be popular. But approaching worldwide economic depression reduced all shipping companies' passenger traffic. On her April 1930 eastbound crossing, *Olympic* carried just 185 passengers in all classes.

That year White Star inaugurated a cruise programme employing *Homeric*, no longer needed on the Atlantic run. These two- and three-day cruises from British ports proved so popular they were continued the following year. Also during 1931, to capture what they viewed as a lucrative American market, White Star scheduled several short cruises out of New York: four-day cruises to Halifax by *Olympic* and *Majestic*, and weekly six-day cruises to Nassau by *Homeric*.

Olympic took the 6 August and 27 August 1931 Halifax trips, returning to one of her wartime ports-of-call where she had long been regarded with sentiment and respect. Military units *Olympic* had transported held on-board reunions.

The Depression curtailed an ambitious 1932 cruise programme. Americans no longer sought 'pleasure cruises,' but *Olympic* did make two three-day cruises from Southampton on Whitsun and the August bank holiday.

Whatever White Star's 1933 plans may have been, damage to *Olympic*'s engines changed them. During a routine examination at Southampton 14 October 1932, a small fracture was discovered in a journal of the port high-pressure crankshaft. It was hoped repairs could be completed to permit a 23 November sailing date. But further examination disclosed other, unsuspected repair problems, and it was decided to overhaul the ship completely, Harland and Wolff's Southampton works performing the three-month task.

Many of the liner's public and private rooms were refurbished. Additional private baths were installed, further reducing first class accommodation. During *Olympic*'s four major overhauls, first class capacity was reduced from 1910's 1,054 cabins to 750 during the 1912/13 refit, to 675 in 1928 and finally to 618 in the 1932/33 refitting.

On 9 March 1933 *Olympic* arrived at New York on the first post-overhaul voyage, White Star describing her engines as '...better than new and able to drive her at 23 knots,' though little speed improvement actually had been observed. Further

engine trouble occurred in September, necessitating premature lay-up for routine overhaul. By mid-December, however, *Olympic* returned to service.

One of six sister ships built at Charleston, South Carolina, the 630-ton Nantucket lightship, or, as she was known officially, *117*, was moored by 2-in cast steel chain cables to her station 41 miles southeast of Nantucket Island and about 200 miles from New York Harbor. Guarding ships from Nantucket's notorious shoals and providing radio navigation aid, *117* had been on station since May 1931. Because some ships 'rode the beam' (zeroed in on *117*'s radio signals), the light vessel had suffered several near misses. Indeed on 4 January 1934 the 24,500-ton American liner *Washington* sideswiped her and tore away her boat davits, wireless rigging and mast grating.

In the early morning of 15 May 1934 *Olympic* was westbound from Southampton to New York and had set course to provide a safe distance on her starboard beam to the Nantucket light vessel. Fog had beset the liner for all but one day since departure.

Aboard *117* wisps and patches of fog appeared throughout the night. Twice that night, passing vessels had nearly run her down, and as was routine in fog, her lifeboats were unshipped to permit a quick emergency getaway. The lightship's powerful siren sounded dolefully through the thick night air.

At 5.00 am fog thickened and *Olympic*'s speed was reduced from $19\frac{1}{2}$ to about 16 knots. Regulation fog signals sounded from her immense steam whistles. On the bridge, a tired Captain John W. Binks was assisted by the staff captain and two watch officers. Binks had had but one night's sleep since leaving Southampton.

A double lookout was stationed at the bow and another in the crow's nest. As the fog's density increased, *Olympic* slowed to about 12 knots.

At about 10.55 am *Olympic* received a radio signal indicating the lightship bore slightly ahead on her starboard bow. Shortly thereafter *117*'s fog signal was heard. Binks ordered further speed reduction to 10 knots. Though officers reported hearing the lightship's siren, Binks could not hear

Above *January 1934* — Olympic *speeds past the Nantucket lightship in a dramatic photo taken from the lightship's deck. Four months later,* Olympic *was to approach even more closely...*(First District US Coast Guard.)

Below *On 16 May 1934 in dense fog off the Massachusetts coast* Olympic *rammed and sank the Nantucket lightship number 117 with the loss of seven lives* (pen and ink sketch ©Michael V. Ralph 1988).

it himself at first. When he did, he ordered *Olympic* to port to provide an extra safety margin.

As the turn began, lookouts shouted a warning. There, dead ahead, lay the light vessel, her name emblazoned in white across her red-painted plates: NANTUCKET.

Binks' commands were swift and certain. *Olympic*'s rudder was immediately put hard left, her port engine full astern. As she began to swing, her starboard engine was put astern. But collision was unavoidable.

Olympic's swinging bow struck the light vessel's port side amidships. The blow was not a heavy one. Binks later estimated that at impact, the liner's forward speed was just two or three knots. It was *Olympic*'s massive weight, not speed, which crushed the smaller vessel in an instant.

As *Olympic*'s watertight bulkhead doors closed, their alarm bells brought passengers hurrying to the decks. Spars, deck fittings and debris from *117*'s ruptured interior dotted the sea amid a sickening smell of oil and acetylene. A red fishing dory — one of *117*'s unshipped lifeboats — floated by silently.

Between sighting and impact, *Olympic*'s port emergency boat, in charge of Sixth Officer Arthur C.I. Anson, was manned and lowered away. The starboard emergency boat soon followed. Before *Olympic*'s momentum carried her into the fog and beyond further view, passengers glimpsed several floating human figures, toward whom the liner's small boats were pulling.

Olympic drifted to a stop in the fog, her whistles still sounding periodically. The small boats were away for 45 minutes, lost in the impenetrable fog. During the search, Captain Binks radioed the New York office with the barest of details: 'Please inform all concerned. In collision with the Nantucket lightship and sank same. Standing by to save crew.'

Gradually the fog lifted and the two lifeboats returned. Bodies of three of *117*'s crew were recovered; four men were missing, their bodies never found. Of the Nantucket light vessel's eleven-man crew, four survived.

As *Olympic* sailed at reduced speed to New York, the United States Department of Commerce, *117*'s nominal owners, ordered that a $500,000 (£100,000) claim be placed on her. The bond was served ('tacked to the mast,' as one crew member put it) as *Olympic* docked at Pier 59 on the morning of Wednesday, 16 May. That afternoon divers examined her stem plates below the waterline but found minimal damage.

The US Bureau of Navigation and Steamship Inspection's preliminary hearing began at New York's Customs House at 10.00 am the next day. White Star accepted responsibility for the loss and requested the removal of the bond to allow *Olympic*'s scheduled departure on her return voyage. Permission granted, she sailed at midnight 17 May for Southampton, arriving a week later.

White Star challenged the £100,000 payment to the United States government, saying it wanted the latter to prove the lightship was worth that figure. The Department of Commerce's Bureau of Lighthouses contacted each contributor of material for *117*'s construction, asking for replacement cost estimates. Eventually an undisclosed sum rumoured to be $350,000 ($70,000) was accepted and paid.

Through the United States Employees' Com-

pensation Act, dependents of those lost received remuneration. And as part of Memorial Day services at the Women's Titanic Memorial in Washington, DC, the men's names were read out and a moment of silence observed.

Pier 59 had been *Olympic*'s customary New York berth since her maiden voyage. Her 30 June 1934 departure was her last from this pier. The merger between Cunard and White Star companies, effective 1 July, moved her subsequent arrivals five blocks southward to Cunard's Pier 54. *Olympic* now flew Cunard's red flag with golden lion and globe, but below the White Star pennant.

Once more *Olympic* experienced the result of sailing through crowded sea lanes with limited visibility. Outbound on Sunday 26 August 1934, in fog near the Grand Banks, Captain John W. Binks had to alter course abruptly and go full speed astern to avoid colliding with another vessel. No sooner had *Olympic* done so than another vessel, the 200-ton Spanish freighter *San Sebastian*, suddenly loomed out of the fog off *Olympic*'s port bow, so close that passengers could read her name. *Olympic* cleared both ships.

With the great Depression considerably reducing Atlantic passenger travel, *Olympic*'s days were numbered. On 25 January 1935 Cunard-White Star announced she would be retired upon completion of her spring schedule. A planned series of short July cruises from New York were given to *Mauretania*. To fill *Olympic*'s place, the new *Georgic* and *Britannic* would be transferred from Liverpool to Southampton service.

On 27 March 1935 *Olympic* departed Southampton on round trip number 257, her final Atlantic crossings. She arrived at New York 3 April, perhaps not so new-looking as on her 21 June 1911 arrival, but just as proud. Her final departure on 5 April was on schedule, without special ceremony. Yet there must have been many misty-eyed officers and crew aboard 'Old Reliable' when the lights of New York City faded into the night as *Olympic* headed for open sea.

Arriving at Southampton 12 April she discharged passengers and cargo, and then was towed to Berth 108 at the new Western Docks. Laid up through the summer of 1935, her officers and crew

After being tied up since April 1935, her fate a source of constant rumour, Olympic *departed Southampton for the last time 11 October for the scrapyards at Jarrow* (Authors' collection).

were discharged or transferred elsewhere.

For a week rumours abounded regarding her disposition: would she be refurbished once again and return to service? Had she really been sold to Italian shipping interests? Was the government considering her conversion into a troop carrier to be berthed permanently at Southampton?

Olympic's fate was sealed with her owner's 20 August announcement that prospective shipbreakers could inspect her the following Monday. Sir John Jarvis purchased her for £100,000 in September and re-sold her almost immediately to Thomas W. Ward, Ltd., stipulating that she would be scrapped at Jarrow to provide work in one of England's most depressed regions.

One week before *Olympic*'s scheduled 11 October departure for Jarrow, rumour again suggested postponement of her demise. With military distur-

bances in Africa and the Middle East, it was thought *Homeric* and *Olympic* might be used as troop ships should conditions worsen. Alas the rumour proved unfounded and as scheduled, *Olympic* departed Southampton for the final time before the sad gaze of thousands.

Even in her final voyage there was drama. Her arrival at Jarrow on 13 October was to coincide with the Tyne's highest tide. But *Olympic* arrived several hours early. The words of the local newspaper, the Shields *Gazette*, described the saddest of all events in a liner's life, her last moments afloat...

'*Olympic* had to wait until there was sufficient water to permit navigation of the channel. She idled to and fro outside the harbour, her pinky-beige funnels resplendent in the sunshine. Then at five minutes to three her bow turned westward and under her own steam she entered the Tyne on the last lap of her journey.

'Then the liner spoke. A rusty trawler, caked with North Sea salt, started her off. From the Fish Quay moorings she screamed and shrieked her whistle for dear life and it was the signal for every craft for miles around to join in the chorus of welcome. The sound died and silence fell. Then, heralded by gushing plumes of white steam from the forward funnels, came *Olympic*'s reply — three long blasts in a deep and tremulous bass — so low as to be just audible to the human ear, full of sadness and melancholy.

'There was nothing pathetic in *Olympic*'s progress up the Tyne. Instead, there was a quiet dignity, a solid and defiant serenity about the great liner as, surrounded by pushing and pulling tugboats, she glided to her berth up-river.'

Olympic arrived at Palmer's Yard at 3.50 pm, the moment of high tide. It took almost an hour to secure her to the wharf. Barely minutes after she tied up, the tide had fallen sufficiently to cause *Olympic*'s hull to settle, upright and perhaps wearily into the river bottom's mud.

Dismantling began on 6 November with auctioning of *Olympic*'s furnishings and fittings, made even more doleful by being conducted in the cold, cavernous rooms of the dying ship's interior. Some 4,456 lots were offered before the final gavel fell on 18 November.

Demolition began several weeks later and continued for almost two years. Finally on 19 September 1937 all that remained of her dismembered hull was towed to Inverkeithing, Scotland, where it arrived the next day for final demolition at Ward's.

In a short but superb article, 'The Great *Olympic*, part of his 'Steamers of the Past' series in *Sea Breezes* magazine, February 1956, J.H. Isherwood best summed up *Olympic*'s passing and provided a suitable salute to 'Old Reliable':

'She will always be remembered for her magnificent war service and as a very fine-looking, reliable, comfortable and steady "old lady" — although she was only 24 when taken out of service. Four years more and she might have been of enormous value to her country in the Second World War. Her hull was still sound as a bell. But the great and rapid strides in marine engineering had made her uneconomical by modern standards and the slump rendered her redundant. The dreary flattened hulk towing up to Inverkeithing was, I think, rather specially pathetic. Besides being all that remained of a very proud ship, it brought back memories of the terrible disasters that had befallen her two sisters and was a symbol not only of the end of a great ship but also one of the greatest transatlantic companies.'

Accidents and incidents

22 June 1911	While docking at New York's new Chelsea piers, *Cedric* ran into a temporary pier extension, which was badly damaged. *Cedric* emerged unscathed.
30 June 1911	Fires in different parts of *Arabic* were discovered five times in a single afternoon while she was docked at Liverpool. Apparently started by incendiary devices they were discovered in storerooms and cabins. They were extinguished after causing minor damage.
13 November 1911	While coming alongside the *Philadelphia* in Cherbourg Roads, the new White Star tender *Nomadic* collided with the liner and had her bows crushed, her stem twisted and several plates stove in.
5 December 1911	During a voyage from Liverpool to Halifax and Portland, Maine, *Teutonic* experienced heavy weather. A broken ventilator allowed water to flood a hold, damaging cargo.
28 December 1911	*Arabic* was delayed 36 hours on a Liverpool-New York crossing. Water found its way into the ship and for forty consecutive hours a dozen stewards did nothing but mop it up.
17 January 1912	*Cedric* encountered high winds and strong gales for six days of her $8\frac{1}{2}$-day passage to New York. Great waves smashed a lifeboat and sent a shower of glass into a stateroom. On the lower deck two companion ladders were swept away with such velocity they pushed a vertical iron ladder two inches out of plumb.
29 February 1912	*En route* Southampton to New York, *Oceanic* dropped a propeller blade.
1 April 1912	Fire broke out in *Titanic*'s coal bunker number six while at the shipbuilder's yard. The fire was extinguished 13 April, the high temperatures causing some slightly bent and twisted bulkhead plates.

CHAPTER 10

Titanic, 1912

DEFIANCE AND DISASTER

The Titans: twelve offspring of Uranus and Gaea to whom were imparted control and implementation of the primal forces shaping Earth. In classical mythology, the Titans generally are characterized as wild, powerful and obstructive. Twice they rose in rebellion, first against their father Uranus, and later against Zeus. Truly, the Titans challenged the gods... Through civilization's eons, defiance of the gods — of fate — has been a means by which man challenges his own insignificance. Sometimes the risk succeeds. New worlds are discovered, new inventions created, great financial empires founded. But far more often defiance ends in disaster.

Perhaps nowhere is this audacity better typified than in the past century's great construction and transportation disasters: the 1879 collapse of the Tay Bridge, whose construction defied design and material strength; the 1893 loss through collision of HMS *Victoria*, whose commander challenged a complex naval manoeuvre's intricacies; the ghastly 1915 Quintinshil railroad wreck, whose unwitting perpetrators could not meet the challenge of limited, war-strained facilities; the 1930 explosion and crash of dirigible *R-101* whose passenger cabins lacked evacuation instructions because 'the airship was held so safe that no emergency could possibly occur.' But few disasters of any era involve fate's defiance by so many groups and individuals as that which befell the newest, largest safest ship of its age. Indeed, the new ship's very name threw down a challenge and evoked recollection of fates and gods defied: *Titanic*...

Constructed as yard number 401, the second of a trio of great liners with which Bruce Ismay hoped to capture the cream of North Atlantic passenger trade, *Titanic* was launched on 31 May 1911 at Harland and Wolff's Queens Island yard. Her sister, *Olympic*, was turned over to her proud owners that same day and entered commercial service with her 14 June 1911 maiden voyage from Southampton to New York.

On 2 April 1912, ten months almost to the day following her launch, *Titanic* was tested in day-long trials in the Lough and Irish Sea off Belfast, and upon their successful conclusion was handed over. Departing Belfast that evening, *Titanic* arrived at her home port, Southampton, around midnight April 3/4, and moored at berth 44. In the morning preparations began for her maiden voyage to New York, to commence 10 April.

For a week the freshly-painted liner dominated Southampton's waterfront. It appeared that Mr Ismay's wish for a weekly New York service would be handsomely realized. To command *Titanic*'s maiden voyage, Ismay selected White Star's senior captain, Captain Edward John Smith. It was rumoured that this was to be Smith's final voyage before retirement at age 62. Actually, the company hoped to have him command *Titanic* another year or two, perhaps until the contemplated third liner joined the Atlantic service.

Titanic's officers had joined her at Belfast. Now, while she was at Southampton, White Star assigned to her Henry T. Wilde, *Olympic*'s chief officer, allowing him to learn about the new ship while bringing his expertise to the shakedown trip. Wilde 'bumped' the previous chief, William M. Murdoch, to First Officer; former First Charles H. Lightoller moved to Second, previously held by David Blair. Blair, somewhat reluctantly, left the

Left *Spectators crowd the stands at Harland and Wolff's Queens Island yard in Belfast 31 May 1911 awaiting* Titanic's *launch (Sphere).*

Below left Titanic *approaches the fitting-out basin following her successful launch (Sphere).*

were jammed. The coal strike's end meant places for all, and they rushed to sign aboard the new ship under command of Captain Smith, a perennial favourite among Southampton crew.

During the week tons of supplies — thousands of individual pieces — were taken aboard, where they were checked by the chief purser's representatives. Andrew Latimer, *Titanic*'s chief steward, was one of the busiest aboard, charged not only with loading supplies but scheduling newly hired stewards. At 54, 'Andy' Latimer had a genial personality which won him many friends among passengers and crew aboard every ship on which he served. He had been appointed *Titanic*'s chief steward before the Belfast departure, and had been aboard several weeks.

At last, supplies and cargo stowed, furnishings installed and polished, machinery in working order and coal bunkered, *Titanic* was ready for her maiden voyage. Wednesday 10 1912, departure was scheduled for noon.

Just before 6.00 am, crew began streaming aboard, arriving from all over Southampton. Around 8.00 am they mustered. Department heads read ship's articles as men stepped up to sign them and surrender seaman's books to the purser's representative. The completed sign-on sheets were approved by Captain Smith, then handed to Captain Maurice Clarke, Board of Trade representative, who would forward them to London.

Clarke then observed boat drill. Two of *Titanic*'s boats, numbers 11 and 15 on the starboard side, were manned, lowered, pulled around the dock and hoisted back aboard. In defiance of reality *Titanic* carried twenty lifeboats, sixteen under davits, and four 'collapsible' boats, scarcely more than rafts. The boats provided 1,178 seats — somewhat short of the 2,228 (1,324 passengers and 904 working crew) expected on this voyage, and yet further short of the 3,547 passengers and crew she was certified to carry.

ship. The remaining officers — Pitman (third), Boxhall (fourth), Lowe (fifth) and Moody (sixth) were unaffected.

A British miners' strike, begun 12 January, had deeply curtailed shipping schedules. The strike was settled 6 April as *Titanic*'s crew signed on. Some engineering officers and department heads had also joined at Belfast, and now assisted with recruitment of the crew. Union and company hiring halls

This discrepancy, this defiance, was neither fault of the owner nor the builder. Board of Trade regulations — last revised in 1894 when the world's largest vessel was about 13,000 tons — were not based upon numbers aboard, but upon cubic footage devoted to their accommodation. When *Titanic* sailed, upward revision was under consideration, but had not been acted upon. Nor was there strong motivation to do so. Rescue of *Republic*'s and *Florida*'s passengers just three years earlier clearly had demonstrated the unwritten principle that lifeboats were intended only to ferry a liner's complement to other vessels which, with wireless's aid, would surely come to the rescue.

In providing sixteen lifeboats with 980 seats, White Star exceeded then-current regulations permitting seats for slightly more than 700. The company had gone even further by adding the four Englehardt collapsible boats with their 196 additional seats. But simple arithmetic demonstrated that even with every boat loaded to capacity and safely launched, 1,052 would have to be left behind. Crew? Passengers? Defiance.

The morning passed. Departure time approached. Passengers began to board. Some had arrived at Southampton several days earlier; others had come

The voyage that was not to be... Titanic*'s original maiden voyage date was announced prior to the* Olympic/Hawke *collision. Diversion of manpower to* Olympic*'s repairing resulted in a three-week postponement of* Titanic*'s first trip (Authors' collection).*

The schedule that was not to be ... Titanic*'s projected 1912 voyages (Authors' collection).*

"OLYMPIC" (Triple-Screw), 45,000 Tons.
AND
"TITANIC" (Triple-Screw), 45,000 Tons (Launched May 31st, 1911).
THE LARGEST STEAMERS IN THE WORLD.

SOUTHAMPTON-CHERBOURG-QUEENSTOWN-NEW YORK SERVICE
Calling at QUEENSTOWN (Westbound) and PLYMOUTH (Eastbound).

"OLYMPIC" (Triple-Screw), 45,324 Tons.
AND
"TITANIC" (Triple-Screw), 46,328 Tons.
THE LARGEST STEAMERS IN THE WORLD.

SOUTHAMPTON-CHERBOURG-QUEENSTOWN-NEW YORK SERVICE
Calling at QUEENSTOWN (Westbound) and PLYMOUTH (Eastbound).

The only known photograph of Titanic's bridge telephones shows the instrument by which Sixth Officer Moody learned of the iceberg from Lookout Frederick Fleet (The Electrician).

In Titanic's wireless cabin, pneumatic tubes sped messages to and from the purser's office (The Electrician).

that morning from London's Waterloo Station aboard the 7.30 boat train, arriving shortly before 9.30. Mainly third and second class, they were directed to their cabins, then explored their designated areas in the great new ship. Many gathered on deck to watch others board. At 11.30, with the arrival of the 9.45 boat train from London, first class passengers trooped up the gangway to the main entrance on B deck amidships. There

were comparatively few members of British aristocracy, but American millionaires in profusion.

Absent were several prominent Americans who, for various reasons, had cancelled passages: Henry Clay Frick, J. P. Morgan, George W. Vanderbilt. Others, less well known, were not aboard because of premonitions, while still others were, despite them. A few minutes past noon — officers and

Titanic was moored at berth 44 in Southampton's new White Star Dock (Smithsonian Institution).

Shortly after noon, 10 April, Titanic *left the dock and headed down the River Test toward Southampton Water and the open sea* (Authors' collection).

crew at stations, captain and pilot on the bridge, tugs standing by — *Titanic* sounded her mighty whistles, cast off and, engines turning slow ahead, pulled away from her dock. Until now the fates had been kind. But ahead lurked disaster.

Early in September 1911 White Star had announced 20 March 1912 as the date of *Titanic's* first Southampton departure. But collision between her sister *Olympic* and the cruiser *Hawke* on 20 September necessitated *Olympic's* return to her Belfast builders. *Titanic's* completion was delayed as men were diverted to repair *Olympic*. *Titanic's* first voyage began on the date scheduled for her second: 10 April. All subsequent events occur at times completely altered from what *might* have been. Even within the modified time frame, further distortion and shifting occurs.

As *Titanic* departed White Star Dock she swung

into the Test River and began her majestic sweep toward the open sea. As she passed berth 38, where the liners *Oceanic* and *New York* were moored in tandem (the latter outward, facing downstream), hydrodynamic forces caused by *Titanic*'s immense bulk and gathering speed snapped *New York*'s mooring lines. Her stern arced out to meet the passing *Titanic*. Immediate action by Captain Smith, Pilot George Bowyer and Captain Gale of the nearby tug *Vulcan* averted collision.

But their backing, clearing and manoeuvring delayed *Titanic*'s departure more than an hour. No effort was made to regain the lost time. To the three weeks already altering *Titanic*'s time frame now were added these minutes, making even more certain the fateful rendezvous that lay in the future.

No longer impeded, *Titanic* crossed the Channel to Cherbourg, where she anchored in the roadstead

As she passed berth 38, suction generated by Titanic's *immense bulk causes the American liner* New York *to break her hawsers and pivot toward* Titanic's *port side. (Father Francis M. Brown collection, Society of Jesus).*

As the Alexandra Towing Company tugs Hector *and* Neptune *nudge* Titanic *away from* New York, *whose stern crosses* Titanic's *bow, disaster is averted (Father Francis M. Brown collection, Society of Jesus).*

about 6.30 pm. After discharging 22 local passengers and taking aboard 274 from the tenders *Traffic* and *Nomadic*, *Titanic* departed at 8.10 pm, speeding off into the night towards Queenstown, Ireland. During the passage around Land's End and through the Atlantic's eastern reaches, *Titanic*'s machinery underwent additional trials. Several sweeping turns tested her steering gear.

Arriving at Queenstown at 11.30 am, *Titanic* an-

chored off Roches Point. The tenders *America* and *Ireland* brought out 1,385 sacks of mail and 120 passengers. Seven local passengers were taken ashore, as was stoker John Coffey, who deserted by hiding under several mail bags.

At 1.30 pm, *Titanic*'s anchor was raised, and three stentorian whistle blasts announced her departure. As she turned into the lowering afternoon sun, a lone passenger high on her after deck

Departure delayed more than one hour, Titanic *crosses the Channel to Cherbourg without further incident. White Star tenders* Nomadic *(left) and* Traffic *ferry the liner's Continental passengers to* Titanic's *roadstead anchorage (Authors' collection).*

Titanic *sails through the night to Queenstown. Arriving 11.30 am 11 April, she takes aboard passengers and mail by tender. As local passengers leave the ship, one takes this stern view of the* Titanic *(Father Francis M. Brown collection, Society of Jesus).*

sounded the haunting strains of 'Erin's Lament' on his bagpipes. The dirge seemed to echo through the green Irish hills long after the ship had vanished.

Thursday, Friday, Saturday... *Titanic* sped westward through gentle Atlantic swells. With calm seas and good visibility, officers had little reason to heed the few wireless messages advising of ice in the waters ahead. The first warnings directed to *Titanic* arrived on Friday 12 April, one in the morning from *Empress of Britain*, the other in the evening from *La Tourraine*, both eastbound.

Through 12 and 13 April *Titanic*'s wireless operators quite likely heard many messages from other ships describing or warning of ice. *Hellig Olav*, *Amerika*, *Montcalm*, *Trautenfels* ... it is not recorded how many were overheard by *Titanic*'s wireless station, or how many — if any — were passed to the bridge. By Sunday 14 April, however, *Titanic* was receiving and acknowledging ice warnings. *Caronia*'s 9.00 am message was the first.

At 1.42 pm, another arrived from *Athinai* via *Baltic*. It was delivered to Captain Smith while he talked with Bruce Ismay. Smith read the message, then handed it to Ismay, who pocketed it and later showed it to several passengers. The message was not posted in the chart room until 7.15 pm, after Captain Smith had requested its return. At 1.45 pm *Amerika* transmitted an ice warning; she received *Titanic*'s acknowledgement.

Californian's message to *Antillian* was overheard by *Titanic*'s wireless. Junior Operator Harold Bride delivered it to the officer of the watch. The message was never shown to Captain Smith, who was attending a dinner party in the restaurant. At 9.40 pm, *Titanic* acknowledged an ice warning from *Mesaba*. It never reached the bridge. Senior Operator John Phillips was working alone, unable to leave the Marconi room. He 'spiked' the message, intending to deliver it later... Defiance.

Ignoring an even more obvious warning helped seal *Titanic*'s doom. From *Titanic*'s bridge at about five bells (10.30 pm), the eastbound freighter *Rappahannock* was sighted, bound from Halifax to London. She had just passed through a great ice field. Her acting master, Captain Albert E. Smith, signalled via Morse lamp: 'Have just passed through heavy field ice and several ice bergs.' After a moment came *Titanic*'s response, also by Morse light: 'Message received. Thanks. Good night.' Defiance.

Seven bells. 11.30 pm. *Titanic*'s knife-like bow parted the dark waters, a barely discernible hiss indicating a $21\frac{1}{2}$ knot speed. The sea was calm, without a ripple. The night sky, dark as the waters below, was moonless but pierced with the sparkle of a thousand stars.

Eleven thirty-five... Eleven thirty-six... the seconds, the minutes passed. High in the crow's nest lookouts Frederick Fleet and Reginald Lee peered into the onrushing darkness. A few minutes earlier, what seemed to be a haze appeared on the horizon ahead. Before they had come on duty at 10.00 pm they had been warned to keep a sharp watch for fog, and now they strained to see what lay ahead.

Suddenly, without a word to his partner, Fleet reached behind him and gave three quick tugs to

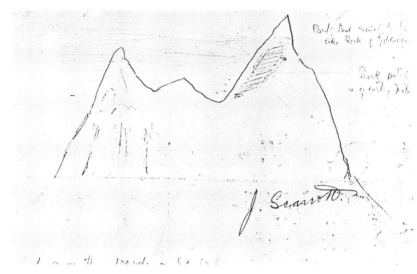

the warning bell's lanyard. He grabbed the telephone that connected directly to the bridge, paused, then waited for what seemed an eternity for acknowledgement. Sixth Officer James Pell Moody responded from the bridge: 'What is it?'

'Iceberg! Right ahead!'

'Thank you.'

Fleet slammed down the telephone and, with Lee, gripped the crow's nest rail and stared in horrified fascination as out of the blackness where sea and sky merged, there loomed an even darker shape: an immense iceberg. Fleet and Lee sensed the beginning of a port turn and a slackening of speed. In moments the berg was at *Titanic*'s bows. Just as a head-on collision appeared inevitable, the ship began to turn away. The berg's dark mass slipped past *Titanic*'s starboard side. The two lookouts gazed after it, noticing at its crest a tip of white which seemed to emit an almost-luminous haze.

On *Titanic*'s bridge, after what had seemed to Fleet an almost casual response to his warning, there had been hasty though deliberate action. Moody, junior officer of the watch, instantly and loudly repeated the message: 'Iceberg. Right ahead.' William M. Murdoch, the watch's senior officer, responded instinctively. He rushed to the telegraph to order engines stopped and reversed, calling simultaneously to Quartermaster Robert

Hichens at the wheel, 'Hard-a-starboard!' Murdoch then quickly activated the lever that closed the watertight doors while simultaneously sounding the alarm bells. It was 11.40 pm — just a bit less than one minute after Fleet had first sighted the iceberg.

Titanic, still turning to port, still moving ahead, missed colliding with part of the berg that Fleet had seen. But a thick, flint-hard spur protruding from the berg's huge bulk struck and raked along the liner's fragile shell, bumping, cutting, tearing open a lethal path of intermittent perforations, an interrupted incision extending along 300 ft of *Titanic*'s

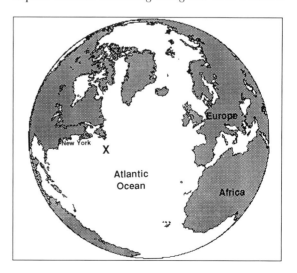

hull, 15 ft above the keel, from forepeak tank to boiler room number five. The blow was mortal. As Captain Smith learned after hasty consultation with Thomas Andrews, the ship's designer on board for her shakedown voyage, *Titanic* had about two hours to live.

Between this moment of immutable truth and the moment of sinking were born heroes and heroines, myths and legends: a panoply of stories to be told in kaleidoscopic profusion through the years.

With destruction's challenge issued, men, women, entire groups rose in defiance. Their courage and determination, their calm in the face of certain death, their unselfish devotion to duty shall endure as long as honour lives. The pages, bell boys, lift attendants: none out of their teens, many scarcely more than children. This night they became men. Told to stand back, to wait, not one survived. Defiance.

The postal workers — two Britons, three Americans. Plain, simple men not given to heroic behaviour, their last hours of life were spent strug-gling to save mails entrusted to their care. With selfless devotion they pulled dozens of heavy registered mail sacks up four flights of steep metal stairs to the open deck, where they awaited boats that surely would arrive to remove their precious burden. Defiance.

The engineering officers. Perhaps nowhere is their story better related than in *Engineer* magazine, which published the statement of Frederick J. Blake, White Star's superintendent engineer at Southampton:

'...In a case like the disaster to the *Titanic* all the engineers would be required below to endeavour to stop any leak that might take place in the watertight bulkheads, and perhaps to take steps to support the bulkheads. All the pumps would be working to their ut-most capacity, and the electrical engineers would be keeping their dynamos running as long as possible. The emergency dynamo would be kept running as long as there was steam to supply it.

'When this accident happened and the telegraph bell rang from the bridge either to stop or reverse the engines, a call bell would be rung from the engine room

WHAT SHALL IT PROFIT A MAN

! IF HE SAVES HIS OWN LIFE, AND GAINS THE WORLD'S CONTEMPT? ·

Below far left *First class Chief Steward Andrew Latimer assists many passengers into lifejackets. Later he gives up his own lifejacket to a female passenger* (Mrs J.H. Walmsley).

Right *Among the saved are Mr and Mrs Anton Kink and their daughter Louise* (Louise Kink Pope).

Below left *Also among the saved is the managing director of White Star Joseph Bruce Ismay. Though villified by the American press, he found many in England who recognized his role in assisting women into the boats* (Baltimore American).

to the engineers' quarters intimating that all engineers were wanted below. At sea and at such a time this would at once be recognised by the "watch off" as being an emergency call, and they would be down below in a few minutes.

'They would be then under the direct orders of the chief engineer, who would depute the engineers to different duties necessitated by the exceptional circumstances, and at such duties the men would remain until ordered out of the engine room by the chief engineer. They would be working surrounded by miles of live steam pipes, and they would be superintending or assisting in drawing out the fires or doing other work where everything was under pressure of steam of 200 lb. The engineers of the *Titanic* were the pick of the service. They were second to none and were chosen from the finest boats in the company's fleet on account of their excellent record. There can be no doubt that it was entirely due to the heroic devotion of these engineer officers that the ship remained afloat as long as she did.'

Titanic's engineer staff numbered 35. Not one survived. Defiance.

Individuals, too, played significant roles in *Titanic*'s saga. Thomas Andrews, after issuing his beloved ship's death warrant, assisted women passengers into the lifeboats; he encouraged stewardesses not only to appear calm, but to wear lifejackets so that passengers also would do so.

Chief Steward Andrew Latimer, mindful of his wife and three young children back at Liverpool, removed his lifejacket and fitted it to the shoulders of a female passenger, remarking as he did so, 'Here, take this. There may not be enough to go around for all.' John Jacob Astor, after assisting his pregnant eighteen-year-old wife into a lifeboat and waving a brave farewell as the boat was lowered, repaired to the F deck kennels and set free the dogs caged there, including his own dear Airedale, Kitty. Isidor Straus would not enter a lifeboat before any other man. Ida Straus would not leave her husband of forty years. Proudly, adoringly, they met death together. Miss Edith Evans, about to enter collapsible D, the last boat to be lowered, stepped away from the deck's edge and urged her companion, Mrs John Murray Brown, 'You go first.' She helped Mrs. Brown over the railing, 'You have children at home,' she said. Defiance.

Collapsible D was lowered at 2.05 am. But a few brief moments remained. High on the boat deck, in a space adjacent to the second funnel, *Titanic*'s bandsmen paused in their music making. Earlier they had played rags, gay pieces from musical theatre, brave marches. The deck beneath them began a slow, almost imperceptible slant forward.

Left *After exhaustive inquiries by American and British authorities, safety measures were enacted to prevent recurrence of disasters at sea. Among the reforms was the establishment of an international ice patrol, whose first sailing was by the British vessel* Scotia. *Subsequent patrols have been conducted by US Coast Guard vessels* (Liverpool Central Libraries).

Below left *Himelf a last-minute cancellation from* Titanic's *tragic voyage, Guglielmo Marconi's wireless telegraph was ordered installed aboard all passenger-carrying vessels: yet another safety measure after the disaster* (Liverpool Central Libraries).

Cold hands gripped instruments tightly; chilled fingers groped for taut strings. Bandmaster Wallace Hartley tapped his bow and spoke a title. The strains of the well-loved *Londonderry Air* ('*Danny Boy*' to many) drifted across the calm waters now dotted with drifting lifeboats.

The slanting decks grew steeper, more slippery. Footing became difficult. The music ceased, then began again, thinly, as Harley, perhaps in reverie, pulled his bow across ths strings for the final time. He was joined as, one by one, the other players picked up the familiar tune — the hymn played at gravesides for brother musicians departed, and Harley's own favourite, *Nearer, My God. To Thee.*

It is impossible to stand. The music's sounds are lost in an increasingly thunderous roar. *Titanic's* stern rises high out of the water. Lights that have stayed lit for so long — at the price of many lives — flicker, turn red as current fails, then go out for ever. Dark, now, against the starlit sky *Titanic* rises almost upright, pauses, then begins a low, inevitable slide.

Roar and clatter pile upon crash and rumble as everything movable slides forward and downward to the vanished bow. The growing thunder yields to the screech and agony of twisted metal as the ship wrenches and tears in two before going under.

At 2.20 am, 15 April 1912, 7,670 hours after her launch, *Titanic*'s stern slips beneath the Atlantic's cold, dark surface. The churning, bubbling sound of air roiling and foaming to the ocean's surface gives way to the shrieks of the dying, the calls for help which gradually, surely diminish. Then there is the dark sea, the starry sky, the silence of eternity. One thousand, five hundred twenty-three dead.

Disaster.

One might imagine that as Captain Smith struggled to keep his footing on the bridge's slanting deck, his eyes touched upon the framed regulations, provided by *Titanic*'s management, that hung on a bridge bulkhead. His eyes dwelled briefly on Regulation Number 2, its first word underlined in red:

'*Overconfidence*, a most fruitful source of accident, should be especially guarded against.'

Accidents and incidents

5 August 1912	*Oceanic* was delayed six hours on her voyage from Southampton to New York when her port engine broke down. Repairs were effected at sea.
1 December 1912	One crewman was killed, three were injured during a lifeboat drill on board *Adriatic* while at Funchal, Madeira.
28 December 1912	Table racks were used for the first time in two years as *Celtic* battled a severe storm during a westbound voyage. One wave caused the ship to lurch, bringing her stern clear out of the water. The racing of the port screw caused an air valve to collapse; as repairs proceeded, *Celtic* proceeded 'at a snail's pace.'
18 September 1913	*Cretic* arrived at Gibraltar with a broken crankshaft. She was drydocked at Naples where repairs were made.
14 October 1913	*Canopic* broke one of her starboard propeller blades and bent the other two when she collided with and sank a lighter at Naples.
18 December 1913	While moving from the Liverpool Landing Stage, *Cedric* struck the overhead gangway with her stern, doing considerable damage to the former. The liner proceeded to New York.
13 January 1914	Bridge ports were smashed, the bridge supports were bent or carried away, and steering gear was rendered inoperative as *Oceanic* was struck by gales on the way to New York.
14 January 1914	In leaving Cherbourg for New York, *Majestic* was run into by a tender, breaking one of her coaling ports. After repairs were made, she proceeded.
16 January 1914	*Cretic* had a fire in mid-ocean *en route* from Genoa to Boston. Damage was not disclosed.

24 January 1914   As *Majestic* docked at her New York pier, her propeller struck and sank the tug *John Nichols*.

7 February 1914   A giant sea smashed six portside portholes in *Olympic*'s first class dining saloon during lunch; several passengers were cut by flying glass and drenched with water. Twelve, including Purser Claude Lancaster and a governess, required the surgeon's attention for cuts. Bits of glass were found firmly embedded in the dining saloon's woodwork.

18 February 1914   *Celtic* collided with the Fabre Line's *Madonna* at Naples. The *Madonna*'s anchor chain was broken and considerable damage was done to her bow and stern, forcing cancellation of her voyage to New York. *Celtic* was seriously damaged on her counter, but only slightly injured below the water line. She proceeded to New York.

CHAPTER 11

Britannic, 1916

SHIP OF A THOUSAND DAYS

The date her keel was laid, her original name and the manner of her loss have never been determined conclusively. During 246 days' service as a commissioned hospital ship she made six voyages; departure dates for two remain undocumented. Why for almost sixty years did she lie beneath the Aegean Sea five miles from officially-recorded loss coordinates? How could the Germans justify their sinking of her?

Of all the great liners, none generates such an aura of mystery as *Britannic.* When J. Bruce Ismay met with Lord William Pirrie to discuss construction of two (and possibly three) immense Atlantic liners, contracts and designs for two were drawn up almost at once. It was not until summer 1911, when *Olympic* was already in service and *Titanic* approached completion, that agreement for a third vessel was concluded. Pleased with *Olympic*'s performance and *Titanic*'s potential, Ismay now envisioned a weekly three-ship Southampton-New York schedule, rather than the original fortnightly, two-ship service.

On 23 November Royal Mail Line's *Arlanza* was launched from number 2 slip at Harland and Wolff's Belfast yard. One week later on 30 November, as best as can be determined, yard number 433's keel was laid in the vacated slip which had served as *Olympic*'s construction site.

Construction photographs of *Olympic* and *Titanic* show painted boards bearing the ship's names near each vessel's bows. No similar photograph for number 433 is known; documenting the name first given her is difficult. There is evidence, however, to support contentions the new liner's name originally was to be *Gigantic.* This name appears in

a brief-but-speculative *Journal of Commerce* article dated, coincidentally enough, 15 April 1912.

'THE GIGANTIC
Another World's Largest Vessel

Our Belfast correspondent telegraphs tonight: — With the departure of the *Titanic* attention is now being centred in the great ship for the White Star Line, the keel of which was laid last week [*sic*] in Messrs. Harland and Wolff's Belfast yard. This monster, which will be fittingly named *Gigantic,* will, it now transpires, be 924 feet long, 94 feet broad and nearly 54,000 tons gross register. The *Gigantic* will thus be considerably larger than either the new Cunarder *Aquitania* or the Hamburg-American *Imperator.* But for the lack of dry dock accommodation and the Belfast channel depth she would have been much larger.'

C.C. Pounder, a Harland and Wolff managing director (department head) and and chief technical engineer stated in the Society of Naval Architects and Marine Engineers' *Transactions* for 1959 that *Britannic*'s original name was to have been *Gigantic.* In later correspondence with a *Britannic* historian, Pounder wrote, 'The original conception was three mammoth ships bearing names suitable for such vessels, namely *Olympic, Titanic,* and *Gigantic.* After the catastrophe which overtook the *Titanic*...it was decided to drop the name of the third vessel.'

Yet several United Kingdom newspapers reported on 16 May 1912 that J. Bruce Ismay denied any consideration of naming the new liner *Gigantic:*'...The White Star managers never had any intention of calling the new ship *Gigantic* and she certainly would not have been so named,' he insisted. Two weeks after Ismay's declaration, the

Her keel laid around 30 November 1911 as Gigantic, *the new White Star vessel's ribbing was completed and plating had begun when this photograph was taken in 1913* (Liverpool Central Libraries).

Her name changed to Britannic *in September 1912 as the result of* Titanic's *loss, the liner, ready for launch, is depicted in a contemporary postcard* (Authors' collection).

new liner's name appears in a 30 May 1912 story reporting *Majestic*'s New York arrival as a substitute for *Titanic*. '...It is understood that *Majestic* will stay on the Southampton-New York service until the new 50,000 ton White Star liner *Britannic* is ready. This ship the company expects will be in service by the fall of 1913.' It was not un-

til 1 September 1912 that White Star itself officially announced that the new liner's name indeed would be *Britannic*.

Britannic's construction had not progressed far when it was abruptly halted. With *Titanic*'s tragic loss came recognition that structural deficiencies which had contributed to her demise might well be

Britannic's machinery takes shape in Harland and Wolff's Belfast shop (Liverpool Central Libraries).

Her construction delayed, her launch twice postponed, even by launch day Britannic's *builders and owners had not released details of her tonnages and dimensions to the public* (Harland and Wolff collection, Ulster Folk and Transport Museum Photographic Archive).

incorporated into the new ship. Work on *Britannic* was suspended as, quite literally, her builders went back to the drawing board.

Modifications reflected conclusions reached at American and British investigations into *Titanic's* loss. The most obvious was in *Britannic's* lifeboat provisions. The clean, dignified profile which would have resembled *Olympic* (for which other lifeboat arrangements were made) was somewhat marred by installation on the boat deck of eight giant gantry davits, each capable of lowering up to six 34-ft lifeboats: twelve forward and 24 aft on the promenade and twelve on the poop deck. The 48 boats 'under davits' could accommodate all 2,572

Above *Following her launch,* Britannic's *completion was slowed because construction materials were diverted to Admiralty orders* (Harland and Wolff collection, Ulster Folk and Transport Museum Photographic Archive).

Below left *One tragedy which befell her sister* Titanic *is impossible aboard* Britannic. *During the ship's outfitting, eighty gantry davits, each capable of lowering up to six lifeboats, are designed for installation at various points on the boat and poop decks* (Authors' collection).

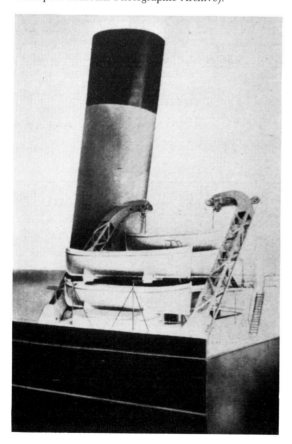

passengers and 950 crew of *Britannic*'s designed capacity.

Edward Wilding, Thomas Andrews' successor as Harland and Wolff's chief designer, headed the company's investigation into improving passenger liner safety and directed *Britannic*'s design changes.*

Between 10 October 1912 and 22 March 1913 *Olympic* was at Belfast to have a new inner skin fitted and her bulkheads heightened and strengthened. *Britannic*'s double bottom was extended to 4 ft above the load line (6 ft around machinery spaces). Watertight subdivision was increased to standards proposed by the *Titanic* inquiries. Five of her sixteen transverse bulkheads extended to 40 ft above the waterline. It is likely *Britannic*'s modifications were incorporated in *Olympic*. It was said *Britannic* and *Olympic* would float with any six compartments flooded.

Like *Olympic* and *Titanic*, *Britannic* was propelled by two reciprocating engines exhausting into a low pressure turbine. Her triple-expansion recipro-

*Wilding became a managing director of Harland and Wolff in January 1914. He resigned under pressure from Lord Pirrie in 1924.

Requisitioned in November 1915 and ordered completed as a hospital ship, RMS Britannic *became HMHS* Britannic. *During conversion the gantry davits on the poop deck and portside boat deck were eliminated* (Imperial War Museum).

cating engines, the largest ever built, weighed more than 990 tons each, while her turbine weighed 500 tons. The 50,000 hp output (32,000 from the reciprocators, 18,000 from the turbine) would provide a 21 knot cruising speed.

Britannic's proposed passenger accommodation more closely resembled *Titanic*'s than *Olympic*'s. Passengers' maids and valets were, as on *Titanic*, provided with their own dining room. But dog kennels were moved from F deck to the boat deck. In contrast to both sister-ships, almost all of *Britannic*'s first class cabins had adjoining toilets, although not always private. As on *Titanic*, second- and third classes surpassed those aboard other period liners, though third class still contained some open, dormitory-style berths.

Published details were few, perhaps because of impending competition from German liners under construction, perhaps from post-*Titanic* paranoia, more likely because of usual business practice. Thus, imaginative figures such as '950 ft long' and '60,000 tons displacement' appeared in popular press and technical journals.

Even figures distributed on launch day, 26 February 1914, contained several uses of 'about' and 'over' when referring to size. Despite heavy overcast and drizzle, thousands gathered for *Britannic*'s launch, which was completed without difficulty and, in White Star custom, without ceremony. The grey-painted, 24,800-ton hull took 81 seconds to slide through its 2,000 ft launch run, reaching $9\frac{1}{2}$ knots before stopped by drag chains.

In May 1912 White Star had announced that it expected *Britannic* in service by the fall of 1913. One year later, in May 1913, it stated she would be ready for launching by November. When that event occurred in February 1914 the company reported that she might be ready for her maiden voyage to New York by the end of September. But on 2 July 1914 the company announced she would not enter service until spring 1915.

Through the summer of 1914, even before war with Germany commenced on 4 August, Harland and Wolff, with no Admiralty orders, found raw materials being diverted to yards building naval vessels. Yet work on *Britannic* continued, though more slowly than her builder or owners might have wished.

During May 1914 boilers were installed, her steering telemotor and bridge telegraphs placed. When, during September's first week, *Britannic* was drydocked for propeller installation, it was reported she was '...still far from finished,' though this may have referred to interior appointments.

The war, originally anticipated to be short-lived, proved otherwise, and labour and materials became scarce. Until the government employed the nation's civilian shipbuilding facilities, work at these yards slowed or was suspended. With many new naval vessels required for victory, the Admiralty and the Shipping Controller soon embarked upon a massive building programme using every possible facility, including Harland and Wolff's yards.

Through the fall of 1914 and most of 1915 incomplete merchant hulls, including *Britannic*'s, languished at fitting-out basins. But upon completion of the initial Admiralty work and a possible hiatus in future government orders, *Britannic*'s work resumed by November 1915. But now there was another change in plans.

Olympic arrived in Belfast 2 November for conversion to a troopship. Moored beside her was *Britannic*. In their 1915 annual report, apparently ignoring *Olympic*'s in-progress conversion, White Star stated,

'...Since November last both *Olympic* and the new steamship *Britannic*, which could have been made ready for service at that time, have been unemployed...It has been suggested to the Admiralty that these vessels should be utilized for military or transport services, as by this means other vessels more useful for trading purposes might be released, but although a vessel of similar type owned by another company [*Aquitania*] was requisitioned, the suggestion has not been viewed with favour...'

By October 1915, White Star's wish was fulfilled. Her conversion completed, *Olympic* departed England carrying 6,000 troops for the eastern Mediterranean.

In January 1915 Russian commanders had appealed to Britain to create a diversion which would relieve Turkish pressure on Russia's army in the Caucasus. The War Council decided upon a purely naval operation against Turkey's Dardanelles fortifications. The naval action was unsuccessful and in April a joint sea-land attack was launched against the Gallipoli peninsula. With serious problems in providing adequate troops, reinforcements and supplies, this operation also failed. In December 1915 the brave forces were withdrawn after incurring severe casualties during the fruitless fighting.

Meanwhile, Germany had stepped up Mediterranean submarine warfare. Four 'U.B.' and four 'U.C.' submarines were shipped by rail from Germany to Pola, on the Istrian coast, where they were re-assembled and put into operation.

As 1915 ended with *Lusitania* sunk, *Aquitania* and *Mauretania* in service as hospital ships, and *Olympic* carrying troops, it was no surprise when on 13 November 1915 *Britannic* was requisitioned and ordered completed as a hospital ship. In a 6 December note to Berlin through the neutral United States, the Admiralty announced *Britannic*'s status, requesting safe passage.

Conversion began immediately with removal and storage of furniture and fittings, and installation of medical equipment and supplies. Time prevented completion to pre-war drawings' appearances. Gantry davits on the poop deck and the portside boat deck were not fitted. Instead, the boat deck's open spaces were filled with fourteen lifeboats under conventional Welin davits, with fifteen additional collapsibles beneath, for 58 boats in all.

Funnels were painted all buff, the hull and superstructure white with a five-foot-wide green band running her length about 15 ft above the waterline. On either side three red crosses interrupted the band, while two smaller red crosses hung forward from the boat deck's bulwarks. These were lighted at night, each outlined by more than 120 electric bulbs, while green lights along the boat deck's railing also were lit.

Britannic's boat- and promenade deck public rooms were converted to operating suites with adjacent sterilization rooms. X-ray, dental and opthomological facilities were added. Large areas became hospital wards containing cots and fittings for mounting stretchers. Wards of 'pipe rack' bunks were prepared for less-seriously wounded. A special section with quiet rooms and 'padded cells' was provided for troops with mental conditions. *Britannic* had 2,074 berths and 1,035 cots.*

On 8 December 1915 *Britannic*'s sea trials were conducted, lasting for one day, as had *Titanic*'s. Returning to Harland and Wolff's yards for three days, her outfitting was completed and her engines

---

**Britannic's planned peacetime accommodation would have provided for 2,572 passengers: 790 first class, 830 second and 952 third, with 950 crew.

adjusted. On 11 December, $21\frac{1}{2}$ months after launch, she departed for Liverpool where she arrived the next day. *Britannic* was handed over to the Admiralty and commissioned His Majesty's Hospital Ship (HMHS) *Britannic*.

For ten days, medical equipment and supplies were hastened on board, a crew mustered and a medical staff assembled. Her crew numbered 675. The medical staff consisted of 52 officers (mostly surgeons and doctors), 101 nurses and 336 orderlies. *Olympic*'s former master Herbert James Haddock had been tentatively selected as *Britannic*'s first master. But because of her construction delays and war's intervention, he now commanded the Admiralty's 'Suicide Squadron,' merchant ships disguised as naval vessels to confuse enemy intelligence. *Britannic*'s command was given to Commodore Charles A. Bartlett, with White Star since 1894 and their marine superintendent since 1912.

She departed Liverpool 23 December for Mudros, on the Aegean island of Lemnos. Reaching Naples 28 December she departed the next day, and after four days at Lemnos, returned directly to England. She arrived at Southampton 9 January 1916, bringing 3,300 sick and wounded from the Gallipoli and Salonika campaigns.

After departing Southampton 20 January 1916 on her second voyage, *Britannic* reached Naples 25 January. The deep draughts of the three immense British liners in Mediterranean hospital service (*Mauretania*, *Aquitania*, and *Britannic*) made it impossible to enter small ports closest to battlefields. Therefore they moored in larger harbours such as Naples and Mudros, where smaller vessels brought casualties out to the giants for the voyage home.

Arriving at Naples 7.00 am 25 January *Britannic* took on water and coal, and was prepared to depart next day for Mudros to embark casualties. Late in the afternoon of 25 January Captain Bartlett received a signal from the Principal Transport Naval Officer at Cairo to remain at Naples and take aboard casualties then *en route* via smaller hospital ships to Naples.

Britannic's activities on this voyage are reflected in this précis of a dispatch from His Majesty's Consulate General at Naples to the Foreign Office in London:

'COALING

Commenced   January 25th – 9.30 a.m.
Finished   do. do.   – 6.50 p.m.
Quantity taken 2,510 tons

WATER

Commenced   January 25th – 10.30 a.m.
Finished   February 2nd – 8 a.m.
Quantity taken 1,500 tons

PATIENTS

Ex H.M.H.S. "GRANTULLY CASTLE" - 438 souls
Commenced embarking 1.18 p.m.   January 27th
Finished   do.   4.22 p.m.   do.   do.

Ex H.M.H.S. "FORMOSA" - 393 souls
Commenced embarking 5.25 p.m.   January 27th
Finished   do.   8.41 p.m.   do.   do.

Ex H.M.H.S. "ESSEQUIBO" – 594 souls
Commenced embarking 9.10 a.m.   February 1st
Finished   do.   1.35 p.m.   do.   do

Ex H.M.H.S. "NEVASA" – 493 souls
Commenced embarking 9.40 a.m.   February 2nd
Finished   do.   1.30 p.m.   do.   do.

Ex H.M.H.S. "PANAMA" – 319 souls
Commenced embarking 9.15 a.m.   February 4th
Finished   do.   11.45 a.m.   do.   do.

The Consul ended his report stating:

...Feb 3rd. Personal arrangements were made with Port and Customs to waive all formalities in regard to hospital ships which are to be treated as warships.

Feb 4th. *Britannic* left at fifteen o'clock bound westwards.'

Britannic arrived at Southampton 9 February where she remained laid up until 20 March. It is likely additional work on her was now completed. Due to her hasty conversion, many upper deck partitions were merely canvas. These were replaced — probably at this time — with more substantial materials. The Dardanelles' evacuation ended early in January 1916, substantially reducing hospital ship requirements. On 1 March the government discharged *Mauretania* from service, followed on 10 April by *Aquitania*.

Now the only large hospital ship, *Britannic* began

On 23 December 1915 HMHS Britannic *departed Southampton for the Aegean island of Lemnos via Naples. She was to make five round trip passages. Joining* Britannic *on her fourth Southampton departure was a 26-year-old nursing sister Sheila Macbeth* (Sheila Macbeth Mitchell).

In 1988, Sheila Macbeth Mitchell recounted her adventures during Britannic*'s final three voyages* (Authors' collection).

her third Mediterranean voyage on 20 March. After coaling at Naples, she proceeded to Port Augusta, Sicily, where she embarked Egyptian campaign wounded from smaller hospital ships, including *Dunluce Castle. Britannic* returned 4 April to Southampton. With several Mediterranean campaigns now resembling attrition rather than aggression, reduced casualties caused the War Department to lay up *Britannic* on half-hire with fittings intact, effective 12 April. She anchored off Cowes, Isle of Wight where she served as a naval hospital for five weeks.

Over Department of Transport objections, the War Department discharged *Britannic* on 21 May, and paid £76,000 ($385,000) for her reconditioning. After returning briefly to Southampton to discharge medical staff and ship's crew, she proceeded to Harland and Wolff's Queens Island outfitting basin. On 6 June dismantling of hospital equipment and re-fitting for Atlantic service began.

While *Britannic* was at Belfast, an incident occurred which, while perhaps having no direct bearing on future events, presents the possibility that Germany could have regarded her as legitimate prey.

On 12 June 1916 an attempt by the Romanian Military Purchasing Commission was made to acquire the 5,900-ton steamer *Britannic*, owned by Messrs. W.H. Cockerline & Co. of Hull. Once purchased the ship would transport munitions

Peering from inside the ship, Sheila's face is surround by the paint of one of six large red crosses on Britannic's *hull (Sheila Macbeth Mitchell).*

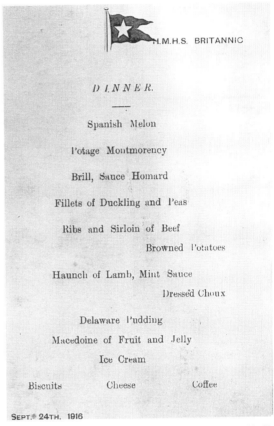

Dinner is served on the fourth voyage's first full day out (Sheila Macbeth Mitchell).

between Spain or France and Vladivostok in support of Russian forces.

Permission for the vessel's purchase was denied by the government. That ended Romania's quest for the ship which, perchance, bore the name of Britain's largest merchant vessel.

Built in 1904, Cockerline's 350-foot-long *Britannic* was sunk by submarine gunfire in the Mediterranean off Tunisia 30 July 1916. Does the loss of this *Britannic* so soon after her attempted purchase imply the Germans learned the vessel's name and intended use? Could the enemy have been misled into believing the hospital ship *Britannic* was engaged in questionable activity? Until a thorough search of German records can be made, questions remain.

Conversion had not progressed far when *Britannic* was recalled to military service. Mediterranean action had intensified, particularly in Egypt and Palestine, and increased casualties required return to England. On 28 August *Britannic* returned from Belfast to Southampton, where she took aboard stores, medical supplies and a hospital staff. She then anchored off Cowes for two weeks.

After signing on a crew *Britannic* departed Southampton 23 September on her fourth voyage and returned without incident from her voyage to Mudros on 11 October. But already clouds had darkened her horizon.

On 31 July the British Deputy Naval Transport Officer at Port Said had signalled the Admiralty's London office with a significant concern: He had

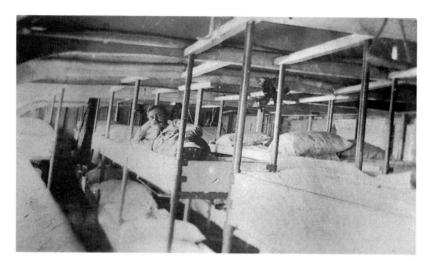

On the return voyage, while there are sick to tend in the ship's capacious wards... (Sheila Macbeth Mitchell).

...there are also moments of recreation. Sheila recalls many visits to Britannic's *pool (Harland and Wolff collection, Ulster Folk and Transport Museum Photographic Archive).*

Right *Aboard* Britannic *on her sixth and final voyage was the Rev John Fleming, one of the ship's two chaplains* (Sheila Macbeth Mitchell).

observed two hospital ships leaving port two days earlier, and in each case, khaki-clad Royal Army Medical Corps lined the rails. The officer suggested they resembled troops; an unscrupulous enemy might draw the same erroneous conclusion and torpedo the hospital ships.

Even as *Britannic* prepared for her fifth Mediterranean voyage, the Admiralty and the Foreign Office exchanged notes concerning permissible cargo and personnel aboard hospital ships. *Britannic*, imminently outbound, was granted specific dispensation. But lack of clear definition persisted.

On 20 October 1916 *Britannic* again departed Southampton for Naples and Mudros. After coal-

ing 25 October at Naples, and picking up many sick and wounded at Mudros, she headed home for Southampton on 31 October. After a non-stop voyage, she arrived 5 November, the voyage's conclusion made extremely uncomfortable by a severe storm through which she had to reduce speed.

Among those who had boarded at Mudros was Austrian opera singer Adelbert Messany. Interned in Egypt at war's outbreak, he was being invalided to England for repatriation, and transferred to *Britannic* from HMHS *Wandilla*. During *Britannic*'s homeward trip, Messany observed what he described as '...2,500 English soldiers, wearing their ordinary uniforms,' in the ship's hold. He added that when *Britannic* reached Southampton, these men marched off in a military formation after the wounded had been taken off.

The Germans refused to believe these were Royal Army Medical Corps men being rotated home, and felt they could challenge the questionable legality by which such men, though non-combatants, were carried aboard hospital ships, including *Britannic*. In less than a month, this unresolved situation was to have tragic consequences.

At noon, Sunday, 12 November *Britannic* slipped out of Southampton on her sixth voyage, again bound for Naples and Mudros. Aboard were 673 ship's crew and 392 hospital staff. She reached Naples on Friday 17 November, moored, and completed coaling. A Friday night departure was delayed by a great storm which raged through the entire following day and night. Finally on Sunday morning it abated briefly and *Britannic* left Naples before heavy weather returned.

Britannic's sixth voyage was recorded through the eyes of a 26-year-old nurse, Sheila Macbeth — now Mrs Sheila Mitchell, who has most kindly granted permission to publish these extracts from her *Pages from a Nursing Sister's Diary.*

'Sunday afternoon was bitterly cold so instead of staying on deck to see the last of England, we gave a tea-party in our cabin.

'Our days were well filled. One of the sergeants gave us a gymnastic class each morning on the boat deck, much to the amusement of the M.O.'s (medical officers), who come up and take snapshots of us when looking most ridiculous and unable to retaliate. Each afternoon we have a lecture by the bacteriologist, and, as soon as we can get away, we fly down to have that precious hour in the swimming bath…After our swim, we have tea and then either play cricket or some other game on deck.

'Having no passengers to help us, we were kept busy getting our 3,000 beds made before reaching Naples — which we did at breakfast time on the Friday. As soon as we got our passes, we went on shore…'

Miss Macbeth then describes her day in Naples. Her eyes still sparkle as she recalls the day of driving about the city and its outlying areas and having lunch at a little country inn, '…where I could not eat for watching the natives shovelling in spaghetti by the yard — a wonderful sight!' Then, back in late afternoon to the ship.

'The next two days were so stormy that we could not get out of the harbour until late on Sunday afternoon. As it was, the pilot had great difficulty in getting off…

'Monday morning found us in the Straits of Messina, which looked nicer than ever. It is always my favourite part of the journey.

'From breakfast time until our afternoon swim, we worked like factory hands, tying up all the kits ready for the next evening — what a day of rest it was!!

'*Tuesday 21st November 1916*: Up late — so only managed to get two spoonfuls of porridge before Bang! and a shiver right down the length of the ship. Of course we all knew what it was! We had thought too much about torpedoes to be surprised to have met one at last. Everyone jumped to their feet, and afterwards I learnt that many went straight off to their cabins for their emergency kit.

'Major Priestly took command and told us to sit down

Returning with friends from a sightseeing trip at Naples, Sheila snaps a photo of Britannic *two days before the ship's loss* (Sheila Macbeth Mitchell).

again as the sirens had not sounded. It was quite the best thing to do, as the doors were few and narrow and there might easily have been a panic. As it was, there was only a most unnatural silence. When the siren sounded, I went off to my cabin for my [life]belt...'

After leaving behind in her cabin her dispatch case containing, among other things, Christmas gifts purchased at Naples (for fear of crowding the boat), Sheila arrived on deck to find that,

'Everyone was very quiet. We kept hanging over the side of the ship for a long while, as the vice-captain, who was looking after the lowering of the boats, had to dash off in the middle to call back some fourteen or fifteen firemen, who had gone off from the poop deck in a boat which should have held about eighty-four persons. They were made to come back to pick up a number of men who had jumped overboard.'

Chief matron of *Britannic*'s nurses was Mrs. E.A. Dowse, described by one of her nursing subordinates as, 'a sixty-year-old "dug out" with a red cape and a row of South African medals.' Mrs Dowse had been one of four nurses who had been in the 1885 Egyptian campaign, serving in relief of Khartoum. During the seige of Ladysmith in the Boer War, she was in charge of the hospital, despite constant danger from stray bullets.

Now she stood calmly on the sinking *Britannic*'s deck, counting each of the nurses as they filed into boats, not leaving the slanting deck herself until certain all her charges were safely away. Sheila recorded her evacuation from *Britannic*:

'We did not realise that while we were hanging over the side of the ship, the whole of the fore part of her was under water — we might have been more frightened if we had seen it. The captain called out to hurry as she was sinking fast. Several of our boats had no seamen in them, and it was rather difficult for the orderlies and sisters to see to the shutting of the water-traps and the getting away from the side of the ship, as all instructions were given from so far above us [by megaphone] and were about things of which we knew little or nothing.

'Fortunately several nurses knew how to row, and in several cases may be said to have saved their boats from being drawn into the propellers. The engines were working until practically the end, doing all they could to beach the ship which unfortunately proved impossible, and she sank about a mile from land.

'Many boats were drawn into the propellers and two were cut in half by them and destroyed. In one of these, a stewardess (formerly of the *Titanic*) was the only survivor. [This was Violet Jessup.] Other boats were capsized by the occupants jumping from them, when they realised that they, too, were being drawn into the propeller swirl.

'Practically all the casualties were caused directly or indirectly by the propeller, and the wounds and fractures were terrible. Of the 299 orderlies, only eight were not in the water — besides many of the M.O.'s, ship's officers and crew.

'In our boat we got well away from the sinking ship and busied ourselves with the wounded, whom we picked out of the water. Our brandy flasks were invaluable, also aprons and pillow cases, which were torn up as bandages. Some boats had only men in them, and if any of these contained wounded, we always went alongside and gave them sisters to help them.

'The *Britannic* disappeared exactly fifty minutes after she had been hit, but as help had not yet come in answer to the SOS calls, we waited until there was no likelihood of any more explosions and then sailed to where the ship

had gone down, to see if we could find any other survivors.

'After some time we saw three trails of black smoke in the distance and knew that help was coming. These three ships were all British — the *Foxhound*, *Scourge* & *Heroic*. After three hours in our lifeboat, we were taken to the *Scourge*, a torpedo-destroyer...We had to wait some time whilst the sailors rowed round to make a final search for survivors. During this time, we saw the captain's bridge and other familiar objects float by...'

Not four hours earlier, Captain Charles A. Bartlett, White Star's commodore and *Britannic*'s commander, had stood on this very bridge and, at 8.12 am, had heard 'a tremendous though muffled explosion, and had felt the ship trembling and

Britannic's Captain Charles A. Bartlett, shown here in yet another Macbeth photo, was on the liner's bridge at 8.12 am 21 November 1916 when the ship struck a mine (Sheila Macbeth Mitchell).

Chief Engineer Robert Fleming did not leave the sinking liner's engine room until all his officers and crew were safely topsides (Marine Engineer).

Left Britannic*'s engineering officers and engine room staff are shown following their rescue* (Marine Engineer).

Below left *Medical officers, nursing sisters and corpsmen pose at Athens for a group photograph* (Sheila Macbeth Mitchell).

vibrating most violently fore and aft, continuing for some time.' In his official report to the Admiralty's director of transport, Bartlett continued,

'...The ship fell off about 3 points from her course. Emergency quarters were sounded on all alarms throughout the ship, the engines stopped, and orders rung below to close watertight doors, at the same time sending out the SOS signal by wireless.

'My first impression was that we had struck a mine and would probably be safe. I gave orders to clear away all boats and have all possible ready to be sent away. After an interval [the] steering gear appeared to have failed. I turned the ship round to port to head for land by the engines, but the forward holds filled rapidly and water was reported in Nos. 5 & 6 boiler rooms, so I stopped the engines and ordered all boats possible to be sent away, but to stand by near the ship.'

Two points in Bartlett's report require consideration: the first, '...My impression was that we had struck a mine.' This has never been proven or disproven. But predominant expert opinion, borne out by accessible documents, is that *Britannic* was sunk by a mine. Two reliable witnesses on deck at the time of the explosion reported they had observed torpedo trails prior to impact. Also it was believed mines could not have been 'laid' because the channel's bottom was too deep and subject to strong currents which would move mines from their charted positions.

From the explosion's appearance, it would appear a torpedo did not strike *Britannic*. Torpedoes send up water geysers as their explosive heads strike a vessel's hull. No such water column was observed in *Britannic*'s case. Portions of the inquiry into *Britannic*'s loss are, in 1989, still closed to the public. But the final accessible document is addressed to the Foreign Office from a British diplomat in Greece, dated 9.10 pm, 25 November:

'Rear Admiral [probably Rear Admiral Cecil Hayes-Sadler] tells me that enquiry respecting "Britannic" led to no definite conclusion but experts inclined to believe in mine not torpedo. Two mines have since been dragged and destroyed in the Zea [*sic*] Channel.

A 2 January 1917 French intelligence report describes October 1916 mine-laying activities of German submarine *U.73*, then describes *U.72*'s November cruise:

'*U.72* Other mines have been laid in the Archipeligo: 10 have exploded or have been swept into Zea [*sic*] Channel (1 struck by "BURDIGALA," 1 struck by "BRITANNIC," 8 raised and destroyed); 4 have been discovered in the Mykoni Channel (1 struck by "BRAEMAR CASTLE" and 3 swept); 1 was struck by "MINNEWASKA" at the entrance of Suda, but we do not know the result of the sweeping in this last zone.

'In all 15 mines...

'We attribute these various mine-layings to *U72* which was reported to us as having left Pola on the 7th November...*U72* probably returned to her base by the end of November.'

The second point to consider is Captain Bartlett's description of *Britannic*'s post-explosion movements. At 7.52 am 21 November, while four miles off Angalistros Point, Makronisos Island, her course was set for N 48° E (magnetic) so as to enter Kea Channel. At 8.12 am, four miles west (magnetic) of Port St. Nikolo light, Kea Island, and steaming at 20 knots, the ship was wracked by explosion. Captain Bartlett quickly issued several orders, including the following:

1. Stopped the engines.
2. Ordered the SOS signal transmitted. [The signal:] '*SOS. Have struck mine off Point Nikola* [*sic*]'.
3. Using the engines, '...turned ship round to port to head for land'.
4. Ordered engines stopped [so that lifeboats could be lowered].
5. 'Again attempted to work ship toward the land'.

The final order never was countermanded. Lifeboats were exposed to the still-turning propellers and were smashed. These movements —

and *Britannic*'s drift after the 'Stop engines' orders — caused *Britannic* to sink several miles from her distress message's position (which contained no latitude or longitude). The wirelessed location was accepted as *Britannic*'s wreck site until French explorer Jacques Cousteau's 1975 discovery of the wreck.

The first British Navy rescue boats arrived at 10.00 am. They found 35 *Britannic* lifeboats spread across the northern part of Kea Channel. Other

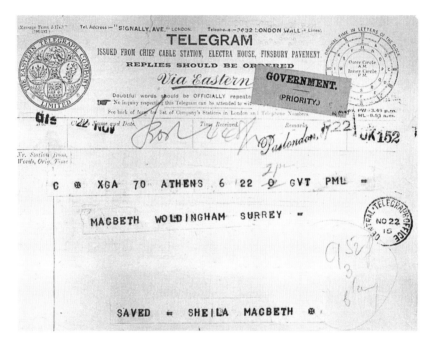

Sheila is permitted to advise her family of her survival by priority telegram (Sheila Macbeth Mitchell).

The day after Britannic*'s loss, the medical staff boards the hospital ship* Grantully Castle *for the trip from Athens to Malta* (Sheila Macbeth Mitchell).

Above far right *On the way to Malta, they are offered a substantial luncheon* (Sheila Macbeth Mitchell).

naval vessels soon appeared and, assisted by Greek fishing boats, searched for survivors. *Britannic*'s personnel were taken to Piraeus where they were brought ashore aboard the ferry *Marinos*. There, injured were taken to the Russian Hospital, while uninjured were taken by taxi to several hotels at nearby Phalerum.

The next day was a sad one as funeral services were conducted for those lost. In his book *The Last Voyage of HMHS Britannic*, Rev John A. Fleming, one of her two chaplains, described the scene:

'We gathered in the afternoon amid glorious sunshine on the grain quay of Piraeus. The friends on the flagship had added to their many kindnesses the gifts of lovely wreaths inscribed, ''To the heroes of Britain''. Surely there never was a stranger or more touching funeral procession! The allied fleets were represented there, and a firing party was furnished from the flagship. Greek sympathisers joined, and our own fellow-countrymen whose homes were in these parts came down to mingle with ours their sorrow for the loss of the brave.

'The streets were packed with men who looked on with strangely conflicting expressions; but all were reverent toward us as we carried our burden to the tomb. The great wreaths which had been sent in sympathy our orderlies carried in front of the coffins. These men and the other orderlies who followed were a touching sight, dressed in all varieties of uniform — naval and military, French and British, a strange reminder of the losses and the trials of the day before; and so we wended our way to the quiet cemetery on the hill and after a simple service we left these brave men sleeping...'

Britannic's crew and officers returned directly to England aboard HMT *Ermine* and HMT *Royal George*, arriving at Southampton 4 December. Around 28 November medical staff were transported to Malta aboard the hospital ship *Grantully Castle*. Ten days later transports took officers and orderlies from Malta to Marseilles; there they boarded a troop train for a three-day trip across France to a port where they embarked for the short voyage to England.

The nurses remained another week in Malta, despairing that they would miss Christmas at home. Finally they were hurried aboard HMHS *Valdivia*, a former French cargo ship, *en route* to a

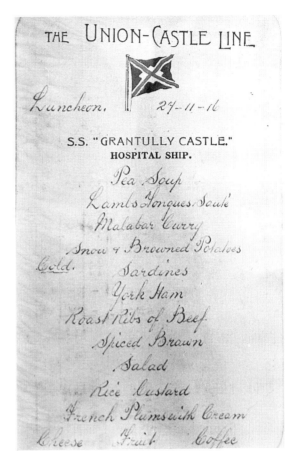

THE UNION-CASTLE LINE

Luncheon. 27-11-16

S.S. "GRANTULLY CASTLE."
HOSPITAL SHIP.

Pea Soup
Lambs Tongues Sauté
Malabar Curry
Snow & Browned Potatoes
Cold. Sardines
York Ham
Roast Ribs of Beef
Spiced Brawn
Salad
Rice Custard
French Plums with Cream
Cheese   Fruit   Coffee

Channel port in France via Malta, Gibraltar and England. Their transportation, lacking cargo or ballast, made the nursing sisters' voyage uncomfortable, and further discomfort was caused by an acute on-board water shortage. But morale was high for they were homeward bound. As Sheila Macbeth described it, 'The thought of getting home on the morrow made everyone hilarious and the "stodgy girls" were teased and put in the ice chests for not being excited, too.'

Valdivia docked at Southampton on 26 December, discharged its 'cargo' of nurses, and left at once for France. The nurses departed for London's Waterloo Station, where their matron-in-chief ordered them to go home, rest and await further orders.

There appears to have been no 'formal investigation' into *Britannic*'s loss, merely Rear Admiral A. Hayes-Sadler's inquiry aboard HMS *Duncan* on 23 November. Upon receiving Sadler's report, Vice Admiral Cecil F. Thursby, commanding the Eastern Mediterranean, interrogated several witnesses himself, then forwarded the report to the Admiralty on 1 December. Five days later the required report to the Board of Trade's Shipping Casualty Wreck Register was filed at Southampton; the Board took no apparent action.

And here — except for several inquiries concerning lost men, lost pay books and remuneration of several Greeks who aided the survivors' rescue — *Britannic*'s official story seems to end. The 28 injured men were treated and returned to England. The 21 dead lay in their 'corner of a foreign field', a white cemetery overlooking the sunny Aegean. For those who planned and built her, or sailed in her, for those whose lives she eased, or even saved, there would be remembrance of a beautiful ship denied the chance to live her own life.

Propellers still turning, as though reluctant to accept the inevitable, *Britannic* sank in the Aegean three days short of one thousand days afloat. Her completion had been delayed for more pressing matters. She never sailed her intended Atlantic route. Yet when called upon, *Britannic* proved her worth. In the livery of mercy, she completed five voyages, bringing home more than 15,000 sick and wounded. Upon one voyage's conclusion, casualties discharged from her wards filled fifteen hospital trains.

Her brief history ends with a question: what might her contribution, so well provided in war, have been in time of peace?

Accidents and incidents

14 February 1917

Outbound from Liverpool, *Celtic* struck a mine off the Isle of Man, creating a 30-ft gash in number 1 hold. She managed to return to port under her own steam.

26 October 1917

Shortly after leaving a Mediterranean port, fire was discovered in *Cretic*'s number one hold, which contained a shipment of Turkish tobacco. The hold was flooded, putting her down by the head. Upon reaching a port in the Azores, land-based fire apparatus pumped in additional water. As *Cretic* resumed her voyage, fire broke out again, and was extinguished only upon reaching Liverpool.

26 January 1918

While tied up at Pier 60 in New York, fire was discovered among several oil barrels on *Adriatic*'s deck. City firefighters flushed the deck and swept burning oil into the North River, minimizing damage.

29 January 1918

Fourteen miles from the Mersey Bar, *Cedric* collided with Canadian-Pacific's liner *Montreal*; the latter sank the following day.

31 March 1918

While outbound in the Irish Sea, *Celtic* was torpedoed. Six were killed. This time damage was serious enough to force her beaching. Eventually refloated, she was taken to Belfast for repairs.

12 September 1918

With 2,800 American soldiers on board, *Persic* was torpedoed about 200 miles off the English coast. All on board were rescued, and the ship was beached, and subsequently repaired. The attacking submarine was reported sunk.

CHAPTER 12

1914–1918

PERILS OF WAR

With routes to Canada, Australia and New Zealand, as well as to the American ports of Portland, Boston and New York, the White Star Line played a vital role in Britain's wartime supply and transport arrangements. Of 35 sea-going vessels White Star owned, controlled or managed at war's outbreak, all saw war service, either directly (as commissioned H.M. ships) or indirectly (operated under the Liner Requisition Act.) Ten were lost.

8 September 1914: *Oceanic*

In common with many other passenger liners, *Oceanic*'s construction was partially subsidized by the Admiralty. As a result, her decks were strengthened to accommodate gun mounts; passenger spaces could be converted readily to troop transport; coal bunkers and bulkheads were placed for maximum protection from gunfire, and specific speed and cruising range requirements were met.

Launched 14 January 1899, *Oceanic*'s luxurious appointments, size and cleanswept appearance gave her the titles 'Ship of the Century' and 'White Star's Millionaires' Yacht.' At 705 ft overall she was the first vessel to exceed the 690 ft of the *Great Eastern*. Sailing from Liverpool and later from Southampton in company with *Majestic*, *Teutonic* and *Adriatic*, *Oceanic* was a substantial and profitable addition to her company's fleet.

At war's outbreak 1 August 1914, *Oceanic* was at sea between New York and Southampton. At the Irish coast she was met by two Royal Navy cruisers and escorted the rest of the way. Upon arrival at Southampton she was quickly converted to war ser-

vice and commissioned HMS *Oceanic*. Her captain for the past two years, Henry Smith (no relation to *Titanic*'s 'E.J.') stayed aboard, but was joined by the Royal Navy's Captain William Slayter. The latter was in nominal command of the ship and her officers and crew, while Smith served in an undefined advisory capacity. Similarly the merchant seamen who remained aboard were joined by a large complement of naval officers and ratings. Initially there was considerable misunderstanding and confusion between the two crews.

Oceanic's conversion took about two weeks. Encouraged by rumour she was to patrol in some exotic (and safe) port in the Far East, her civilian crew volunteered to remain aboard. They must have felt keen disappointment when on 25 August, HMS *Oceanic* departed Southampton to proceed north and join the 10th Cruiser Squadron at Scapa Flow.

Upon arrival at Orkney, *Oceanic* was detached to patrol the Western Approaches to the west of Fair Isle. After a brief courtesy call to Reykjavik, Iceland, *Oceanic* returned to Scapa Flow where gunnery practice for her inexperienced crews commenced. Her civilian staff now was augmented by several Shetland Island fishermen who filled the ship's roster.

Oceanic resumed war patrol in a 150-mile stretch of sea from north of the Scottish mainland to the Faroe Islands, making spot checks on shipping, their cargoes and passengers, assuring that no contraband or German sympathizers entered British waters.

To accommodate gun crews whose watch endings would not otherwise have coincided with each morning's general alert, Captain Slayter soon

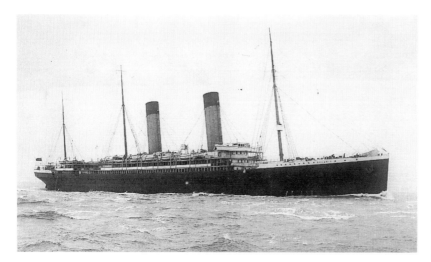

At the time of her launch in 1899, Oceanic was called the Ship of the Century. Until 1914 she had a successful career (Captain Jens Nilsen collection, Steamship Historical Society of America).

Below left *Requisitioned for Admiralty service at war's outbreak, by 25 August 1914 Oceanic was on her way to patrol the Northern Approaches. By 8 September she was hopelessly aground off Foula, Shetland Islands, a victim of misunderstanding between civilian and military command. As HMS Forward stands by, HMS Oceanic, her boats in the water, evacuates her crew (Steamship Historical Society of America).*

Right *The final entries in Oceanic's log demonstrate possible attempts to correct navigational errors. The final lines describe futile efforts to work the ship free with her engines (Public Record Office document MT53 53135).*

ordered the ship's clock put back forty minutes. To the confusion resulting from two captains and — literally — three crews now was added the complexity of two times, ship's time and Greenwich Mean Time.

Although still at odds over ship management, Captains Smith and Slayter had informally agreed that the former was to be in charge during the day and Slayter at night. But *Oceanic* was now in His Majesty's Navy and Slayter, a Royal Navy Captain, was in overall command, his decisions final.

Slayter decided *Oceanic* should search for possible German submarines or patrol craft near the tiny Foula Island, a bleak though inhabited aggregation of rock and reefs lying twenty miles west of Shetland. Through the day and night of 7 September, *en route* to Foula, *Oceanic* steamed continuous zigzag courses to evade submarine attack. It was the duty of *Oceanic*'s navigator, David Blair (who had been displaced from *Titanic*'s roster of officers by Charles Lightoller) to plot and record each complex course change.

Foula came into sight early in the evening of 7 September, and Blair had taken accurate bearings from the island's northern and southern ends. During the night the liner continued to zigzag and at one point encountered thick fog that had cleared somewhat by dawn of 8 September. According to Blair's calculations *Oceanic* was well south of Foula. Before retiring from the bridge, Captain Slayter ordered a course that would take *Oceanic* back toward the island; he was to be called when land was sighted. Blair plotted the course and then, exhausted from many hours of arduous duty, he, too, retired for a brief nap.

While Blair was off duty, Captain Smith arrived, scrutinized the chart and determined that their northeasterly heading, based on Blair's calculations, would place *Oceanic* about fourteen miles to the south and west of Foula. Worried lest the liner foul the island's treacherous reefs, Smith changed

Oceanic's course without consulting Slayter. He turned the ship due west, toward open sea, away from the island's danger. Blair, now back on the bridge, suggested that soundings be taken to determine the ship's position accurately, but Smith vetoed the idea.

About a half-hour later, Foula was sighted dead ahead. Blair's calculations, either because of his fatigue or their complexity, had been in error. Estimating that the island was four miles off, Smith turned the ship several points to starboard, intending to sweep around the southern end of a large reef known as Da Shaalds ('The Shallows') and bring *Oceanic* up the narrow channel between reef and island.

At this moment, Slayter appeared on the bridge, alerted by the lookout's cry. Realizing that the ship was closer to the island than Smith apparently thought, Slayter ordered a sharp starboard turn to leave the area as quickly as possible. But at that moment fast-running tides swept her onto Da Shaalds. Grinding and crunching to a halt, with her stern toward the island, *Oceanic* was driven ever more firmly onto the reef by the tide.

Efforts to free her were unsuccessful. First the trawler *Glenogil* from Aberdeen, and then the Royal Navy cruiser HMS *Forward* put lines aboard *Oceanic*. But the liner's own great weight and the firmness of her grounding snapped the tow lines. Soundings showed *Oceanic*'s double bottom to be so badly breached that even if she were towed off, she would quickly sink.

Late that afternoon, orders were given to abandon ship. The evacuation of the 600-man crew was completed without incident by evening, the men leaving in lifeboats and then transferring to and taken ashore by larger vessels standing by.

Oceanic stood astride the reef for three weeks. During this period the Admiralty salvage vessel *Lyons* recovered all guns, all but one of the gun shields, most of the ammunition and many other naval fittings.

After what was considered an amazingly long quiet period, the area was swept on 29 September by one of the fierce storms for which the region is so well known. By morning *Oceanic* was gone.

At first it was thought that she had been driven into deeper water where she had sunk. But it soon was found that the storm's force had pounded the strong vessel with such fury that she was reduced to pieces and lay, torn to scrap, in relatively shallow water. (The subsequent salvage of much of *Oceanic*'s metal is well recounted in Simon Martin's book, *The Other Titanic*, David & Charles, 1980.)

Captains Smith and Slayter and navigator Blair were court-martialled. Though *Oceanic*'s log, her course as plotted by Admiralty bearing, and her last movements as witnessed by Foula's inhabitants are all at variance with one another, Smith and Slayter were exonerated and Blair released with a mild reprimand. The hearings led to considerable change in armed merchant cruisers' administration, far more responsibility being given their mercantile officers.

And so, after a relatively short fifteen years of commercial life, and an even shorter naval service of just hours more than a single month, *Oceanic*, one of White Star's proudest ships, sadly ended her career.

19 August 1915: *Arabic*

Laid down as *Minnewaska* and launched 18 December 1902 as *Arabic* the 13,801 ton liner had plied her course between Liverpool and Boston or

Below left Arabic's loss by German torpedo 19 August 1915 almost brought America into the war (Authors' collection).

Right Torpedoed and sunk 8 May 1916 Cymric met her fate at the hands of Commander Walther Schwieger and his submarine U.20, which had sunk the Lusitania on 7 May 1915 (Authors' collection).

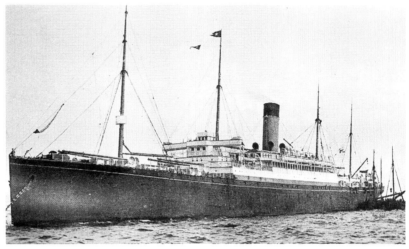

New York without major incident since 1903. On 19 August 1915 *Arabic* was outbound from Liverpool for New York. Under command of Lieutenant Will Finch, RNR, she carried 253 crew and 181 passengers, including 25 Americans.

When opposite Ireland's Old Head of Kinsale and steering a zigzag course, *Arabic* was attacked without warning by German submarine *U.24*, a single torpedo striking the liner's starboard side about 100 ft from the stern.

Arabic sank in just eleven minutes, and it was her crew's remarkable discipline and seamanship that resulted in rescue of all but 44 of the 434 on board. Of the lost, only six were passengers. The 390 saved were taken to Queenstown where, three months earlier, *Lusitania*'s 761 survivors had landed.

Though ordered not to sink passenger ships without warning, *U.24*'s commander, Lieutenant Commander Schneider, justified his action, saying he mistook *Arabic*'s zigzag course as an attempt to confuse him and then run him down. Germany eventually dropped its contention that the attack was necessary, but it was only through exchange of diplomatic notes that American neutrality could be secured for another year.

9 May 1916: *Cymric*

Launched 12 October 1897, the 12,553-ton *Cymric* was no stranger to war. Less than two years after her 1898 Liverpool-New York maiden voyage, she made the first of two round voyages between Liverpool and Cape Town, transporting British troops to the Boer War. After returning to regular service in the spring of 1900, *Cymric* spent her next sixteen years on Liverpool-New York or Liverpool-Boston runs.

On 29 April 1916 *Cymric* departed New York for Liverpool under Captain Frank E. Beadnell's command. Though fitted to carry 258 first and 1,160 third class passengers, this voyage she carried only cargo and 110 crew. At about 4.00 pm on 8 May, when 140 miles west-northwest of Fastnet, she was attacked by Commander Walther Schwieger's submarine *U.20*. (One year earlier, almost to the day — 7 May 1915 — Schwieger and *U.20* had sent *Lusitania* to the bottom of St. George's Channel with a single torpedo; she had sunk in less than twenty minutes.)

Cymric was struck by three torpedoes, but remained afloat almost a full day, sinking at about 3.00 pm on Tuesday 9 May. All but five of her crew survived; four were killed in the explosion, and a steward drowned leaving the ship.

21 November 1916: *Britannic*

The story of White Star's greatest single war loss — and Britain's largest vessel prior to the *Queen Mary* — has been recounted in Chapter 11.

Left Britannic's loss through striking a recently-laid German mine was a great blow to White Star's intended post-war plans (Charles Dixon for the White Star Line).

Right Laurentic's Commander Reginald A. Norton, RN personally searched his sinking vessel for possible injured survivors before leaving the ship himself (Daily Mirror).

Left The German surface raider Moewe counted the freighter Georgic as her largest merchant victim (Private collection).

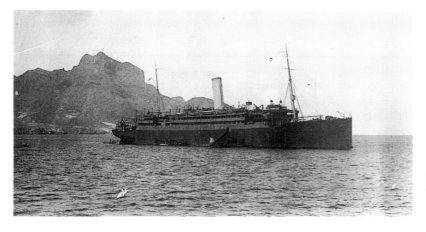

Left On 25 January 1917 during a westbound voyage, Laurentic steamed into a minefield off Malin Head and sank, taking with her 354 crew and almost £5 million in gold. After the war, all but a small portion of the gold was salvaged (National Maritime Museum).

10 December 1916: *Georgic*

Built to replace the lost *Naronic* (*qv*), the 10,077-ton *Georgic* was the largest livestock carrier yet constructed when launched 22 June 1896. After her 16 August 1895 maiden voyage from Liverpool to New York, *Georgic* remained on that route until pressed into war service.

Built in 1914 by the Laeisz Line for its fruit trade between Hamburg and South Africa, the 4,778-ton *Pungo* was appropriated for German naval service in 1915. Disguised as a Swedish merchantman, complete with Swedish colours on her sides, she was renamed *Moewe* ('Gull'), and placed under command of Count Nikolaus zu Dohna-Schlodien, whose instructions were to lay mines and then, supplies and other conditions permitting, engage in raiding merchant vessels.

Moewe was armed with four 5.9 in and one 4.1 in gun, torpedo tubes and 500 mines; collapsible sides concealed her armament. She carried a crew of 235.

Dohna departed Kiel 15 December 1915 and upon his return 4 March 1916 he could claim one battleship (the 16,350-ton HMS *King Edward VII*) and sixteen merchant vessels sunk, and one captured.

Moewe's second voyage was even more successful. Departing Germany 22 November 1916 Dohna spent three weeks cruising the North Atlantic. He returned to Germany 22 March 1917 after sinking or capturing 24 vessels comprising 120,000 tons.

Georgic, meanwhile, had departed Philadelphia, Pennsylvania 3 December 1916 for Brest, France and Liverpool. She carried 1,200 horses and a general cargo, primarily wheat and 10,000 barrels of oil. On 10 December 1916, when 590 miles east-southeast of Cape Race, she was intercepted by *Moewe*. Enforcing his order to heave-to, *Moewe*'s commander ordered shells fired at *Georgic*: one man was killed. After *Georgic*'s crew was taken off, the ship was sunk by torpedo and became *Moewe*'s largest merchant victim.

25 January 1917: *Laurentic*

Laid down as Dominion Line's *Alberta*, but launched

9 September 1908 as White Star's *Laurentic*, Harland and Wolff's yard number 394 was the first ship fitted with triple-screws powered by combination reciprocating/turbine engines. Her 29 April 1909 maiden voyage from Liverpool inaugurated White Star's service to Quebec and Montreal.

She remained on this route (with winter cruises to the West Indies) until 13 September 1914 when requisitioned as a troop carrier for the Canadian Expeditionary Force. Then converted to an auxiliary cruiser, she served in this role for more than two years.

Under command of Captain Reginald A. Norton, *Laurentic* departed Liverpool 23 January 1917 on a voyage to Halifax. On board was £5,000,000 ($25,000,000) in gold bars, as payment for munitions, and a crew of 722 officers and men. After a brief stop, *Laurentic* departed Lough Swilly, on Ireland's northern coast, at about 5.00 pm Thursday 25 January 1917 in fine but bitterly cold weather.

At 5.55 pm, when opposite Malin Head and about to turn toward the Atlantic, there was a loud explosion on the port side near the foremast. Twenty seconds later, a second explosion on the port side rocked the ship, this one next to the engine room. Dynamos stopped almost at once; the

Already a veteran of the Boer War, Afric's World War service was ended when, inbound from Australia, she was torpedoed and sunk 12 February 1917 when 12 miles off the Eddystone Light (Library of New South Wales).

ship was plunged into darkness and there was no power for the wireless.

Laurentic had steamed into a minefield laid by German submarine *U.80* and had struck two mines moored 20 ft below the surface. With splendid discipline, the ship's company took to the lifeboats; Captain Norton personally searched below with an electric torch, ensuring no one remained behind.

Fifteen boats cleared the ship, but only seven were saved. The rest were swamped or blown out to sea where their occupants died of exhaustion and exposure. Altogether, 368 were saved, but 354 were lost.

Laurentic sank in 23 fathoms. After the war, operations to retrieve her gold began. Of 3,211 gold bars aboard, 3,186 valued at £4,958,708 ($24,793,540) were recovered in a series of 5,000 dives from the salvage ship *Racer*. The operation — one of history's most remarkable cargo salvage feats — cost just £128,000 ($640,000).

12 February 1917: *Afric*

Following *Afric*'s 8 February 1899 maiden voyage from Liverpool to New York, she returned to her builders for alterations. Her first voyage on her intended route, Liverpool to Sydney, Australia via Cape Town, began 11 February 1900. On board were horses and troops for the Boer War. After another New York round trip in August 1900, she returned to and remained on the Australian run.

On 12 February 1917, inbound from Australia and Cape Town, *Afric* was torpedoed and sunk by German submarine *UC.66* in the English Channel, twelve miles south-southwest of the Eddystone Lighthouse. Five crewmen were killed by the explosion, and seventeen drowned during evacuation. The 145 survivors included *Afric*'s pilot and her captain.

4 June 1917: *Southland* (ex Red Star Line *Vaderland*)

Built in 1908 for the Red Star Line, the 17,540-ton *Vaderland* ran on the Antwerp-Dover-New York service for five years. Transferred in December 1914 to White Star, she ran on that company's Dominion service between Liverpool and Halifax for several months before requisitioning as a troop carrier. Because of her German-sounding name, she was renamed *Southland*.

Right *Before her loss to submarine* U.70's *torpedo 4 June 1917 off Northern Ireland* Southland *had already suffered torpedo damage when she was nearly sunk in the Aegean Sea 15 September 1915. Judging from the warm-weather dress, this evacuation appears to be during her earlier encounter* (Imperial War Museum).

Below *Another Boer War veteran, the twenty-year-old freighter* Delphic *was sunk by a German submarine on 16 August 1917 when bound for Uruguay with a cargo of coal* (Authors' collection).

Used for trooping in the Salonika campaign, *Southland* was torpedoed in the Aegean Sea 15 September 1915 but managed to reach a safe port where she was repaired. In August 1915 she re-entered White Star-Dominion service, this time on the Liverpool-Quebec-Montreal route.

Southland was sunk by German submarine *U.70* on 4 June 1917 when 140 miles northwest of Tory Island (Northern Ireland) with the loss of four lives.

16 August 1917: *Delphic*

The 8,273-ton freighter *Delphic*, launched 5 January 1897, was another White Star vessel to which war was no stranger. After a maiden voyage from Liverpool to New York, and one voyage from London to New York, she entered the London-Wellington, New Zealand route for which she had been intended.

In 1900 *Delphic* was chartered for Boer War transport service, making voyages in March 1900 from London and April 1901 from Queenstown. After almost sixteen years on the New Zealand run, *Delphic* was taken up 10 March 1917 under the Liner Requisition Act.

On 16 August 1917, bound from Cardiff to Montevideo with a cargo of coal, *Delphic* was torpedoed and sunk by a German submarine 135 miles southwest of Bishop Rock, Scilly Isles, with a loss of five lives.

20 July 1918: *Justicia*

Built and launched in wartime, *Justicia* never sailed in peace. But her war service was significant.

Harland and Wolff's yard number 436 was laid down in 1912 as *Statendam* for the Holland-America Line. Launched 9 July 1914, war's arrival on 1 August delayed her completion. The new liner was 740 ft 6 in long, and 86 ft 5 in wide; she measured 32,234 gross and 19,801 net tons. *The Shipbuilder* magazine said of the new vessel,

'There are nine steel decks and eleven watertight bulkheads, the latter being carried up to the bridge deck at the fore part of the vessel and up to the saloon deck in the after part.

'Accommodation is provided for over 3,000 passengers including 800 first, 630 second and about 2,000 third class...

'The emergency lighting set, consisting of a Diesel engine and dynamo, is arranged in a steel house at the after end of the saloon deck, with storage tanks on the bridge deck. The propelling machinery consists of two reciprocating engines of a combined horsepower of 12,400 driving the wing shafts, and a turbine of 6,300 S.H.P. actuating the center shaft. We hope to deal more fully with this interesting vessel in a subsequent issue of *The Shipbuilder*...'

But the periodical never had the chance. In October 1914 the British Admiralty offered *Statendam*'s owners £1,000,000 for the vessel 'as is,' without fittings and lacking the upper promenade deck. Two Holland-America directors went from Rotterdam to London to discuss the purchase. Ultimately, it was agreed to allow the Admiralty to oversee *Statendam*'s completion and then charter her at a low rate, with the understanding that at war's end she would be returned. *Statendam*'s fittings, 'of the latest and most elaborate kind,' were put into storage in the company's Rotterdam warehouse.

Completed as a British troop carrier, the new vessel was renamed *Justicia* ('Justice'). The government wished her to sail under Cunard colours as replacement for the lost *Lusitania*, thus her name's '-ia' ending. But *Lusitania*'s crew had long since dispersed, while White Star's crew from the more recently lost *Britannic* was still relatively intact. *Justicia* was given over to White Star management, and IMM, White Star's parent company, acted as the Admiralty's agents on a 10 per cent commission basis.

Because of wartime secrecy and censorship, little is known of *Justicia*'s early activities. Her first

Above right *Laid down as* Statendam *for the Holland-America Line, the 32,000-ton liner was launched 9 July 1914* (Harland and Wolff collection, Ulster Folk and Transport Museum Photographic Archive).

Right *Soon after launch,* Statendam *was chartered by Admiralty, completed as a British troop carrier and renamed* Justicia. *When Cunard was unable to muster a crew, the vessel was put under White Star management using remnants of the recently-lost* Britannic's *staff* (Harland and Wolff collection, Ulster Folk and Transport Museum Photographic Archive).

trooping voyage was in April 1917. After several round trips to Halifax, *Justicia* changed to the Liverpool-New York run and carried American troops.

She could accommodate 5,000 troops comfortably, though on occasion she transported as many as 12,000 with their gear. Simultaneously she could carry 15,000 tons of cargo in her holds. With an 18-knot speed, *Justicia* could not out-run some enemy submarines, and therefore travelled frequently in convoy.

Initially painted wartime grey, early in 1918 *Justicia* received a dazzle camouflage designed and supervised by artist and Royal Navy reservist Norman Wilkinson. The prismatic decoration — patches of black, blue and grey — was intended to disguise the three-funnel 32,000-ton liner as a single-funnelled freighter.

Justicia's first direct contact with the enemy occurred on 23 January 1918 when she escaped an attack by German submarines in the southern Irish Sea.

During winter and spring 1918, under White Star Captain Arthur E. S. Hambleton's command, *Justicia* made three round trips to New York, returning filled with cargo and troops. After a 19 June arrival, *Justicia* departed New York 27 June 1918 for the fourth and final time. Because enemy attacks were more readily controlled along a so-called

northern route, most British war-time shipping, both east- and westbound, sailed around Northern Ireland, using Liverpool as principal arrival and departure point.

Justicia was scheduled to leave Liverpool 16 July 1918, but was held in port thirty hours so that mines and submarines could be cleared from North Channel, the approach to Ireland's northern coast. Finally on 18 July *Justicia* departed in convoy with eight other steamships, protected by six destroyers. Aboard were the customary 525 crew. Captain Hambleton, in command since *Justicia*'s first trip, had been replaced on this voyage by Captain John David.

Shortly after 2.00 pm on Friday 19 July, when about twenty miles off Skerryvore Rock in the Inner Hebrides, *Justicia* was attacked by German submarine *UB.64*. A single torpedo struck the liner's port side in the engine room, which immediately flooded, as did the next compartment aft. Crew hastily mustered on deck.

Soundings showed the watertight doors were

After a number of 1917 and 1918 round trips to Halifax and New York, Justica's luck ran out when she was torpedoed repeatedly off the Inner Hebrides on 19 July 1918. She sank the following day, with a loss of sixteen lives (Steamship Historical Society of America).

holding well, and other compartments were un-damaged. It appeared the ship could float long enough to be towed to port or to shallow water. The convoy's other vessels scattered, and the destroyers converged on the stricken liner. Ten depth charges were dropped around the spot it was thought the submarine lurked. The attack ceased with no sign of a periscope.

But at 4.30 pm two more torpedoes were fired at *Justicia*: one missed and the other was exploded by gunfire from *Justicia*'s crew. A rescue tug accompanying the convoy, HMS *Sonia*, got a line aboard and attempted towing, but could make no headway. A second tug was summoned and at about 8.00 pm the tow began. It was hoped *Justicia* could be towed to Lough Swilly and, if necessary, beached at Buncrana. As the tow commenced, a fourth torpedo was fired, but it was diverted by gunfire, again from *Justica*'s decks.

For safety's sake, some crew were evacuated before the tow resumed. Through the night the procession moved smoothly at a steady three knots: progress became increasingly difficult as the ship continued to take on water.

At 4.30 am another torpedo was fired, passing just ahead of *Justicia*'s bows. The slowly moving liner was again attacked at 9.30 am with torpedoes fired at her port quarter by *U.54*. One struck number three hold, the other, number five hold. *Justicia* began settling more rapidly, and remaining crew were ordered to abandon ship as the tugs cast off their lines. At 12.40 pm, to the hiss of escaping air and a clutter of broken debris, *Justicia* sank stern first. Lost were the third engineering officer and fifteen ratings, killed in the first torpedo's explosion.

Estimates regarding the number of torpedoes fired at *Justicia* vary between seven and ten, the number of submarines engaged in the attack between two and four. Several torpedoes were exploded by gunfire. And while a third submarine — the *UB.124* — was sunk 21 July by HMS *Marne* near the site, it had merely surfaced routinely and had not attacked *Justicia*.

Germany's High Command was initially elated when they believed their submarines had sunk not *Justicia*, but the three-funnelled *Vaterland*, which

had been impounded, requisitioned and renamed *Leviathan* by the Americans. When the German press corrected the misconception, they expressed hope that '*Vaterland* will be caught yet — sooner or later.'

By 12 August 1918 submarines *UB.64* and *U.54* had returned to their German base. By 11 November 1918 the war was over.

Holland-America was eventually compensated for its loss with 60,000 tons of steel, from which was constructed a fleet of modern, mid-sized freighters.

White Star vessels performed actively and gallantly through the Great War, 1914–1918. Some, including the great *Olympic*, had survived. But in addition to the 48,138-ton *Britannic*, the company suffered loss of eight of its own ships, a total of more than 100,000 tons.

Teutonic (1889) was sold to the Admiralty in 1915 as a troopship. *Cevic* was requisitioned early in the war and converted to the dummy battleship *Queen Mary*. After several false starts caused by running aground, she finally joined the North Atlantic patrol where her appearance off New York was instrumental in the *Kronprinz Wilhelm*'s surrender and internment. *Cufic* (1904) served as an armed merchant cruiser and a troop ship. *Megantic*, *Zeeland* (renamed *Northland*), *Ceramic*: all were engaged in troop transport. *Lapland* was damaged in 1917 when she struck a mine off the Mersey Bar lightship; during her repairs she was converted to a trooper.

Celtic, first of the 'Big Four,' was twice damaged: once in February 1917 when she struck a mine in the Irish Sea; again in March 1918 when she was torpedoed, also in the Irish Sea. *Celtic*, *Cedric* and *Baltic* all saw service as troop transports. Together with their sister *Adriatic*, all carried fuel oil for naval vessels in their deep tanks. According to an article in *Marine Engineer*:

'...The practice was inaugurated by *Baltic* on her voyage to New York 8 August 1917. She and her sisters were able to carry from 2,500 to 3,500 tons each voyage and brought altogether no less than 88,000 tons of this indispensable commodity at a time when the country was in great need of all that could be got.'

All White Star ships — those not engaged as armed merchant cruisers, hospital ships or troop transports — served under the Liner Requisition Act, bringing from the corners of the Empire the goods to support the Mother Country in years of need. At perhaps no other time in its history did White Star Line's star shine quite so brightly or proudly.

Accidents and incidents

28 March 1914	Several passengers were injured in four days of gales as *Oceanic* sailed for Plymouth. One passenger, becoming distraught at the ship's incessant rocking, jumped overboard and drowned.
26 July 1914	*Baltic*'s number 13 lifeboat fell from its davits during boat drill at New York, killing one and injuring nine.
16 September 1914	*Arabic* arrived at Liverpool from Boston with fire in numbers one and two holds. Captain Finch's crew were able to extinguish the blaze with help from land-based fire brigades.
26 September 1914	*Cretic* had a fire in number three hold while docked at New York. With help from two fireboats, it was extinguished after 'slight loss.'
19 November 1914	While leaving New York's Ambrose Channel for Liverpool *Baltic* collided with the steamer *Comal*, bound for Galveston, Texas. *Baltic* was undamaged and proceeded. *Comal* had several portside bow plates damaged, requiring drydocking. As she left the scene, *Baltic*'s passengers gathered on deck and shouted to *Comal*, 'Leaving so soon? Awfully sorry!'
19 January 1915	Four city firemen were overcome by smoke while fighting a smoky fire in a hold aboard the freighter *Georgic* docked at New York. Discovered at 8.00 am by second officer Bertram Hayes, the fire spread so quickly that ship's crew could not contain it and a fireboat and land-based apparatus were summoned. The blaze caused $2,000 in damages.
27 February 1915	During a gale at Naples, *Canopic* broke from her moorings and fouled the steamers *Gianicolo*, *Tellus* and *St. Ninian*, inflicting slight damage above the waterline to all three vessels.
23 March 1915	White Star's *Baltic*, under Captain Ranson, collided in the Mersey with the British steamer *Iberian*, both vessels sustaining damage. The next day, as she was leaving her pier, *Baltic* badly damaged her rudder, and had to go into drydock for repairs. Her passengers were transferred to other vessels.
27 April 1916	Far from her peacetime London-Wellington route, *Corinthic* had a fire in her fo'c'sle while berthed at New York's Pier 59. Damage was estimated at $500.

16 December 1918	An explosion in *Adriatic*'s engine room delayed her sailing from New York for two days.
5 April 1919	*Adriatic* arrived at Liverpool with a fire in one of her holds. Damage was slight.
7 May 1919	On her next eastbound voyage, *Adriatic* again arrived at Liverpool with fire in a cargo hold. The space was sealed, and steam injected. Damage was 'trifling.'
9 July 1919	Bound to Liverpool from New York, a porthole burst aboard *Lapland* during heavy weather, flooding the forward lower hold. Some cargo was damaged.
24 July 1919	Twenty city firemen and several of *Cedric*'s crew were trapped in number six hatch while fighting a 'treacherous' fire at New York. At great personal risk, a squad of policemen, firemen and crew struggled into the smoke-filled compartment and dragged the unconscious victims to safety. One crewman fell into the hatch, breaking his left leg and suffering contusions. Two city fire boats, the West 20th Street police station, New York Hospital ambulances, and *Cedric*'s entire crew participated in the operation. After ninety desperate minutes, the blaze was extinguished, having caused $25,000 damage to the hold.
20 September 1919	White Star's emigrant liner *Vedic*, returning from Archangel with 1,000 British troops aboard, went ashore in the Orkney Islands, north of Scotland. Warships and tugs soon arrived, and with their assistance she was pulled into deep water and proceeded on her voyage.
29 November 1919	Outward bound for Southampton, *Adriatic* and the British steamer *St. Michael*, bound for Brazilian ports, collided near the Statue of Liberty. The latter vessel had to return under tow to Brooklyn for repairs.
21 January 1920	Attempting to tow the disabled steamer *Powhattan*, *Bardic* broke her tow line and fouled her propeller. Subsequent damage required her to put into Halifax for repairs.
20 February 1920	*Celtic* damaged her port quarter in a collision with a Liverpool dock.
6 March 1920	While backing out from her New York pier in a 60 mph gale, *Cedric* collided with a float under the dock, jamming her helm and breaking the rudder. Repairs required lay-up for several days before she could depart for Liverpool.
14 August 1920	A boiler valve exploded on board *Cretic* at Genoa, severely injuring several workers.
24 October 1920	During a heavy sea, *Adriatic*'s lifeboat number 50 was carried away on a voyage from New York to Southampton via Cherbourg.

6 January 1921   *Megantic* dented two portside plates when she collided with the anchored ship *Berkelstroom* at Liverpool.

30 March 1921   *Baltic* sustained propeller damage while in tow of the tug *Blue Ridge* at New York's Robins Dry Dock. One week later she suffered unspecified fire damage at Fletcher's Dry Dock.

30 March 1922   *Pittsburgh* was struck by an enormous wave 600 miles east of Sable Island, disabling her steering apparatus and doing considerable deck damage. She was *en route* from Bremen to New York via Halifax.

11 August 1922   Five men were killed by an explosion and fire in *Adriatic*'s number two hold at 2.00 am as the liner sailed for New York from Queenstown. Some $1,000 in cargo was damaged, and hatch doors on three decks were shattered.

22 December 1922   Bound for Liverpool, *Celtic* encountered a North Atlantic gale that smashed lifeboats and deck fittings, and flooded the third class saloon, forcing removal of passengers to other quarters.

23 December 1922   Docking during severe gales at Southampton, *Majestic* collided with *Berengaria*. Railings on the latter's starboard quarter were torn away.

12 February 1923   While on a cruise from Syracuse to Alexandria, *Homeric* collided with an unknown brigantine off Chanak Kalesi, Turkey. *Homeric*'s gangway ladder was carried away, and the second class deck windows were broken.

10 June 1923   *Baltic* struck an unknown object off Ireland's southern coast, forcing her return to Liverpool for repairs. She sailed three days later.

19 September 1923   The American steamer *West Arrow*, bound from Liverpool for Boston, collided with White Star's *Haverford* at sea, sustaining broken plates and a crushed forepeak tank. Upon drydocking in Boston, it was found she had dented plates from her forecastle head to below the waterline and a twisted stem. Repairs to *West Arrow* cost $50,000.

30 September 1923   In dense fog near the Tuskar Light, off Ireland's southern coast, the *Cedric* collided with Cunard's *Scythia*. Three passengers and one crewman aboard the Cunarder were hurt through falling. While White Star's vessel had only minor damage, a large hole was punctured in *Scythia*'s starboard side, forward, above the waterline. She returned to Liverpool for repairs.

24 February 1924   A 'slight' fire, believed to have been started by strikers, broke out on board *Majestic* at Southampton. It was quickly extinguished.

26 August 1924   More than 100 *Arabic* passengers were injured as a devastating hurricane smashed the ship on her first voyage from Hamburg to New York via

Southampton, Cherbourg and Halifax. Four liferafts and one lifeboat were swept away, while nine other boats dropped from their davits, broken and useless. Hundreds of smashed ports and windows were stuffed with pillows in a futile attempt to prevent flooding.

Some 100 persons were in the library when a single wave shattered all the windows and sent a torrent of water into the room. 'Men, women and children were sent headlong the entire width of the room, to land amid a wreckage of tables and chairs and to be slewed back again as the ship rolled in the other direction.' Cargo shifted; lights went out; the wireless was out of action, and passengers in alleyways were all knocked flat. Unable to get their footing, they sat in the corridors with feet braced against the opposite wall, arms shielding their faces. An A deck skylight shattered, followed by a waterfall that flooded cabins and corridors. One passenger was thrown through the wall separating his cabin from the next, rendering him unconscious. One woman in a deck chair was halfway over the railing when a sailor grabbed her by the hair and pulled her back.

All of *Arabic*'s seventeen engineers, forty firemen and six greasers were injured in being thrown off their feet and into operating machinery. Even at full speed *Arabic* could make no headway against the high winds.

Casualties were so numerous that the injured lay, swathed in bandages, on improvised cots in alleyways under ministrations from the ship's surgeon and six doctors among her passengers. Upon her New York arrival, *Arabic* had a ten degree port list, 'a mass of sodden, broken wreckage inside, her passengers and crew bandaged and weary.' She was met by seven ambulances.

Homeric arrived in New York just behind *Arabic*, after having been hit by an 80 ft wave from the same storm. Seven people were injured, ports and windows were smashed, one lifeboat was lost, and chairs snapped from their fastenings in *Homeric*'s lounge and elsewhere.

CHAPTER 13

Bardic, 1924 and Celtic, 1928

SHIPS ASHORE

As the First World War concluded on 11 November 1918, the world's shipping companies were eager to resume normal passenger and cargo services as quickly as possible. New orders, repairs and conversion work for war survivors jammed the shipyards. Slipways occupied by navy or government-ordered vessels had to be cleared for more profitable contracts from the private sector.

War Priam, one of three 8,000-ton 'G-class' cargo ships ordered by the Shipping Controller in 1918, was nearing launch when the Armistice was signed. With an uncertain peacetime future, she went down the ways at Harland and Wolff's Belfast yards on 19 December 1918. White Star soon purchased *War Priam* for its war-depleted cargo service. She was renamed *Bardic*, was handed over 13 March, and sailed from Liverpool to New York on her maiden voyage five days later.

Other International Mercantile Marine companies were also experiencing post-war difficulties in re-establishing service. In June 1918, *Bardic* was temporarily transferred without name change to the Atlantic Transport Company and sailed for almost two full years on their London-New York route. She made her last Atlantic Transport voyage in April 1921. White Star then resumed her operation, transferring her to the Australian cargo service.

Above left *In fog on 30 April 1924, the White Star freighter* Bardic *went aground off Lizard Point, Cornwall, several hundred yards from where* Suevic *had grounded in 1907* (Authors' collection).

Left *The Lizard Point lifeboat returns to shore carrying some of the stranded* Bardic's *crew.* (Mariners Museum, Newport News).

Sydney, Australia's spacious harbour, receded astern as *Bardic* left with a large cargo of baled wool, wheat, frozen beef and lead on 6 August 1924. Her twin triple-expansion engines drove her at a stately 14 knots for the long voyage to England.

Arriving at Liverpool on 26 August after an uneventful run, she discharged a portion of her cargo. At 10.45 pm on 29 August she sailed for London where the remainder would be unloaded. Fog and drizzle obscured everything soon after departure. As *Bardic* moved southward, there was a close call when an inbound transatlantic liner — identity unknown — cut across her path. A collision was narrowly averted.

Rounding Cornwall's southernmost point, the Lizard, *Bardic* was forced to reduce speed further as the fog thickened and it began to rain heavily. White Star's own *Suevic* had already met disaster there, and many other vessels' wreckage enhanced the area's dangerous reputation. Wise mariners gave the region a wide berth; but excessive distance from shore needlessly lengthened voyages, a practice managements didn't appreciate.

Bardic's lookout strained to see through the night, every nerve on edge seeking a danger sign. Shortly after 1.00 am, he heard a foghorn almost directly ahead. He called out at once, but it was too late. With a grinding, rumbling sound, *Bardic* impaled herself among the Maenheere rocks, just several hundred yards east of *Suevic*'s disastrous position below the Lizard Point lighthouse.

An attempt was made to dislodge the ship using the engines but without success. Crew reported that *Bardic* was taking on water in numbers 1, 2 and 3 holds, and now the engine room began to

Salvage efforts are underway as pumps send cascades of water from Bardic's *port side. A lighter behind her starboard bow unloads cargo* (Mariners Museum, Newport News).

Lightened through discharge of cargo and pumping, tugs pull Bardic *free of the rocks after a month of salvage efforts* (Shipbuilding and Shipping Record).

Down slightly at the bow, Bardic *is escorted toward Falmouth* (Authors' collection).

flood. With each wave, the grinding sound returned; the ship's bottom was being mercilessly pounded against the rocks.

The master radioed his ship's plight to the company, and requested aid from tugs. Lizard Point's motor lifeboat took off eighty of the crew, while the captain and several engineers remained aboard to keep pumps running. The crew were lodged in a local hotel as two local tugs continued efforts to get the ship off. Already, observers and press had marked *Bardic* a doomed ship. With damage increasing with each passing hour and shipboard efforts unsuccessful, White Star again contacted the Liverpool and Glasgow Salvage Association, whose *Suevic* rescue seventeen years earlier had amazed the world.

The next day, the salvage ship *Ranger* arrived under Captain I.J. Kay's command. He found *Bardic* well down forward with a severe port list. Several holds contained as much as 22 ft of water. Virtually the entire double bottom was flooded, the tank tops exposed to the sea. Kay immediately ordered two 60 ft coasters to come alongside and lighten the freighter. Six days of calm, clear weather permitted unloading of much of the wool and beef.

Ranger, now supplemented by *Trover*, began supplementing *Bardic*'s own pumps with several brought from shore. While the ship's lower boiler furnaces were under water, the upper furnaces were fired to drive the ship's pumps. The combined assemblage could send 1,160,000 gallons of water overboard each hour. Powerful compressors could flood a space with air, driving water out. The equipment was necessary, for divers had discovered an 11-ft hole in *Bardic*'s bows and extensive damage along virtually her entire 450-ft length. Periodically, Kay sent progress reports to White Star; one pertaining to a refrigerated cargo hold sounded more like a hospital report; 'No apparent change in condition. Temperature 31°.'

Work on lightening the ship was frequently interrupted by storms, which drove the lighters back to shore. Eventually *Bardic*'s crew returned to assist in stiffening the hull and making tank tops watertight.

On 9 September a gale swept the area, and salvors had to be evacuated for safety's sake. Captain Kay re-flooded the *Bardic*, undoing all the pumping, to minimize grinding on the rocks and further bottom damage. Storms continued for more than a fortnight. On 25 September salvors returned with additional pumps and air compressors.

On 29 September, almost a full month after *Bardic*'s grounding, a flood tide offered good prospects for refloating her. *Trover* was tied up to *Bardic*'s starboard quarter to provide extra buoyancy. The freighter's stern anchor was attached to a rock behind her, to steady the ship. Full steam was produced from the available boilers and all pumps were operating. Four tugs and the *Ranger* tied up with wire hawsers.

At 3.45 pm, the tide reached maximum, and the salvage fleet and *Bardic*'s starboard engine exerted power. With a shuddering series of bumps, *Bardic* floated free, heavily down at the head and listing 11° to port. *Ranger* now tied up forward of *Trover* and the trio began to move slowly for Falmouth where repairs could be made. Upon arrival, no drydock space was available; manoeuvring on her starboard engine, the ship moved to Falmouth's eastern breakwater where she was beached. Work resumed on clearing remaining cargo and again pumping out tons of water, as all compartments except the engine and boiler rooms had been permitted to flood with the tide.

On 3 October drydock space opened and *Bardic* entered using one screw and her own steering gear. Examination revealed that 140 plates had been destroyed on the rocks, and large sections of framing had been twisted or smashed. Temporary repairs were completed on 17 October, and *Bardic* sailed at 11 knots for Harland and Wolff's Belfast yards, where full repair facilities were available.

Bardic's salvage was considered one of the most difficult operations in thirty years. By the end of 1924 she returned to White Star's Australian service, but not for long. In August 1925 she was sold to the Aberdeen Line and renamed *Hostilius*, and within a year was again renamed as *Horatius*.

The Shaw Savill Line with whom White Star had co-owned its New Zealand service for many years, purchased her in 1932, renaming her

Celtic
10 December 1928

Bardic ——
30 April 1924

English Channel

Above *At a Falmouth dock, water gushes overboard as pumping efforts continue prior to* Bardic's *repair* (Shipbuilding and Shipping Record).

Kumara. In 1937 Greek ship owner John S. Latsis purchased the freighter, renaming her *Marathon*. On 9 March 1941, the former *Bardic* met her end, sunk by the German battle cruiser *Scharnhorst* off the Cape Verde Islands. Men had succeeded in sinking what nature could not.

For another White Star ship, nature was to prove the superior force, but only after more than a generation of outstanding service. *Celtic* was the last ship to be ordered by White Star's founder, Thomas H. Ismay prior to his death in 1899. Launched 4 April 1901, the 20,880-ton vessel was the first to exceed the legendary *Great Eastern* in tonnage. Indeed at the time of her launch, newspapers expressed doubt that sufficient passengers or cargo would ever be found to fill her. *Celtic* was the world's largest ship, but certainly not the fastest: her exceptional steadiness, not her $16\frac{1}{2}$ knot cruising speed, quickly earned her a large and continu-

Above Celtic *was the first of the famous 'Big Four' on the Liverpool-New York service* (Everett E. Viez collection, Steamship Historical Society of America).

Right *The magnificent dome over* Celtic*'s first class dining saloon typified her spacious accommodation* (Authors' collection).

ing following from transatlantic passengers.

Offering comfortable accommodation for 347 first class, 160 second and 2,350 third class passengers, she was the first of the 'Big Four' designed for White Star's Liverpool-New York service, with occasional voyages to the Mediterranean or the Orient during winter months.

Her peacetime career punctuated by several incidents and accidents, *Celtic*'s first significant mishap occurred on 19 February 1914 when she collided with the Fabre Line's *Madonna* in the Bay of Naples. Both ships were seriously damaged.

On 20 October 1914 *Celtic* and her sister-ship *Cedric* were commissioned as auxiliary cruisers, fitted with 6-in guns and assigned to the 10th Cruiser Squadron. By January 1916, following *Oceanic*'s loss in the Shetland Islands, the Admiralty realized such huge ships were unsuitable as armed cruisers, and *Celtic* became a troopship instead.

On 14 February 1917 *en route* to New York from Liverpool, she struck a mine near the Isle of Man. The forepeak and number one hold flooded, but Captain Bertram Hayes was able to return to Liverpool. Fourteen months later on 2 April 1918 she was torpedoed twice in the Irish Sea. The first torpedo caused her to settle by the stern; the second caused her to straighten up, and she was safely beached on an even keel, though six men had been killed in the explosions.

She began her first peacetime voyage on 8 December 1918 in her wartime configuration and did not return to Belfast for re-conversion until late 1919. For almost three years she sailed from Southampton; accommodation had been reduced to 350 first class, 250 second and 1,000 third.

Celtic's postwar years were marred by several collisions. On 21 April 1925, *Celtic* crashed into the 787-ton coastal steamer *Hampshire Coast* while docking at Liverpool, both ships sustaining damage. On 29 January 1927, she collided with the US Shipping Board's *Anaconda*, and two C deck staterooms were demolished.

On 12 November 1928, in rough seas off the Maryland coast, the overloaded Lamport and Holt liner *Vestris* capsized and sank after a prolonged struggle with the elements. Some 68 passengers and 44 crew, including her captain, were lost. The 213 saved were soon landed at various east coast American ports. Thirty survivors, many *Vestris*'s crew, immediately booked passage aboard *Celtic*, then in New York. A large cargo was loaded aboard, hundreds of mail bags were placed in the post office, and with 300 passengers and 350 crew aboard, *Celtic* left for Cobh via Boston on 1 December. Passengers took part in lifeboat drill under Captain Gilbert Berry's supervision soon after departure.

The voyage was a splendid one, with calm weather and seas. About midnight on 9 December, however, the weather began to deteriorate. The wind freshened, and soon a very heavy swell developed. As *Celtic* began the final hours of her crossing, the winds continued to increase.

At 3 o'clock the next morning, she arrived off the Daunt's Rock light ship near Roches Point in a howling southwesterly gale with heavy rain. With weather making it impossible to take a pilot on board, Captain Berry reluctantly decided to omit the call at Cobh and proceed directly for Liverpool. Slowly the ship steamed away; then, almost miraculously, the storm abated and the seas calmed. With seventy passengers and 750 post bags having Cobh as their destination, Berry rescinded his decision and returned to Cobh.

Meanwhile, White Star's pilot boat had been waiting an hour for *Celtic*'s arrival. As the giant liner passed by the harbour and headed eastward, the pilot assumed Berry had decided on a direct voyage to Liverpool. With his services apparently no longer required, the pilot returned to Cobh, three miles away.

Again the weather deteriorated, and as *Celtic* returned, she was forced to heave to awaiting another lull, a pilot, and the tender that would transport his passengers to Cobh. Minutes passed, Berry pacing the bridge. The powerful twin beams of the Roches Point lighthouse, marking the entrance to Cobh Harbour, could easily be discerned off to starboard. At last the pilot boat arrived, but the sea did not permit him to board. With dawn approaching, Berry decided to move closer to the harbour entrance, perhaps to create a lee permitting the pilot to board.

And then at about 4.55 am, it happened. A swell and a gust of wind buffeted the ship's exposed seaward side. With a firm bump, *Celtic* was carried upward and inward onto the twin pinnacles of the Cow and Calf Rocks, some 400 yards west of Roches Point and 300 yards offshore, her bow facing west. Captain Berry sounded his whistle, alerting lighthouse keeper F. Hill to *Celtic*'s danger, then tried futilely to get *Celtic* off. Hill immediately notified authorities and several shore-based lifeboats.

Vestris hospital attendant Hugh Jones, experiencing his second shipwreck in a month, said:

'When I got on to the *Celtic* to come home I did think that I was all right, and last night a crowd of us stayed up all the night to have a bit of a farewell, as some of us

Above *Disaster strikes as* Celtic *grounds off Roches Point lighthouse near Cobh, on 10 December 1928* (Arnold Kludas collection).

Right Celtic*'s proximity to land is demonstrated in this newspaper photograph* (Cork Examiner).

were getting off at Cobh. I was in the lounge when the ship gave a sort of bump. We all ran on deck and found that the *Celtic* was on the rocks. I wondered what the deuce was going to happen next. A few minutes later one of the bedroom stewards came along with orders for all hands to get on deck and all passengers to put on their life belts, with the usual women and children first order.'

Despite the gentle impact, there was some on-board damage visible: glasses and other debris were strewn around the floor, and the smoke room door's wood panelling was smashed. With *Celtic* flooding in at least one hold and the ship rocking from side to side, apparently threatening to cap-size, Berry sounded the ship's whistle six times, signal for abandoning ship. Another passenger, an Irish priest, said:

'All the passengers were called and ordered to boat stations. This manoeuvre was carried out expeditiously and without the slightest trace of panic owing to the fact that shortly after leaving New York we were all made to take part in a general lifeboat drill. At this time the bum-ping was considerable, as every sea lifted the ship slight-ly, then it receded, and she crashed down on the rock again.'

It all seemed quite routine to her crew. Said one steward:

'When the alarm was given we stood by our stations and the [28] lifeboats were swung out without the slightest panic. It was more like a Board of Trade demonstration than a mishap. Everyone put on life belts and a breeches buoy was rigged up from the lighthouse in case of emergency.'

Those not awakened by the impact were aroused by stewards and stewardesses. An American novelist on board said she was awakened by her stewardess:

'I was told not to stop even for money. It was a very terrible awakening and the terror was added to by the fact that there was no life belt in my room. A passing steward took off his own and gave it to me. We all went to our boat stations and remained there, wondering what was going to happen, until eventually the ship's officers reassured us and told us we could go below and pack.'

There was no panic, merely confusion. That, too, soon subsided as stewards and stewardesses reassured jittery passengers. As the tide continued to recede, the ship settled hard aground and in no immediate danger of sinking. Nevertheless, passengers were told to keep life belts handy. In about an hour, they were offered a hot breakfast in the dining saloons. 'We were jolly glad to get that news, I can tell you,' said one passenger later.

As daylight arrived, so, too, did assistance, in-cluding the Dutch tug *Gelezee* and the Cork-based tug *Morsecock*. They put lines aboard and tried to pull *Celtic* off, again failing. The tender *Failte* (Gaelic for 'welcome') then took passengers to Cobh, a job made difficult by *Celtic*'s placement amid the rocks, by the seas sweeping her port side, and by the port list. Because the ship's own gangways could not be used, special ones were im-provised between the ship and the tenders. As the passengers waited their turn, they sand *It's a Long Way to Tipperary* and *Pack Up Your Troubles*.

Ashore, White Star's manager W.R. Harman and his assistants spent some sixteen consecutive hours arranging recovery of the mails and for physicians' services, hotels and transportation for passengers and crew. By 3.15 pm, more than 300 had been put aboard the mail train for Dublin.

The crew then departed, leaving behind only those essential to continuing salvage operations. By nightfall, the ship was held firmly in place amid-ships, with a large amount of water in the stoke hold and number 3 hold. With boilers flooded, her engines and salvage gear were inoperative. Passengers' luggage was off-loaded.

By the next morning, *Morsecock* and *Gelezee* had been joined by the German salvage tug *Seefalke* and the Liverpool and Glasgow Salvage Association's tug *Restorer*. HMS *Sesame* and HMS *Scythe* stood by to assist.

A *Cork Examiner* reporter managed to go aboard and recorded the eerie atmosphere of an en-dangered liner:

'The first impression on getting on board the *Celtic* was a difficulty experienced in walking the decks. It was then that the list became more apparent...There is a limited electric light service along the corridors, in the of-

Right *Listing slightly to port,* Celtic *is visited by a salvage vessel* (Arnold Kludas collection).

Below *A workman on a scaffold begins dismantling* Celtic's *forward funnel, which has been obstructing the beam of Roches Point lighthouse.* Celtic's *lifeboats have already been removed* (National Maritime Museum).

Bottom *The Roches Point lighthouse overlooks the dismantled* Celtic, *her funnels now removed* (Smithsonian Institution).

ficers' quarters and other parts of the vessel, but the main machinery is out of action.

'It was a sorrowful sight to walk along the decks and become aware of a great sense of loneliness everywhere. The cabins were deserted and, in fact, except where an odd officer or member of the present skeleton crew was met with, the *Celtic* had all the appearances of a deserted ship.

'At intervals, as the slight swell of the sea affected the vessel, one heard a creaking sound, due to straining amidships where she is caught on the rocks. On the rails of the stairways were a number of life belts and jackets. At that particular time, when the tide was at its highest point, it was learned that there was 25 ft of water in the stokehold, engine room and number three hold.

'In the dining saloon a private conference was being held by officials of the White Star company. Amongst these were Commodore Bartlett, chief marine superintendent; Captain Howe of the London Insurance, Mr Thomas of the Liverpool Insurance, both salvage officers, Mr Dunlop of Messrs. Harland and Wolff, Belfast, and Captain English, White Star marine superintendent at Cobh.

'...Commodore Bartlett expressed the view that the ship could not be in a worse position. They were hopeful for the best when they got the salvage people there.'

On 13 December another salvage tug, *Ranger* (a veteran of *Suevic*'s salvage), arrived. But conditions aboard *Celtic* had already worsened considerably as a telegram to shore detailed:

'Position very precarious in event of winds from S.E. to S.W. Apparently badly holed under engine space, stoke hold, nos 3 and 4 holds; each compartment tidal. Nos 5 and 6 holds now showing water on port side. Tunnels full. Steamer listed 7° to port. [Rescue] craft able [to] lie [along] starboard side only...In view of position and winter season, prospects not favourable. Have reduced crew retaining only sufficient to assist salvage.'

It became apparent that if there were to be any possibility of refloating *Celtic*, it would have to begin with the discharge of her cargo into lighters alongside. It seemed a losing battle. Within 24 hours, another telegram reported that hold number 2 was beginning to flood. 'Vessel shows considerable signs [of] straining on decks immediately forward of boiler spaces. Lower deck set up and fractured in several places over large area,' it noted.

With each incoming wave, *Celtic* rose and fell, punching another hole in her bottom plates. A reported noted, 'Experienced seafarers display much anxiety about the *Celtic*, and they are unanimous in saying that every hour she remains where she now is increases the likelihood of ultimate and complete disaster.' Weather was favourable for removing cargo, but ocean swells were causing time to run out. Repeated efforts with tugs to pull her off failed.

On 12 December divers completed their survey of her hull, reporting that she was badly holed amidships with the sharp rocks imbedded into her plating. By the following morning, the entire vessel was flooding, with salvage crews' cofferdams, built to contain the water, now starting to leak. A strong southeasterly wind and rough seas eventually stopped cargo discharge. Huge waves broke over the liner's stern and swept forward along her decks. Incredibly, the four automobiles on board were salvaged, as well as 200 tons of fruit. Salvage crews were evacuated at 10.30 pm on 13 December as the weather threatened their safety.

One salvage expert said if the weather did not soon abate, *Celtic* 'would come off the Calf rock, but in two pieces.' Nobly the liner sat upright and seemingly unmoving in her tomb, enduring the punishment. Salvors were unable to re-board on Friday, and watched helplessly as the waves and a full gale continued the assault. Blown spray flew over her funnels and deserted decks. One report said she had been holed in nine different places.

The list increased, and doubts were expressed as to whether salvage would now be economically justifiable. The ship was insured for £230,000, and observers thought repairs were rapidly approaching that figure. Despite torrential rains, the hills around Roches Point were filled with a steady stream of automobiles, buses and wagons filled with sightseers. Salvage crews waited aboard their vessels or ashore for a respite.

On Sunday 16 December, two officers and several salvage crew managed to board from a motorboat, staying only long enough to ascertain damage. In response to numerous expressions of concern from as far away as Scotland, they also located *Celtic*'s cats and brought them ashore in excellent condition. While winds died down, the heavy seas continued.

By now it was clear that attempts to refloat *Celtic* were hopeless. The liner was 27 years old, past her prime. Even if salvagers did get her off, she would quite possibly sink quickly, given the damage. A sad Captain Bartlett told the Cork Harbour Board, 'The accident to the *Celtic*, I must say, is a very sad one...Up to the present we have not had very great success in regard to the salvage of the ship, and I am afraid it will be a very long job before we, if ever, get her off.' On 19 December White Star decided to abandon their veteran to the shipbreakers.

Early the next day, more than 100 men resumed salvaging as much as possible. Some of the cargo, including metal, wheat and 30,000 barrels of apples and pears, was already worthless, but most was insured. As salvagers worked to clear her holds, others loaded ship's stores, crockery, cutlery, bed linens, furniture and fittings into the waiting coasters.

Authorities were concerned that *Celtic*'s funnels, masts and remaining lifeboats were blocking the beams of the Roches Point lighthouse. Priority was therefore given to cutting away her superstructure to eliminate the navigational hazard. To make salvaging more efficient, a bridge was built, connecting the shore below the lighthouse to *Celtic*'s upper decks. At Cobh, '*Celtic* apples' were sold for 1p apiece. Unfortunately, the 'bridge' apparently permitted an influx of rats into the lighthouse.

By 4 January 1929, underwater cargo had commenced to rot, forming pockets of exploding gas. Salvage continued, for on 2 February an exceptionally high tide would provide the best chance of floating her. But gales the night before cancelled the plan.

Fully stripped, *Celtic* lay in a forlorn state, with empty lifeboat davits and rust-streaked plating. Eventually, her hulk was sold to the Danish shipbreakers Petersen and Albeck. Demolition was completed in 1933 after providing significant employment to many Cobh and Cork citizens.

But perhaps a moving ceremony in Birkenhead on Christmas Eve 1928 should provide final words about *Celtic*. At Captain Berry's home, members of *Celtic*'s crew presented their master with a smoker's cabinet inscribed, 'As a mark of our appreciation, esteem and confidence while under your command.'

Steward Alec Sutherland said *Celtic*'s loss was caused 'not by bad navigation, but due to the great elements of the universe.' A tearful Captain Berry replied, 'I thank you and all members of the crew for the splendid manner in which you maintained the tradition of the sea. Your action in the emergency was wonderful. Thank God no lives were lost.'

Accidents and incidents

8 October 1924	The Red Star liner *Finland* was forced by wind and tide against *Baltic* while being placed in her New York berth. Both ships were slightly damaged.
14 November 1924	On a voyage from Southampton to New York, *Adriatic* had three lifeboats smashed and one carried away when she encountered a hurricane.
26 December 1924	Fire broke out in 102 bales of Peruvian cotton that had been loaded aboard *Cedric* in New York. The ship was undamaged but the cotton cargo was destroyed.
27 October 1925	*Celtic* dropped her starboard propeller in Boston harbour, and immediately returned to her pier. Passengers were sent to New York by train. Divers recovered the propeller and replaced it in the Boston Navy Yard's drydock.

9 November 1925	*Arabic* arrived at Hamburg from New York with a fire in a starboard bunker. The fire was extinguished and caused slight damage.
16 February 1926	While on a cruise, *Homeric* collided with the British steamer *Charterhurst* at Constantinople. *Homeric* lost her starboard anchor, while the *Charterhurst* had to be beached.
13 March 1926	*Majestic* partially sank one scow and cut another in two outward bound from New York's Quarantine. *Majestic* proceeded on her voyage late.
12 September 1926	While docking in Boston, *Cedric* drifted down and struck the river steamer *Van* at her wharf. The *Van* had her starboard side planking smashed and a guard rail broken.
3 November 1926	*Regina* was struck by the steamer *Carrabulle* while at Cienfuegos, Cuba on a cruise.
12 January 1927	*Arabic* arrived at Antwerp with a fire in her bunkers. It was extinguished after some damage.
30 January 1927	*Celtic* was rammed by the U.S. Shipping Board freighter *Anaconda* in thick fog off Nantucket Lightship *en route* to Cobh via Boston. *Celtic* had several plates ripped off above the waterline on C deck's port side aft as some passengers attended divine services in the dining saloon. 'Passengers were hurled from chairs, tossed from berths in their cabins and shaken up but not injured seriously.' *Anaconda* was not seriously damaged.
27 March 1927	During a voyage from Southampton to New York, *Majestic* encountered heavy weather and seas, and had two cargo booms wrenched loose; one was broken, the other smashed a ventilator.
9 July 1927	While leaving Southampton for New York, *Homeric* collided with the Italian schooner *Giacomo* at the entrance to the English Channel. While the liner was uninjured, the schooner's masts were carried away. *Homeric* left one lifeboat with the schooner in case of need.
14 September 1927	The British steamer *Barrie* collided with *Doric* at Montreal. *Doric* had a bow plate damaged, but made temporary repairs before departing for Liverpool. *Barrie* had her stem bent and two plates damaged.
9 December 1927	Several passengers were knocked down and thirteen were injured during a gale that struck *Celtic* as she sailed from New York via Boston to Cobh. One man's head was forced through a glass panel, severely cutting his ear; several other passengers had their fingers crushed. *Celtic* reached Cobh on 12 December.
14 May 1928	While leaving her berth at Montreal's grain elevator, the steamer *Judge Kenefick* brushed *Doric*, damaging the lower blocks of number three lifeboat's falls. No hull damage was apparent.

SHIPS ASHORE

6 July 1928	*Megantic* arrived at Southampton from Montreal with a fire in number two hold. The cargo hatch's paintwork was damaged, the lower hold's ladder was badly blistered, and some woodwork was charred.
26 November 1928	As she sailed from Southampton to New York, *Homeric* was battered by heavy weather. Hatch covers on number two hold were smashed in, and some cargo was water damaged. The fo'c'sle head's railing was torn away, and forward promenade deck windows were smashed.
1 March 1929	On a Mediterranean cruise, *Calgaric* parted her moorings during a high wind at Algiers, and collided with the British steamship *Tintern Abbey*, whose superstructure was damaged. *Calgaric* was able to resume her voyage.
1 March 1929	Fire broke out in *Megantic*'s number two hold as she lay at London's King George dock. Firemen found it necessary to flood the hold, which contained rolls of paper and straw.
21 May 1929	A large pin connected with *Albertic*'s steering gear slipped, putting the liner's rudder out of commission off Cobh. Emergency steering gear brought her to port; a tender rushed from Liverpool to escort her into the Mersey. She was repaired in a Liverpool drydock.
5 June 1929	The tender *Traffic* had two plates damaged and a railing broken when her starboard quarter bumped *Homeric* while at Cherbourg.
8 September 1929	*Adriatic* collided with the coastal steamer *Suffolk* at New York. The *Suffolk*'s bows were stove in, while *Adriatic* had three port quarter plates dented, and six beams and five frames buckled.
4 December 1929	*Homeric*'s orchestra was twice hurled off its platform, and promenade deck windows were smashed as the liner encountered a powerful North Atlantic storm *en route* to Southampton.
9 December 1929	While coming alongside the Atlantic Transport liner *Minnewaska* at Cherbourg during stormy weather, *Traffic* damaged a bulwark plate, a sheerstrake plate and a stringer plate on the starboard bow.
18 January 1930	Just before her departure for New York via Boston, *Baltic* was thrown against her Liverpool pier by a tidal surge and badly damaged her propeller blades. It took divers nine hours to repair the damage.
28 February 1930	A collision with the British tanker *Fortfol* damaged *Calgaric*'s stern at Gibraltar. After temporary repairs both ships proceeded on their voyages.
29 August 1930	While leaving Liverpool for Montreal *Albertic* struck a dock wall. Repairs required drydocking.

| 8 December 1930 | During an overhaul at Liverpool, fire broke out aboard *Doric*. Five C deck cabins burned for 45 minutes before flames were extinguished. |

8 December 1930 — During an overhaul at Liverpool, fire broke out aboard *Doric*. Five C deck cabins burned for 45 minutes before flames were extinguished.

18 December 1930 — While inbound from Fremantle, *Ceramic* collided with the British motor vessel *Laguna* near Gravesend. Damage to both was slight.

29 November 1931 — The tender *Nomadic* collided with the anchored *Minnewaska* at Cherbourg. *Nomadic* had her stem twisted and four plates dented, while *Minnewaska* had one starboard plate dented.

27 September 1932 — *Homeric* collided with the Spanish steamship *Isla de Teneriffe* while the latter was leaving Santa Cruz on the island of Teneriffe. The stem of the 5,000-ton Spanish vessel was badly twisted; *Homeric* was able to continue her voyage.

16 December 1932 — A forecastle bulkhead was smashed and the crew's quarters severely damaged when *Majestic* was struck in mid-ocean by a huge wave that killed one seaman.

2 October 1933 — The British steamship *Lurigethan* was badly damaged at foggy Montreal in a collision with *Laurentic*. *Lurigethan*'s starboard bow was badly torn, five plates were buckled and others were severely dented. She lost one fluke of her starboard anchor and a section of anchor hawsepipe. Deck plating was damaged, the forecastle bulwark was driven backward and parts of her railing were broken. *Laurentic* was not extensively damaged.

Nemesis: Lord Kylsant

Celtic's loss paralleled the disaster overtaking the White Star Line itself as the 1920s ended. In November 1926 the Royal Mail Steam Packet Company, headed by the Rt Hon Lord Kylsant GCMG, purchased all authorized and issued share capital of the Oceanic Steam Navigation Company, Ltd (White Star's parent company) from the International Mercantile Marine Company of New Jersey.

For almost 25 years, since 4 February 1902, American interests had controlled White Star. Now, effective 1 January 1927, it returned to full British control. The £7,000,000 ($35,000,000) purchase price was payable in instalments at 4 per cent, bringing total cost to £7,907,661 (almost $40,000,000). A principal in the management of Royal Mail, Union-Castle, Harland and Wolff, the Southern Railway and the Midland Bank, Kylsant's White Star Line acquisition put his group in control of the world's largest shipping fleet totaling 2,500,000 tons.

Having purchased Oceanic Steam Navigation Company, or at least placing a down payment on it, Kylsant immediately created a new company, the White Star Line Ltd, to finance the deal. Registered on 10 January 1927, the new company had Kylsant as its chairman and Harold Sanderson as deputy chairman.

The purchase furthered Kylsant's obsession to build the world's greatest shipping empire under Royal Mail aegis. Incorporated by an 1839 royal charter, Royal Mail had already absorbed the Union-Castle, Elder Dempster, King, and Shire Lines, the Pacific Steam Navigation Company, the Nelson Line, Lamport & Holt, David M'Iver & Co., and the Argentine Navigation Company. In

Owen Phillips, Lord Kylsant, repurchased the White Star Line from International Mercantile Marine for his Royal Mail group (Authors' collection).

his introduction to *The Royal Mail Case* (Wm Hodge & Co, Ltd, London, 1933), Collin Brooks summarizes the group's status:

'Although it was generally realized by the investing public that shipping since the war years had suffered a severe decline in prosperity, the Royal Mail group, with its ancient standing, its large capitalization, and its famous and trusted chairman, was regarded as a concern in which every confidence could be placed.'

Early in 1928, Kylsant outbid two rivals and for £1,900,000 ($9,500,000) purchased the Commonwealth Line's passenger and cargo ships from the Australian government. Despite surplus tonnage on the Australian route and Commonwealth's continual losses, £250,000 was paid on delivery and the rest in equal yearly instalments with $5\frac{1}{4}$ per cent interest.

Had Kylsant made a risky agreement? 'I believe in the future of Australia' was his response. He put the newly-acquired fleet under the Aberdeen Line's flag.

Barely a month later, Kylsant gained control of the Shaw Savill and Albion Line through purchase of Sir John Ellerman's majority interest. To finance this purchase, Kylsant used £994,000 of the £9,000,000 capital created with White Star Line Ltd's formation. He placed yet another strain on the Royal Mail group's finances, already whirling about as so many juggler's balls, with a £2,550,000 ($12,750,000) loan the British treasury was persuaded to make to fund an ambitious shipbuilding programme.

From 1921 to 1929, Royal Mail Steam Packet Company's public balance sheets failed to disclose whether profit had been earned. Of total dividends paid during this period, more than £5,000,000 came not from current earnings, but from non-recurring revenue and undisclosed transfers of hidden reserves, some from subsidiary companies. Indeed, during 1926 and 1927, when the company allegedly made large trading profits, it had actually incurred serious losses.

If the shipping industry's prosperity had revived, as Kylsant anticipated, his financial plan probably would have succeeded, with his group's stability restored and his foresight hailed as courageous. In June 1928, supposedly to expand operations, but actually to consolidate the rapidly accumulating debt, Kylsant caused £2,000,000 in second debenture stock to be issued by the Royal Mail Steam Packet Company. The new stock's prospectus contained the following statement:

'Although this company in common with other shipping companies has suffered from the depression in the shipping industry, the audited accounts of the company show that during the past ten years the average balance available, including profits of the insurance fund, after providing for depreciation and interest on existing stock, has been sufficient to pay interest on the present issue more than five times over.

Based on present knowledge of ten years of dividend payment manipulations, it is apparent that this statement is false. In 1930 and 1931,

By 1934, Kylsant's White Star Line Ltd stock was replaced with Cunard-White Star Line securities (Authors' collection).

Parliamentary questions regarding his handling of the £80,000,000 Royal Mail group's finances finally sparked a government inquiry into its affairs.

Kylsant tried to maintain his companies' credit, but rumours of irregularities spread. His own brother, Viscount St Davids, resigned from the board and advised shareholders of the group's financial problems. The Royal Mail Steam Packet Company granted Kylsant a leave of absence.

On 13 May 1931, ten days after returning from a two-month South African holiday, Kylsant was charged with falsifying the 1926 and 1927 annual reports, and issuing false statements in the 1928 stock prospectus. John Morland, Kylsant's accountant, was charged with 'aiding, abetting and instigating Lord Kylsant in issuing false statements.'

Tried at London's Criminal Court, Morland and Kylsant were acquitted of publishing false annual reports. But Kylsant, who alone accepted the blame, was found guilty of 'making, publishing and circulating' a false prospectus, and sentenced to twelve months' imprisonment. Upon his return

to ordinary life, Kylsant retired to his residence at Carmarthenshire, South Wales where, except for occasional public appearances, he remained until his 5 June 1937 death at the age of 74.

But irreparable damage to White Star had been done. As early as 1928 Kylsant had begun siphoning off White Star's earnings to support the less-profitable group members. White Star's 1929 profit of £335,155 ($1,775,775) turned into a 1930 loss of £108,556 ($542,780). Allowing even for the economic slump and increased North Atlantic competition, Kylsant's mismanagement was clearly evident.

In July 1930 the government began the Royal Mail group's reorganization. In 1933, Shaw Savill ceased to be a White Star subsidiary. In that year, the Commonwealth Line became an overwhelming burden. With almost half of its £1,900,000 purchase price now due, White Star Line Ltd tried unsuccessfully to renegotiate its debt with the Australian Government. Early in 1933 the latter advised White Star that they had decided to realize their security under the debentures charged to the fleet. The ships were sold for £500,000 ($2,500,000) to a new company, Aberdeen and Commonwealth Line Ltd, formed by Shaw Savill and P&O groups. The transaction's total cost to White Star, including interest and money spent on the ships' improvements, amounted to a catastrophic £2,712,994 ($13,564,790). Less than one-fifth of this amount was received from the ships' sales.

In a desperate attempt to salvage the company's name and reputation, White Star's management asked J. Bruce Ismay, now well over seventy and twenty years retired, to become involved in the company's reorganization. Ismay acceded, and raising capital began. But before the plan could proceed, it was discontinued.

Britain's two largest shipping companies, White Star and Cunard, had each been forced to quit construction of immense liners — though White Star's *Oceanic* was now abandoned totally, while Cunard's number 534 was merely suspended. The government offered Cunard the money to complete 534 if it would agree to merge with White Star.

The two companies' directors agreed on 30 December 1933. Under the Merchant Shipping Act of 1934, HM treasury advanced £9,000,000 to the merged company. Rushed through Parliament, the bill received the Royal Assent on 28 March, and on 10 May 1934 the new company was registered as Cunard White Star Ltd.

White Star Line Ltd brought little dowry to the marriage. Of the £7,000,000 due to International Mercantile Marine for purchase of the Oceanic Steam Navigation Company, £2,500,000 was still owing. In the next fourteen years, various White Star Line Ltd and Oceanic assets were sold off or dispersed. White Star headquarters in Liverpool's James Street closed 1 September 1934. The White Star Line Ltd was ended by High Court order on 8 April 1935; the official receiver reported an astounding £11,280,864 ($56,404,320) deficit. The Oceanic Steam Navigation Co was dissolved 21 August 1939: White Star Line Ltd followed on 16 March 1945.

In 1947 the Cunard Steam Ship Company purchased the balance of Cunard-White Star share capital, the merged company becoming a wholly-owned Cunard subsidiary.

Today, in the 1990s, a single vessel — still afloat and bearing her original name — serves as something of a White Star Line memorial. Her funnel removed but much of her superstructure intact, the 1911 tender *Nomadic* is moored in Paris's River Seine near the Eiffel Tower, converted into a restaurant. It is not difficult to see the original Harland and Wolff lines, nor to imagine her efficiently serving two generations of White Star and Cunard liners at Cherbourg.

Nor is it difficult to recall one warm April evening in 1912 at Cherbourg, when *Nomadic* set out from a wharf with passengers for perhaps the greatest, and certainly the most memorable White Star ship, *Titanic*...

CHAPTER 14

Laurentic and *Doric,* 1935

DOUBLE TROUBLE

The financial shoals into which the White Star Line had been steered did their work quickly, with wrecking ball effectiveness. On 10 May 1934 Cunard-White Star Ltd was officially registered, and immediately assumed operational control of a combined fleet. Within a year, hundreds of White Star employees were discharged, facilities were sold, White Star corporate records discarded.

Faced with excess tonnage, the continuing slump in passenger traffic and the new *Queen Mary*'s forthcoming debut, made possible by the merger, Cunard-White Star immediately began a parade to shipbreakers' yards. Many of the first to go were White Star vessels. The company defended its choices, stating that White Star ships were elderly and in poor condition. Some nautical observers sniffed that the only thing wrong with the ships was their White Star colours.

Albertic from White Star's Canadian fleet went first, after just six years of company service. Sold for £34,000, she left in August 1934 for her longest and last voyage to scrapyards at Osaka, Japan. The veteran *Adriatic*, last survivor of the 'Big Four,' followed *Albertic* to Osaka in December. *Calgaric*, another Canadian ship, was sold for £31,000, again after six White Star years. She departed for a Rosyth, Scotland, scrapyard the day after *Adriatic*'s final voyage began.

Above left *The second* Laurentic *entered White Star service in 1927, and was placed on the Liverpool-Canada run with extensive wintertime cruising* (Everett E. Viez collection, Steamship Historical Society of America).

Left Laurentic*'s cabin class lounge offered simple comfort; it was the site of a shipboard dance that ended with tragedy* (Authors' collection).

The year 1935 found only *Britannic, Georgic, Olympic* and *Majestic* still engaged in transatlantic service, while the remaining survivors were sent cruising. Seemingly wonderful bargains were offered: seventeen-day Mediterranean cruises for just £20; one-day cruises to nowhere for £3. Among the cruise ships was *Laurentic*, which had entered White Star's Canadian service in 1927. The second vessel of the name, she was the only ship not built to White Star's usual 'cost plus shipyard profit' arrangement with Harland and Wolff. Instead, she was built to a strict budget fixed by International Mercantile Marine, already looking for someone to purchase its White Star Line holdings. To some, therefore, she was a 'penny pincher' ship; indeed, she was built as a coal burner with combination reciprocating-turbine machinery, long after oil-fuelled, all-turbine vessels were common. Accommodation for 594 cabin, 406 tourist third and 500 third class passengers was comfortable and 'homey,' if not lavish.

Laurentic's seven years on the Liverpool-Quebec-Montreal run were marked by only one serious accident. On 2 October 1933 she collided with the British steamer *Lurigethan* in the St Lawrence River's Belle Island Strait. Both ships were damaged above the waterline. With transatlantic travel down sharply, she began cruises-only service in 1934.

Her mid-summer 1935 schedule was typical: a thirteen-day Liverpool-to-Mediterranean cruise, departing 13 July. A cruise from London to Sweden with a party of Rover Scouts, departing 27 July. And, on 17 August, a fourteen-day 'North Cape' cruise from Liverpool to German and Scandinavian ports.

For Annette Wolff, a Montrealer working as a

dental surgery assistant in London, the 17 August cruise was an ideal holiday promising cooler weather aboard a ship she knew well and liked. Her grandmother frequently had chosen *Laurentic* for her Canadian visits; 'White Star was our company,' Annette said. She would often meet the liner in Quebec and sail with Granny to Montreal. In her twenties, Annette had already crossed the Atlantic in *Laurentic* twice, once in first class and once in third. For her, the liner was a 'gracious and happy ship.'

The cruise began inauspiciously. Annette and many of the 620 other passengers arrived on the London – Liverpool boat train during a driving rain storm. Told to board immediately, they left their luggage in the pier shed; porters would bring it aboard later. Annette soon found her inside cabin on F deck's port side. Dinner would be served at once: formal dining room seating assignments would be issued later.

During a 'good meal,' passengers began enjoying themselves. Dinner was followed by dancing and mingling with shipmates. Annette found them 'easy to get along with,' predominantly English, Irish and Scottish, with few Americans. Many were on their holidays. The evening assumed a festive atmosphere; passengers went for long strolls around the covered promenade deck or sipped

lemonade offered by ever-attentive stewards. 'We had so much fun; we seemed to be a very lively crowd,' Annette recalled. To everyone's delight, Captain William Sewell Quinn decided that, in view of the vessel's rain-delayed departure, the orchestra could play until 1.30 am, ninety minutes into Sunday, when dancing on board usually wasn't permitted.

Exhausted from a day that had begun at 5.00 am, Annette went to her cabin which was 'a long way down from where we had been dancing,' she said, 'but I didn't mind so long as I had a place to sleep.' It was a tiny, white-enamelled room with a cupboard and a single berth below a folded Pullman upper. Annette stowed her suitcase alongside her life preserver under her bunk, splashed some water in her face, and 'fell into bed'. But before sleeping, she followed her usual practice, placing her eyeglasses, purse and flashlight under her pillow. She was asleep almost at once.

As *Laurentic* sailed westward at about 15 knots from Liverpool to a point south of the Isle of Man, the heavy rains ceased; to *Laurentic*'s officer of the watch, Junior First Officer Oliver Tugwell, the night was clear and cool. He was therefore astounded when at 2.29 am he heard a prolonged blast of a ship's whistle on the starboard bow apparently about two miles ahead, for he couldn't see any other ship. He sounded a prolonged blast on *Laurentic*'s whistle, and ordered 'stand by' on the engine room telegraph. Another 45 seconds passed, still with no sighting.

A second short blast from the other still-invisible vessel was answered with another prolonged blast from *Laurentic*: her engines were stopped. The stranger sounded a third blast, and two seconds later her two masthead lights and red side light appeared. *Laurentic* at once sounded three short whistles to indicate engines were going full astern. At this moment Captain Quinn arrived on the bridge, assessed impending danger, and ordered *Laurentic*'s helm hard-aport.

The stranger — the 10,116-ton Blue Star Line freighter *Napier Star* — had encountered fog at about 2.10 am on her voyage from Glasgow to Liverpool and, according to her Captain James Taylor, had suitably reduced speed to $7\frac{1}{2}$ knots. But to *Laurentic*'s captain and crew, *Napier Star* still had considerable headway as her lights materialized out of the now-apparent fog.

There was no time for *Laurentic*'s Quartermaster Weston to react to Captain Quinn's hard-a-port command. At 2.32 am, with a shattering impact, *Napier Star*'s bow rammed into *Laurentic*'s starboard side forward of the bridge, creating a huge triangular hole from the fo'c'sle to below the waterline, penetrating 15 ft into B deck, 13 ft on C deck, and somewhat less on A deck. *Napier Star*'s bow was crushed for 38 ft from the stem, with another hole further aft on the starboard side. As *Napier Star* turned away, her port anchor was torn loose, jammed in *Laurentic*'s side.

Six *Laurentic* crewmen were killed instantly and five others were seriously injured as the sharp steel prow of *Napier Star* smashed its way in. On board the freighter there were no injuries.

The orchestra which had brought pleasure to so many that night had their cabins in the collision area. Saxophonist D.H. Holcroft was lifted in his bunk and crushed against the ceiling, killing him. 'We felt so badly,' Annette said. 'This poor man had played until 1.30, and by 2.30 he was dead.' Bandmaster Grundy escaped with severe facial cuts caused by a shower of plaster, dust and debris. He then pulled the baggage master, Mr Hewitt, from the latter's splintered cabin woodwork.

Len Backhouse, cellist, emerged unscathed, saying, 'I saw the reflection of light [from *Napier Star*] on the water, and then there was a terrible crash. Sparks flashed across the porthole as the plates were torn apart. The partition of the next cabin crashed towards me, but luckily it stopped a few in-

Above left *At about 2.30 am on 18 August 1935, the 10,116-ton Blue Star Line freighter* Napier's Star's *sharp prow rammed the* Laurentic's *starboard side forward of the bridge* (Uhle collection, Steamship Historical Society of America).

Right *Cruise passenger Annette Wolff snapped a view of* Laurentic's *boats still swung out the next morning, as the damaged liner limped back to Liverpool* (Annette R. Wolff).

Laurentic's starboard bow is rammed inward from the blow; a normally taut rope ladder dangles loosely, indicating the extent of the bow's deformation (Annette R. Wolff).

A Laurentic *motor lifeboat is seen below another as damage inspection continues* (Annette R. Wolff).

ches short of my bunk.'

A fourteen-year-old crewman on his first voyage had a miraculous escape. He was totally enveloped in twisted wreckage and steel, but was utterly uninjured. As efforts to extricate him and others began, concerned colleagues passed in brandy, cigarettes and oranges to keep their spirits up.

Meanwhile, *Laurentic's* passengers were stirring in their cabins. Said Annette Wolff, 'The next thing I knew something had awakened me — I

wasn't sure what, but I knew it had made me turn over. It was a severe jostle. Then I heard the alarm bells and the foghorn blowing. I had had enough boat drills on board to know what this meant.'

Other passengers were confused, but 'stewards and stewardesses seemed to be there [in corridors] in a flash, fully dressed. Everyone opened their cabin doors at once, all inquiring, "What's it all about?" ' Six short rings and one long ring of the alarm bells and a similar pattern on the ship's whistle had sounded. Veteran traveller Annette calmly told them. 'Well that means that you'd better grab your life belt and get to your lifeboat station!'

Throwing a coat over her dressing gown and collecting her purse, glasses, passport and life belt, Annette now found corridors filled with people in various states of dress trying to find their shoes, left there for polishing overnight. Stewards were helping people put on life belts, then sending them to their boat stations above. By now the ship was stopped and on an even keel.

Boat drill had been scheduled for later that day, so the uninitiated had to find their own ways to boat stations. Passengers watched as lifeboats were lowered to the promenade deck. 'One lady was in a terrible state because her daughter was in a cabin on the other side of the ship. Someone found some brandy for her. She was the only person I saw who was really distressed. Everyone was saying what they thought or what they heard or what they felt, and speculating.' There was absolutely no panic.

The cool, damp weather was soon felt by those clad only in pyjamas and nightgowns. Some were barefoot, quite ill-prepared if evacuation became necessary. Many retreated to the warm lounge to wait.

After about a half-hour of wondering, a junior office arrived, and said, 'I have a message from the captain for you, He says, ''All's well for the time being; you may resume your interrupted repose.'' ' The ship's watertight doors had been closed immediately, and her bulkheads were now containing the flooding.

Annette doffed her uncomfortable, old-fashioned life belt at once, and swinging it as she went, happily left for her cabin whistling one of the orchestra's tunes. 'Not another soul was moving anywhere; it was a hollow ship because there was nobody below. I think I saw only one soul on the way down to F deck.' Her steward greeted her with excitement upon her arrival: 'What on earth are you doing down here?' Annette said, 'The captain says all's well. I'm going to sleep! I don't care what's happening!'

No sooner had she returned to her bunk than a stewardess knocked at the door. 'I've got hot cocoa for everyone,' she explained. Annette dismissed her, citing a need for sleep, 'my chief purpose in life at that moment.' The stewardess was followed by her steward, who had appointed himself a one-man news bureau, relaying latest developments. Both seemed somewhat distracted, but very matter-of-fact in asking when others on deck would be returning; after all, the silent corridors needed tidying and the helter-skelter collection of shoes

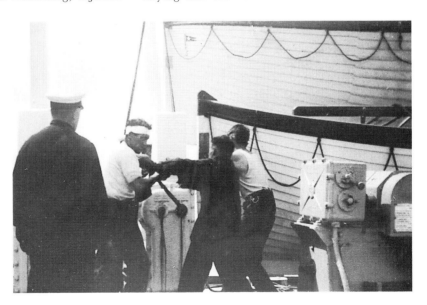

Danger now past, crewmen return a lifeboat to its chocks; one man has had his injured head bandaged (Annette R. Wolff).

Above *The 'other ship,' Napier Star, is observed nearby by Laurentic's passengers* (Annette R. Wolff).

Left *At her Liverpool dock, the full extent of* Laurentic's *damage is evident; the Napier Star's anchor remains embedded in the smashed crews' quarters* (Shipbuilding and Shipping Record).

Right *Annette Wolff,* Laurentic *passenger, recalled her unfortunate-but-exciting voyage in 1988* (Authors' collection).

Far right *The mangled bow of the Napier Star shows significant deflection. A court later apportioned blame for the collision to both captains* (Shipbuilding and Shipping Record).

needed matching before their owners arrived. Sleep returned at once for Annette.

At 5.45 am she was awakened for breakfast; 'I was most indignant about this because we didn't get breakfast until 7 o'clock!' Everyone came to breakfast, some still dressed in pyjamas and night caps. It was announced the ship would return to Liverpool, where further arrangements would be made for passengers.

As the ship slowly steamed toward the Mersey's entrance, two salvage ships equipped with acetylene torches arrived alongside in response to *Laurentic*'s wireless call to the company for assistance. Harland and Wolff men, arriving aboard *Skirmisher* with a medical crew, went to work from outside trying to free men still trapped in twisted and tangled girders. *Laurentic*'s crew had been unable to free them despite twelve hours of desperate efforts with hammers, chisels, blocks-

and-tackle and axes. To permit *Laurentic* to cross Mersey Bar, the other salvage crew began cutting away eight tons of anchor chain dangling from the still-imbedded *Napier Star* anchor. Meanwhile, Annette strolled the deck with her camera, taking photographs of the damage and *Napier Star* standing nearby.

At 3 pm Sunday 18 August *Laurentic* was berthed in Liverpool's Gladstone Dock, where Cunard-White Star officials met her. Passengers were overwhelmed by the assembled press. Some 120 were taken by tender to the landing stage station where they soon boarded a train to London. Others accepted full refunds or transferred to ships. At least one — Annette Wolff — at first refused to disembark. 'I was pretty highly strung by then. I realized that my holiday was over, or it was going to be cut short; my favourite ship was seriously damaged.'

She accepted an invitation to visit her grand-

Doric *entered White Star's Canadian service in 1923* (Authors' collection).

mother's cousins in Liverpool. Upon leaving the ship at 9.00 am on Monday, she sneaked several shots of the bow. 'I could see the whole gash; there were sheets, clothes and other things hanging out of the gash, which went right down to the waterline. I was told that if the gash had been five yards further amidships, it would have hit the boilers and we wouldn't have had such an easy time.'

She resolved immediately to find another ship to continue even a shortened holiday. Forthcoming cruises on *Lancastria* and *Doric* were rejected because they would go to hot climates. With White Star Line's assistance, she booked a week's voyage aboard the *Meteor* sailing from Newcastle to Norway. It provided the holiday Annette required — and as events would soon prove, it was an excellent choice of ship...

With damage estimated at more than $100,000 (£20,000), repairing *Laurentic* began at once, for Cunard-White Star hoped to proceed with a well-booked 6 September voyage of Catholic pilgrims from Dublin to Lourdes. Harland and Wolff workmen toiled around the clock, cutting away large hull sections, reconstructing smashed cabins, and fitting new plates. Within two days much of the twisted debris had been removed. Removal of *Napier Star*'s anchor proved a difficult challenge.

The workers met their deadline, and *Laurentic* sailed as scheduled. But it was to be her last voyage

with fare-paying passengers. Upon her return to Liverpool she was laid up for nearly a year in Birkenhead's Bidston Dock.

Not to be kept ashore, several *Laurentic* passengers now chose *Doric*'s thirteen-day Mediterranean cruise.

Doric had entered White Star's Canadian service in 1923 and remained there ten years before being transferred to cruise duty. She and *Vedic* were the only turbine-driven ships White Star had ordered from Harland and Wolff. On cruise duty she quickly had earned the nickname 'Cupid's Ship,' being especially popular with newlyweds and young people. On one voyage, a record nine couples had announced their engagements.

With 736 passengers and about 350 crew aboard this time, there was plenty of room. The cruise passed quickly, with daily activities and shore excursions. The final port of call, Gibraltar, was reached with regret, for the voyage home now reached its final phase.

Thursday 5 September began with difficult weather conditions. Heavy fog and mist obscured the area off Oporto, Portugal as *Doric* moved northward at reduced speed. Southbound in the same area, the Chargeurs-Reunis coastal steamer *Formigny* was *en route* to Oran, in northwestern Algeria, from Dunkirk.

On 5 September 1935 off the Spanish coast, the Chargeurs-Reunis ship Formigny *crashed into* Doric's *starboard side.* Formigny *is seen here during World War 2* (Mariners Museum, Newport News).

It was now about 3.25 am. *Doric*'s corridors and public rooms had been silent for several hours as passengers finally retired to their cabins. The night crew busied itself with usual nighttime chores aboard ship.

Suddenly lights loomed out of the fog to starboard. A shouted warning on the bridge, a quick turn of the wheel, but too late. In an amazing replay of *Laurentic*'s accident just eighteen days before, the 2,166-ton, 310-ft *Formigny* rammed *Doric* just forward of the bridge, missing occupied crew areas by feet. *Doric*'s cargo hold number three instantly began to fill through a hole 10 ft long and 5 ft wide. A second hole 2 ft in diameter also punctured the hull. Captain A.C. Greig ordered watertight doors closed, but already *Doric* had assumed a strong starboard list. *Formigny*, with only minor damage, disappeared again into the fog. Incredibly, there were no injuries on either ship.

Passenger Mr A.H. Rae from Dublin had been reading in bed and had fallen asleep. He awoke seconds before the collision, which he described as 'a rather violent impact, followed by a shuddering and a list to starboard.' Said Captain Greig later, 'The crash was terrific, and the crew had to work fast and hard to prevent anything from happening

to the passengers who became terrified when they were awakened by the collision.'

With the extent of damage unknown and the list increasing, he took no chances. At once the ship's radio operator was ordered to begin sending out a distress call as preparations for the ship's evacuation began. Almost immediately *Doric*'s whistle began sounding the signal for boat stations. 'Grabbing a dressing gown, a pair of slippers and a life belt I opened my cabin door and followed the hurrying passengers along the promenade deck to the emergency station,' Mr Rae said.

'Everyone showed marvellous coolness and presence of mind. In fact while waiting for the dreaded order to take to the boats, and watching the sailors getting the lifeboats ready and tearing off the canvas sheltering from the starboard deck, a couple waltzed round what little space there was, and the call of "The Doric!" sounding like a football rallying cry was taken up lustily by the majority of those on deck,' he said. There was no panic whatsoever.

The ship's orchestra, life of every *Doric* dance, had soon assembled on the boat deck still dressed in pyjamas, and as people waited for lifeboats to be lowered, they struck up *It's a Long Way to Tipperary* and dance tunes which the passengers joined in singing. In most cases, women and children were placed in the boats first. It all seemed an eerie reminder of *Titanic*'s bandsmen and passengers

Left *Before* Doric's *passengers evacuated their ship as a precaution, they were served breakfast in the ship's dining saloon* (Authors' collection).

Left *Breakfast over, they assembled on the promenade deck as lifeboats were lowered* (Authors' collection).

Right *Somewhat haphazardly,* Doric's *boats descend to the water as the fog finally lifts* (Sphere).

almost a quarter-century before, but no one noticed.

Two boats were filled and sent away immediately, to disappear in fog. Other passengers waited for more than an hour for their boats to leave. Some returned to their cabins for more clothing. After about an hour in the water, the two launched boats were summoned back to *Doric* and their passengers returned on board to await transfer to rescue vessels now speeding to the scene.

Some 35 miles away, Orient Line's brand-new *Orion* was returning from her maiden voyage, a Mediterranean cruise. At 4.00 am she received *Doric*'s distress message, and immediately headed for the position, 41° 19′ N, 9° 34′ W at her full 21 knots. *Orion* had been carrying only first-class passengers and her tourist class accommodation was not ready for unexpected arrivals. But there was plenty of space as crew hastened to put the cabins right. Other crew swung out lifeboats and launches.

Similar activity began on the P & O liner *Viceroy of India* when *Doric*'s message had come in. The *Viceroy* had also been returning from a Mediterranean cruise after many years on the London-Bombay route.

Viceroy of India arrived first at 5.30. Her lights immediately cheered the *Doric*'s passengers. With help now at hand, they were permitted to return to their cabins for small hand luggage and some breakfast, served in the dining room as usual. Transfer of passengers and crew from *Doric* went splendidly. At 6.30 the *Orion* arrived. Boats from the rescue vessels joined those of *Doric* in effecting rescue.

A London *Times* correspondent aboard *Orion* wrote, '...I put my head out of the cabin porthole at 7 o'clock to see the vague outline of a big ship on our starboard bow and one of the *Orion*'s launches coming from that direction... Lifeboats and launches immediately proceeded to the *Doric* to return laden with passengers, fully dressed, each carrying a suitcase and all in good spirits. As they came alongside, the *Orion*'s passengers, who by this time were lining the rails, welcomed them with cheers. One girl passenger from the *Doric* called up, 'Is there dancing on board this evening?' Everything went in the most orderly manner. The task of suddenly dealing with 500 extra passengers aboard *Orion* was cheerfully tackled as though it were an everyday occurrence.'

Fortunately the sea was smooth. In two and one-half hours, *Orion* took on board about 486 passengers and 42 crew with remaining passengers going to the *Viceroy of India*. The rest of the crew stayed on *Doric*. As the last of the passengers boarded rescue ships, the sun began to break through the fog.

Assured by Captain Greig that *Doric* could make her own way to Vigo, Spain for temporary repairs, the two rescue ships left the area in mid-morning. At noon a thanksgiving service was held on *Viceroy of India*'s upper deck, led by Framlingham College's chaplain. Passengers sang *Eternal Father, Strong to Save* and *O God, Our Help in Ages Past*.

Orion's Friday evening radio messages said she was proceeding northward at full speed, officers fearing an on-board food shortage. Both rescue ships arrived at Tilbury on Saturday 9 September. They were greeted by a large crowd. *Orion*'s passengers presented Captain A.L. Owens and the ship's crew with a letter of gratitude which concluded, 'The quietly effective way in which everything was so successfully done will long remain in our memories.' A similar testimonial had been presented on Friday to *Viceroy of India*'s commander.

Meanwhile, the damaged *Formigny* limped into Lisbon where repairs were quickly accomplished. *Doric* arrived in Vigo under her own power on the evening of the collision and immediately entered drydock where she was thoroughly inspected.

Above *The forward end of the boat deck was severely damaged by the collision; a lifeboat dangles over the side as a seaman inspects the damage* (Shipbuilding and Shipping Record).

Left *Her repair economically unjustifiable, Doric is sold immediately; before long, the shipbreakers in Newport, Monmouthshire have begun her demolition* (Private collection).

Already it was apparent that *Doric*'s next Mediterranean cruise, scheduled to depart on 10 September, would have to be cancelled as repairs could not be completed in time. The 800 or more passengers booked on the cruise were issued refunds.

Doric's temporary repairs were completed on 12 September and at 3.00 pm she sailed for Tilbury, where she arrived the morning of 15 September. Passengers' luggage was finally offloaded and forwarded to its owners. A thorough analysis of damage and repair costs resulted in Cunard-White Star's immediate decision to lay *Doric* up. While she was just twelve years old, it was felt uneconomical and unwise to permanently repair her, given the merged company's excess tonnage and diminished passenger traffic. Within two months she was sold for scrap for £35,000.

Meanwhile, on 10 October Cunard-White Star brought suit against the Blue Star Line, for damages in the *Laurentic-Napier Star* collision. Cunard alleged that *Napier Star* was navigated at excessive speed, had improperly turned to starboard, had improperly attempted to cross *Laurentic*'s path, and had not sounded her whistles properly for signalling either her manoeuvres or the presence of fog, and had not stopped upon eharing *Laurentic*'s whislte. Blue Star Line countersued, similarly blaming *Laurentic*'s watch. Each side denied the other's allegations.

During the four days of testimony *Napier Star*'s quartermaster suggested that she did not steer well at low speeds. Other witnesses from the ship denied the problem was serious.

On 24 October 1935 Mr Justice Bucknill found *Laurentic* to blame for excessive speed in fog, not sounding her whistle in fog, and not stopping her engines immediately upon hearing *Napier Star*'s whistle. He further found *Napier Star* to blame for negligently altering course to starboard, saying the ships would have passed starboard-to-starboard if the course change hadn't been made. He pronounced both ships equally liable for the collision.

On 9 November 1935 *Doric* made her last voyage to Sir John Cashmore's scrapyard in Newport, Monmouthshire, becoming the largest vessel to enter the River Usk. Thousands watched the procession of *Doric* and her tugs. Before stripping and demolition began, she was thrown open for a ten-day series of public inspections, luncheons, dinner-dances and a police carnival to raise funds for Newport's Royal Gwent Hospital. On one day more than 9,000 people visited the ship. The activities, together with a four-day public sale of furniture and fittings, earned more than £7,500 for the hospital's building fund. *Doric*'s demolition provided employment to 250 men for a year. It was a quick but premature ending for a ship that had brought cruising pleasure to thousands.

For *Laurentic*, however, a twilight period had begun. On 14 September 1936, in a somewhat-faded condition, she was pressed into temporary troopship service, making a single voyage to Palestine with British troop reinforcements in the face of increasing unrest. In May 1937 she was moved to Southampton. In April 1938 she was moved to the River Fal.

On 24 August 1939 she was commissioned as an armed merchant cruiser, probably the Royal

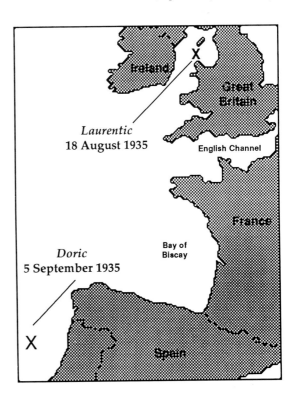

231

Navy's final ocean-going coal burner. Conversion in Plymouth's naval dockyard involved repainting her with black funnels and a light brown superstructure. Several 5.5-in guns were installed, and a portion of the aft superstructure was cut away. *Laurentic* was sent to patrol Icelandic waters looking for German blockade runners.

Soon after conscription, she ran aground on the Island of Islay off Scotland's western coast. Tugs from Glasgow got her off, but six weeks of hull repairs in Belfast followed.

On 3 November 1940, at about 9.00 pm, *Lauren-* *tic* met German submarine ace Otto Kretschmer and *U.99* off Ireland's northestern coast. Four torpedo hits crashed into her, the last at 4 o'clock the next morning. *Laurentic* finally succumbed, sinking with 49 men lost.

When Annette Wolff reluctantly left *Laurentic* in 1935, family members teased her about being a Jonah. When news of *Doric*'s accident arrived just eighteen days later, she was able to say triumphantly, 'See? Jonah sailed on *Doric*!' But Jonah seemed to be aboard several remaining White Star liners...

Accidents and incidents

4 January 1937	Engine trouble held *Britannic* in Quarantine at New York for 45 minutes. Temporary repairs enabled her to dock, and she entered drydock the next day where permanent repairs were made.
15 March 1940	*Georgic* collided stern first with a sea wall upon arrival at Liverpool. The resulting damage caused her sailing to New York to be delayed three days.
19 September 1940	*Georgic* was falsely reported as having been struck by German aerial bombs and severely damaged.

CHAPTER 15

Georgic, 1941

TERROR FROM THE SKY

Work on White Star's largest ship ever, yard number 844, the 60,000-ton *Oceanic*, stopped in September 1929, another casualty of the company's financial entanglements. Britain's answer to the record breaking *Bremen* would have been 1,000 ft long; her diesel-electric propulsion would have driven her at 30 knots.*

But there simply were no funds to complete her. A White Star overture to the British government for a loan to continue construction was refused. *Oceanic*'s huge keel was coated with preservative oil in hopes construction would resume. It did not; White Star had spent £150,000 in her design and production, but could afford no more; the project was abandoned and the slipway in Harland and Wolff's Musgrave yard cleared.

Attention now turned to yard number 896, which would prove a sad milestone: she was to be Harland and Wolff's final White Star commission. Her financing also seemed an insurmountable problem but the Northern Ireland government eventually guaranteed loans to complete the vessel, preserving precious shipyard jobs.

She could not have been born into less auspicious times. In 1930, White Star had lost £379,069. A £450,777 loss followed in 1931. American immigration regulations revised in 1924 had virtually ended emigrant traffic. Laid down in November 1929, just one month after the stock market crash, the new ship was launched at the depression's height on 12 November 1931. She was named *Georgic*, honouring King George V.

In general, she followed the plan of yard number 807, *Britannic*, launched in August 1929. Both vessels were designed for the Liverpool-New York service and were about 712 ft long overall. Each measured about 27,000 gross tons, though *Georgic* was slightly larger, providing accommodation for 1,636 passengers in cabin, tourist and third classes.

In what then was a daring choice for ships destined for North Atlantic service, both were driven by two ten-cylinder Harland-Burmeister & Wain four-stroke, double-acting diesels, generating 10,000 horsepower each and an 18-knot service speed. Their squat motor ship funnels were a radical departure from the usual towering symbols of power and gave *Britannic* and *Georgic* a streamlined look. *Britannic* and, in turn, *Georgic* became Britain's largest motor ship; indeed, only Italy's *Augustus* was larger.

Both set new standards for 'cabin class' liners but in different ways; *Britannic*'s interiors were based on historic architectural styles, while *Georgic*'s were ultra-modern. As the White Star Line optimistically told the press, 'The charming twin sisters of Liverpool will be as distinct as blondes and brunettes and there is every indication that the younger sister will attract an enthusiastic following that is all her own.' Both vessels were triumphs but their company would fail within eighteen months.

On 12 June, after three days of trials, *Georgic* left Belfast for a short cruise with several hundred invited guests. Upon its completion she sailed for Liverpool where she arrived at midday on 13 June. Five days of preparations there culminated in her maiden voyage to New York via Cobh beginning 25 June, with F. F. Summers in command. Despite a rough crossing she arrived twelve hours

*It was not until some sixty years later, when *Queen Elizabeth 2* was converted from steam in 1987, that a diesel-electric ship surpassed *Oceanic*'s projected size.

Left *Workmen rivet Georgic's double bottom during construction at Harland and Wolff's Belfast yard. Georgic was the shipbuilders' final White Star commission* (White Star Magazine).

Right *Dressed in flags, Georgic arrived in New York on 3 July 1932, twelve hours ahead of schedule* (Everett E. Viez collection, Steamship Historical Society of America).

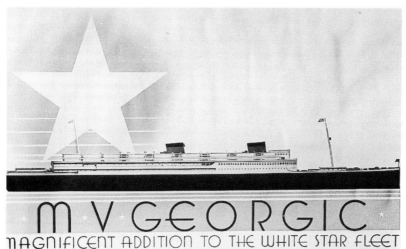

M V GEORGIC

MAGNIFICENT ADDITION TO THE WHITE STAR FLEET

TRANSATLANTIC TRAVEL now has an added appeal—the M. V. GEORGIC has just entered into the field. For in this illustrious addition to a famous fleet of cabin liners is introduced the alluring *moderne* theme of decoration. Startling reds stand in bold relief against demure old ivory. Bold treatments of gold and green create a sustained atmosphere of interest. Even the bridge front has a rakish rotundity which adds both to the streamlining of this new vessel and to the spaciousness of her promenade deck.

The GEORGIC—a 27,000 ton vessel, 712 feet long and 82 feet wide—offers roomy accommodations to 1636 contented voyagers whose days will be filled with action and whose nights will be replete with comfort. Those who have crossed on the Britannic, the Baltic or the Adriatic know what to expect aboard the GEORGIC: cuisine supremely typical of White Star excellence, service both willing and unassuming, appointments which add a new definition to comfort. For these features are expected of vessels flying the pennant of the White Star Line.

Now that the GEORGIC has joined the fleet, you are assured that one of these ships sails at a time which suits your convenience. Your steamship agent will gladly secure for you the precise accommodations you prefer . . . provided you make arrangements sufficiently in advance. Why not consult with him now? Remember — he is the travel authority in your community.

WHITE STAR LINE
INTERNATIONAL MERCANTILE MARINE COMPANY

Left *The company announced Georgic's 1932 entry into service in this contemporary advertisement* (Authors' collection).

ahead of schedule on 3 July. New York City news-papers and her passengers praised her comfortable accommodation at length.

In September she and *Britannic* were sent cruising to the West Indies. Both ships achieved continuing popularity with travellers while many other liners were sailing empty. In January 1933, *Georgic* filled in on the Southampton – Cherbourg — New York route for two voyages while *Olympic* underwent her annual overhaul. Two thousand people visited her at Southampton, the proceeds going to local charities.

In 1934, the inevitable occurred. After a £152,045 loss in 1932 and a further £353,552 deficit in 1933, there was no further future for White Star. The company's collapse and subsequent merger with Cunard had little initial effect on *Britannic* and *Georgic* except that they (and other former White Star vessels) flew Cunard's red-and-gold flag beneath White Star's burgee.

A cotton fire threatened a forward cargo hold while *Georgic* was at New York in January 1935; it was quickly extinguished, but delayed sailing for several hours. On 3 May, Cunard transferred her and *Britannic* to a new Longon – Southampton – New York route, without eastbound voyages calling at Le Havre. Successful winter cruising continued.

Britain declared war on 3 September 1939. Two days earlier, *Britannic* had been requisitioned as a troopship. *Georgic*, however, made five more trans-atlantic round trips. The United States govern-ment prohibited Americans from sailing aboard her, for she was now classified a 'belligerent ship.'

On 11 March 1940, as *Georgic* sailed home, her owners received her requisition papers from the Ministry of War Transport. Arriving at Liverpool she discharged cargo and passengers before proceeding to the Clyde for conversion into a troopship. Like her sister, she was painted a dull grey. All lifeboat davits were filled with double-nested boats, while scores of life rafts added further capacity. Anti-aircraft armament was installed and the ship was equipped to carry 5,000 soldiers or more on a single voyage.

Spring 1940 found her evacuating British troops from Andesfjord and Narvik, Norway and Brest and St Nazaire, France. Repeated air attacks failed to hit her. During the summer, she made trooping voyages to Iceland and Halifax.

Between September 1940 and January 1941, war found *Georgic* in many ports. One voyage took her from Liverpool and Glasgow to the Middle East via Cape Horn. Others took her to Bermuda, New York and Halifax from Liverpool. In May 1941, *Georgic* was ordered to Greenock, Scotland to embark personnel for a convoy trip to Suez via the Cape. Delays ensued and *Georgic* departed on 3 June, about a week late.

The trip southward was uneventful. On the first day, passengers assembled in the beautiful domed lounge for orientation tours. That afternoon, Captain A. C. Greig OBE, RNR and the ship's chief

Left Georgic's *single houseflag in this May 1934 New York departure was soon replaced by the double flags of the merged Cunard-White Star Line.* Georgic *and her sister* Britannic *retained their buff White Star funnels* (R. Loren Graham collection, Steamship Historical Society of America).

Below left Georgic's *low twin funnels were distinctive hallmarks of the Harland and Wolff motor ships of the later 1920s and 1930s. The forward funnel (right), a dummy, housed the engineers' smoking room and the wireless cabin,* (Everett E. Viez collection, Steamship Historical Society of America).

Right *Pre-war comfort is reflected in this view of* Georgic's *cabin class lounge* (Authors' collection).

steward presided over a light-hearted reception in the lounge.

At times, public address announcements informed everyone of news developments, including the battleship *Bismarck*'s destruction. Past Gibraltar and the Azores *Georgic* sailed, occasionally encountering high-level aerial attacks and submarine threats. The convoy docked safely at Freetown, Sierra Leone then proceeded southward off Africa's western coast. A 'Crossing the Line' ceremony appeared on *Georgic*'s foredeck, where those crossing the equator for the first time received 'baptisms' from 'King Neptune.'

The ship put in at Durban, South Africa for supplies, then sailed to Aden with another, smaller convoy. On 7 July she arrived at Port Tewfik, Egypt, anchoring in Suez Roads. Troops and other personnel destined for the African campaign left, 5,000 tons of cargo was unloaded and *Georgic* was readied around the clock for her return voyage.

Some 800 men, women and children now boarded, including *Georgic*'s officers and crew, Middle East evacuees, servicemen, Royal Navy ratings and Arab stevedores. The night of 13 July was hot and humid; sleep came fitfully to the 120 civilian passengers, while *Georgic*'s officers maintained attentive watch.

At 12.30 am on the 14th, air raid sirens' wailed warnings shattered the harbour's stillness. With memories of *Doric*'s evacuation still vivid after six years, Captain Greig again took no chances. He immediately ordered lights extinguished, watertight bulkhead doors closed, guns manned, fire pumps and firefighters readied. Then the waiting began.

The drone of dozens of German bomber engines soon could be heard, matched in its growing intensity by the pounding of the port's anti-aircraft batteries. The din grew as the planes dropped their lethal cargoes, inflicting heavy damage on the shore installations. For two full hours it seemed *Georgic* and the other ships in the harbour somehow were being spared.

But with shore installations destroyed and bombs still available, the Germans' attention now shifted to the harbour, with *Georgic*, the largest ship present, singled out for special attention. First one, then another and another bomb fell near by,

Above *With war's outbreak, Georgic was requisitioned as a troopship. This December 1939 photograph at New York shows her palm court windows covered over, though remnants of her peacetime colours remain. Queen Mary, at the adjacent pier has already been painted grey (David Kreines collection).*

Left *Fully readied for war, Georgic's dummy funnel was covered with sandbags to protect the wireless installation below (Gilbert collection, Steamship Historical Society of America).*

without effect. Five such bombs were released and still *Georgic* seemed charmed.

The sixth bomb struck a glancing blow on her hull, then bounced into the water where it exploded; its concussion severely damaged portside plating forward of the bridge and water began pouring into number four hold.

Another plane dived overhead and dropped a single bomb. It scored a direct hit on the after end of *Georgic*'s sports deck, crashed through the top of an elevator shaft and plummeted through five decks before exploding in number five hold near the swimming pool. The engine room bulkhead was fractured between D and E decks and fires

started simultaneously on five decks aft. Oil fuel forced upward from a ruptured double bottom tank immediately exploded, engulfing accommodation areas as it flowed through companionways and down stairs. Within twenty minutes the fire was completely out of control despite the firefighting crews' best efforts.

In numbers seven and eight holds several thousand rounds of outdated ammunition being returned to England now detonated, adding to the conflagration aft. Fortunately, the explosions went upward, sparing the ship's bottom from additional damage. Further explosions rocked the ship when the fire reached a magazine containing ammunition for *Georgic*'s 6-in stern gun.

By 3.30, Captain Greig faced conditions far beyond those after *Doric*'s 1935 collision: severe flooding forward, more extensive flooding aft, a strong port list. Responsibility for the safety of the ship and hundreds on board rested on his shoulders. But if *Georgic* remained and possibly foundered where she was, her sunken hull would block a vital shipping channel and stop supplies

Above *On 14 July 1941 at Port Tewfik, Egypt, a German plane drops a bomb that strikes the after end of* Georgic's *sports deck, once the scene of pleasant leisure activities* (Authors' collection).

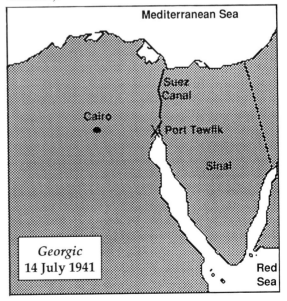

and troops to the Middle East.

Fire or explosion had severed all communication between bridge, engine room and steering gear. Somehow her anchors were raised and Greig began steering the ship to shallow water using her engines. *Georgic*'s gallant engineers remained below though virtually surrounded by fire. The diesel engines continued operating despite flooding.

Heavy smoke made navigation difficult; *Georgic* soon collided with a neighbouring ship and badly damaged her stern. Within ninety minutes of the attack, she grounded on North Reef, with a 17° list to port and 18 ft of water forward. Oil-covered water filled the engine room, completely submerging the diesels. But the critical shipping channel was cleared.

Evacuation now proceeded quickly. Three lifeboats left the ship in the normal manner before spreading flames forced remaining passengers and crew to lower themselves over the side on ropes from the fo'c'sle. Many were rescued by harbour craft. The bridge became uninhabitable; the entire superstructure was engulfed in flames; engine room staff were finally forced to flee. By 5.00 am, *Georgic* lay abandoned.

For two full days, she burned fiercely at her forward end; the after fires had soon burned themselves out. On 17 July Captain Greig and a small party boarded to survey damage. They found an incredible chaos of twisted, charred rubble from the top of her superstructure to the engine rooms. Significantly, the main engines were undamaged

but underwater. Greig wired the findings to the owners, who dispatched their London marine superintendent Captain F. Manley and a London Salvage Association surveyor to the scene.

They arrived on 14 September and ordered divers to inspect the hull. Within 24 hours, and with Admiralty concurrence, the decision was made to try to salvage *Georgic*. The only salvage vessel available, *Confederate*, was totally inadequate for the operation, so improvising was necessary. It further became apparent that permanent repairs were impossible in Suez, so priority was given to preparing her to sail to a more fully equipped port.

Divers plugged all hull openings and closed all open ports. Then the *Confederate*'s pumps were set to work. Their limited capacities barely touched the water inside *Georgic*. Local Egyptian labour began clearing the ship of debris and fuel oil while stiffening bulkheads. Emptying the holds began on 9 October and continued for ten days. It was then determined that stability would deteriorate if the engine room were not emptied, so pumps were redeployed there. As the water level dropped, men immediately began cleaning and greasing exposed machinery parts.

By 24 October, with all hull leaks temporarily patched, the ship began to rise. Two days later she began to respond to tides and on 27 October she was floated. Immediately she was towed to an anchorage, lest her continued racking and bending on the sandbank caused further damage.

In the badly damaged number four hold, the

Left *Within an hour, flames race through Georgic's interior as lifeboats are hastily manned and lowered away* (University of Liverpool Archives).

Right *Run aground on North Reef in Suez Roads, Georgic's stern floods to the tops of her twin diesel engines* (Authors' collection).

Gutted, listing to port, Georgic lies abandoned and half-submerged at Suez (Journal of Commerce).

Corrugated decks and blistered paint abaft Georgic's forward funnel graphically depict the fire's intensity (Journal of Commerce).

Harland and Wolff workmen cut away Georgic's damaged superstructure. The date is 21 September 1943 (Shipping World).

Some thirty months after her destruction in Egypt, new promenade deck plating and riveting is installed at Belfast (Shipping World).

Below *Minus her forward funnel and completely rebuilt as a troop-ship, Georgic bunkers at Liverpool before resuming wartime voyages in December 1944 (Russ Lownds collection).*

men constructed a large watertight cement box inside the port shell plating. At this point, *Confederate* was called to other duty and the resulting loss of electricity meant building the box by the light of kerosene lanterns. Captain Manley protested the darkness and another ship was requisitioned for duty alongside *Georgic*. Two days later, Manley found the 'power ship' to be filled with live shells. He decided he and his men would rather work in lantern light.

After three weeks of searching in Cairo, Manley found a 12-horsepower American tractor engine which he purchased and installed in the ruins of the cabin class dining room. Pulleys and a leather belt connected the engine to a generator, another Cairo find. They powered additional pumps and restored limited lighting.

Attention now turned to finding a means of towing the ship south to Port Sudan, where additional repairs could be made. *Georgic*'s towing gear had been destroyed and Manley had to borrow replacements from other Cunard-White Star ships calling at Suez. *Mauretania* donated an 8-in thick, 120-fathom long tow line.

Requests to other ship owners for assistance with towing met with resistance, for *Georgic* would be an unmanned ship totally at nature's mercy. Eventually, officials arranged for the Clan Line steamer *Clan Campbell* to tow and the Ellerman liner *City of Sydney* to steer. Towing began at 5.00 pm on 29 December.

As *Georgic* and her escorts sailed through the Red Sea at about 6 knots, gales and heavy seas arose. On 3 January, the twin tow wires from *City of Sydney* snapped and *Clan Campbell* now found a wildly veering 'dead ship' behind her. Only Captain Vooght's excellent seamanship aboard *Clan Campbell* averted *Georgic*'s loss. By 7 January, *Georgic* had developed a 10° list; apparently the heavy seas had caused the cement box to leak badly. A boarding party comprised of Captains Manley and Greig, *Georgic*'s senior second engineer and *Clan Campbell*'s second engineer restarted the tractor-powered generator. Volunteers maintained a 24-hour watch on board and reduced listing to 5° by morning.

Fortunately a tug from Port Sudan arrived, for the gales had jammed *Georgic*'s rudder hard-aport making steering virtually impossible. With difficulty, *City of Sydney* reconnected to *Georgic*. The ships arrived safely at Port Sudan at 6.15 am on 10 January. Number four hold was again pumped out, the cement box rebuilt and the rudder freed, then locked amidships. The *Clan Campbell* and *City of Sydney* were released, with thanks, by naval authorities.

Georgic remained in Port Sudan for seven weeks as patching continued. But this port, too, lacked facilities for the liner's rehabilitation. It was decided to tow her to Karachi and from there to Bombay for drydocking. Again it proved difficult to find a tow. At last the Harrison Line's *Recorder* was requisitioned, with the tug *Sampson* providing steering. The trip commenced on 5 March, 1942, with Captains Manley and Greig and their staff aboard *Recorder*. It was to be an incredibly difficult 2,775-mile journey, one of the longest tows on record.

Again disaster struck. On 6 March the *Sampson* had to cut her tow wire when heavy weather flooded her engine room. The tug soon foundered, but her crew was rescued by the Bibby liner *Dorsetshire*. Two days later the British India steamship *Haresfield* replaced *Sampson* and progress resumed at $4\frac{1}{2}$ knots. Throughout the 26-day voyage, *Georgic* was abandoned except for brief inspection visits.

On 1 April five tugs and several dredgers shepherded her into Karachi's harbour. Bombay's drydock could be spared only for repairs requiring such a facility; all other work, including making the ship habitable, had to be completed at Karachi. There was an enormous amount of work to be done.

The ship's generators, immersed in salt water for months, required thorough drying before they could be used. Karachi lacked heavy lifting equipment to remove them, so heating coils from the galley's electric ranges were stripped out and used to 'bake' the generators where they lay. Once the first was dried, it provided power for lighting, heating and pumping.

Some 400 Indian workers removed additional debris and cleaned the main diesel engines and auxiliary machinery which had been heavily coated as oil-covered water was pumped out. Temporary crew accommodation and officers' cabins were arranged and the water supply restored.

The badly bent stem seemed irreparable without drydocking. But improvisation triumphed. With after bulkheads repaired, number eight hold and the aft double bottom tanks were deliberately flooded while forward tanks were emptied. As the ship settled by the stern, the bow rose sufficiently to permit repair. A fire was built in an iron cage around the twisted stem; sledge hammers, block-and-tackle and crowbars then straightened the heated steel as damaged plates nearby were replaced.

After thorough cleaning, the two main diesel engines roared to life in dock trials that revealed another problem: The asbestos insulation around the engines' exhaust pipes had absorbed considerable oil that produced acrid smoke as the pipes heated. The insulation was stripped away and replaced.

After eight months Captain Manley ruled the ship 'fit to travel,' an Indian crew was signed on, and on 11 December Georgic left for Bombay sailing at about 11 knots under her own power. The ship was drydocked in Bombay on 13 December, where another inspection found the hull had twisted and slightly sagged. New port side shell plating was installed with additional stiffeners fastened to the hull's structure. The hull was painted, the propellers and rudder were examined and the machinery was further repaired.

Five weeks later on 20 January 1943, Georgic began the 6,200-mile journey home to Liverpool. Before departure, she accepted a cargo of 5,000 tons of pig iron for ballast. The freight earned the ship a £10,000 fee. She averaged 16 knots on the perilous, unescorted voyage, relying upon speed alone for protection. After stopping briefly at Cape Town for supplies, she proceeded without incident, arriving at Liverpool on 1 March after six weeks at sea.

On 16 March, after another survey, the Admiralty and the Ministry of War Transport decided to rebuild Georgic solely as a troop transport. The Ministry, now the ship's owner, appointed Cunard-White Star as managers. On 18 March she left Liverpool for Belfast, arriving in Bangor

Bay the next day. She remained there, some twelve miles from Harland and Wolff's shipyards, which were filled with wartime construction.

Georgic's repairs could not wait and on 24 March the first boat loads of workmen sailed to Bangor. Within ten days, all deck gear including lifeboats, davits, fans, ventilation casings and piping had been dismantled and cutting away Georgic's superstructure and decking began. By 1 July more than 550 tons of damaged structure had been burned away, cut up and loaded into coasters alongside.

On 5 July, the Musgrave yard's number three berth opened at last and intensive reconstruction work began, including removal of the entire superstructure, most of A and B decks and large portions of the lower decks. Electrical and sanitary systems were found beyond repair. Main and auxiliary machinery required extensive overhaul and lingering signs of fire damage needed removal.

By mid-August 1943, she entered Thompson Graving Dock for rudder, tail shaft and propeller repairs. Inside the hull, all fittings, wiring and tons of debris had been removed and shoring supported the remaining decking. Some 5,000 tons of steel had been removed and much machinery was sent ashore for reconditioning.

In the next fourteen months, more than 2,000 men transformed Georgic's shell to meet Ministry of War Transport specifications. Georgic's trooping accommodation featured superior lighting, heating and ventilation, and even offered a barber shop, two canteens and a cinema. Georgic's grey-painted exterior changed radically. The forward funnel (a dummy housing the wireless room and engineers' smoking room) had been removed. The mainmast was removed and the foremast cut down, while a lightweight signal mast was installed behind the bridge.

On 12 December 1944, reconstruction ended with Georgic the world's best-fitted troopship. After two days of trials, she returned to Liverpool to resume trooping service interrupted 1,252 days ago. She was sent to Italy, the Middle East and India. War's end meant a change to repatriation duties. On Christmas Day 1945 she arrived at Liverpool with several thousand superb 'presents,' troops from the Far East, on board.

The officers' recreation room aboard Georgic, *'the world's finest troopship,' offered comfort* (Shipping World).

During one 1946 voyage, *Georgic* brought home 5,000 former Italian prisoners-of-war and several months later repatriated a like number of Royal Navy and Air Force personnel from Bombay. Trooping and repatriation continued into 1948.

Australia's government launched an intensive postwar drive for emigrants, creating great demand for ships to bring settlers to the 'land down under.' With repatriation duties completed *Georgic* went to the Tyne yards of Palmers Hebburn Company for conversion into a dual purpose emigrant/troop ship. She was given accommodation for 1,962 emigrants and under Cunard-White Star management, began service in 1949 on the long run from Liverpool to Fremantle, Melbourne and Sydney. Ironically, her Suez Canal route passed the site of her near-destruction. Passengers could find other remnants of her past in sections of corrugated decking, sensed more than seen.

In December 1949, the Cunard Steamship Company announced it was assuming all assets and operations of Cunard-White Star Ltd and deleting 'White Star' from the corporate name. Nevertheless, Cunard honoured tradition and *Georgic* and *Britannic* (also a war survivor) continued in White Star colours.

By 1950, other ships could handle Australian immigrant traffic, but a North Atlantic traffic jam had developed. With much of its fleet undergoing postwar conversion, Cunard chartered *Georgic* for six round voyages from Liverpool to New York via Cobh, offering only tourist third accommodation. From 1951 to 1954, she was employed on the summertime Southampton – Havre – Cobh – New York run, with occasional calls at Halifax. On 16 April 1955 she concluded her longest voyage, arriving at Liverpool with troops returning from Japan.

With her hull and machinery now almost 25 years old, and with new tonnage arriving from the shipyards, *Georgic* was offered for sale. No offers were received and in May the Australian government again chartered her for another season of immigrant traffic.

M.V "Georgic"

ON the completion of your voyage, I send you my best wishes for your happiness and good fortune in your new life in the country of your adoption. Should you at any time contemplate re-visiting the Old Country, or having your dependents or relatives join you, the Cunard organisation throughout Canada is, I am sure, at your disposal for information and advice.

CAPTAIN.

Her final voyage ended at Liverpool on 19 November 1955, when she returned from Hong Kong with 800 soldiers on board. In January 1956 she was sold to Shipbreaking Industries Ltd and by 1 February had arrived at their Faslane, Scotland scrapyards.

Totally modernized during her 1948 conversion, *Georgic*'s sister-ship *Britannic* continued plying the Liverpool – Cobh – New York route, with her extensive West Indies and Mediterranean winter cruises enjoyed by many 'repeat customers.' But after a dozen postwar years, time ran out. *Britannic*'s diesel engines, now thirty years old, became increasingly trouble-prone. Cunard was contemplating new tonnage. In its first three years jet travel made a significant impact on transatlantic shipping. A wildcat seamen's strike and its consequent financial losses accelerated *Britannic*'s retirement. In August 1960 Cunard announced that despite a published schedule showing her busy well into 1961, *Britannic*'s last eastbound voyage from New York would begin on 25 November.

As *Britannic* sailed slowly down the Hudson River that day, a city fireboat offered her an unprecedented salute through arching, watery plumes. A tradition reserved for vessels on their maiden voyages, it was the city's farewell to the gracious *Britannic* and to the White Star Line.

She arrived at Liverpool on 4 December. Immediately she was sold to Thomas W. Ward Ltd and on 16 December the lonely voyage to the Inverkeithing, Scotland scrapyard began.

As *Britannic* sailed hull down over the horizon from Liverpool, not a few reflected on the hundreds of voyages White Star vessels had made under the red burgee. They thought of the innovations, now taken for granted, that White Star's management had pioneered. Perhaps they remembered with fondness some of the thousands of dedicated White Star personnel throughout the world who had offered outstanding service to company patrons.

White Star ships were driven hard by demanding masters. While other companies were content with the certainties of a purely North Atlantic service, White Star had dared to call at six of the world's seven continents. Fate had brought great tragedies with the triumphs. Risk was a regretable component of reputation. But for every voyage marked by accident or incident, miscalculation or mishap, many more offered comfort and competence, service and safety. The white star no longer gleamed above ship-studded seas. Instead, it shone in memories, where recollections of happy journeys and beautiful ships endure.

Accidents and incidents

28 January 1950	A 54-day Mediterranean cruise was extended two days when *Britannic*'s engines broke down as she left New York. She returned to her dock where repairs were made and proceeded on 30 January.
1 June 1950	*Britannic* collided with the United States Line freighter *Pioneer Land* while departing New York in dense fog. The freighter's bow was smashed by the head-on collision, but she returned safely to port as *Britannic* continued her voyage.
20 November 1953	Moments before departing on her voyage to New York, the *Britannic* developed a minor leak at Liverpool and the sailing was postponed one day to allow repairs.

30 December 1953   Half an hour after extinguishing a blaze on board the *Winchester Castle*, Southampton firefighters were called to the *Britannic*, moored nearby for overhaul. They found mattresses and lifejackets blazing in a cabin. The ship's sprinkler system quelled the blaze, and using gas masks in the heavy smoke, firemen removed the burning materials.

23 April 1955   A serious fire broke out in *Britannic*'s number four cargo hold three days out of New York and bound for Liverpool. Crew extinguished the blaze after six hours, but fire and water damage destroyed 550 mail bags, 210 heavy pieces of passenger luggage and four automobiles. Three crew members were overcome by smoke.

May/June 1960   Severe crankshaft damage on one of *Britannic*'s two diesel engines resulted in cancellation of several transatlantic voyages at the height of the season. Repairs were attempted at New York's pier 92, but lay-up extended for two full months until parts could be flown in from England. Eventually after a $400,000 (£84,000) expenditure, she departed on 7 July.

August 1960   52 passengers each earned $3.15 (66p) per day plus about $50 (£10.50) in tips by working as volunteer waiters and galley help aboard *Britannic* during a British seamen's strike. At the beginning of the westbound voyage, Cunard announced the liner's retirement.

WHITE STAR SHIPS LOST UNDER OTHER OWNERSHIP

Vessel	Post-White Star history
Asiatic (1871)	1873: Sold to African Steamship Company, renamed *Ambriz*. 1891: Sold to Elder Dempster, placed on New Orleans service. 1895: Sold to Madagascar; became a coal hulk in 1896. 1903 (February): Wrecked on Madagascar coast.
Baltic (1871)	1888: Sold to Holland-America Line, renamed *Veendam*. 1898 (6 February): Foundered in North Atlantic after striking submerged derelict. All saved.
Traffic (1873)	1896: Sold to Liverpool Lighterage Company. 1919: Converted to an engineless barge. 1941 (5 May): Sunk by German air attack while at Liverpool. 1955: Scrapped.
Belgic (1873)	1883: Sold to Cia. de Nav. la Flecha, renamed *Goefredo*. 1884 (26 February): Stranded on Burbo Bank near Liverpool, broke her back.
Doric (1883)	1896: Chartered to Occidental & Oriental Steamship Company. 1906: Sold to Pacific Mail Steamship Company; renamed *Asia*. 1911 (23 April): Wrecked in fog near Wenchow, South China.
Cufic (1888)	1901: Sold to Dominion Line, renamed *Manxman*. 1915: Sold to R. Lawrence Smith Ltd, Montreal. 1917: Requisitioned by British government for trooping; released 1919. 1919: Sold to Universal Transport Company, New York. 1919 (18 December): Foundered in North Atlantic on eastbound voyage. At least 40 lost.
Runic (1889)	1895: Sold to West India & Pacific Steamship Company, renamed *Tampican*. 1899: Transfered to Frederick Leyland & Company. 1912: Sold to H.E. Moss & Co, Liverpool; then almost immediately resold to South Pacific Whaling Co, Oslo; renamed *Imo*. 1917 (12 June): Collided with French munitions ship *Mont Blanc* at Halifax; latter ship exploded, killing 1,500, injuring 8,000, destroying large portion of city.

	Imo badly damaged, beached.
	1920: Sold to Norwegian owners, renamed *Guvernoren*.
	1921 (30 November): Wrecked near Port Stanley, Falkland Islands.
Medic (1899)	1928: Sold to N. Bugge, Tonsberg; converted at Birkenhead into whale factory ship *Hektoria*.
	1942: Requisitioned by British government as tanker.
	1942 (11 September): Torpedoed and sunk in North Atlantic.
Runic (1900)	1930: Sold to Sevilla Whaling Company, London; converted to whale factory ship *New Sevilla*.
	1940 (20 October): Torpedoed and sunk off Galway; two lost.
Traffic (1911)	1934: Sold to Société Cherbourgeoise de Remorquage et de Sauvetage, Cherbourg; renamed *Ingénieur Riebell*.
	1940 (June): Scuttled at Cherbourg; raised by German Navy.
	1941 (17 January): Under German flag, sunk by British torpedo boat in English Channel.
Zealandic (1911)	1926: Sold to Aberdeen Line, renamed *Mamilius*.
	1932: Sold to Shaw Savill Line, renamed *Mamari*.
	1939: Sold to Admiralty; converted to dummy aircraft carrier *Hermes*.
	1941 (4 June): Destroyed in air attack off England's eastern coast.
Ceramic (1913)	1934: Transferred to Shaw Savill Line.
	1940: Requisitioned but continued carrying passengers.
	1942 (6 December): Torpedoed and sunk by *U.515* near Azores; 655 lost, 1 survivor interred in German prison camp.
Majestic (1922)	1936 (May): Sold to Thomas W. Ward Ltd for scrapping. (July) Sold to Admiralty. Converted to training ship HMS *Caledonia*.
	1939 (29 September): Destroyed by fire at Rosyth, Scotland, sank at berth.
	1940 (March): Re-sold to Ward.
	1943 (July): Towed to Inverkeithing for final demolition.
Pittsburgh (1922)	1925: Transferred to Red Star Line.
	1926: Renamed *Pennland*.
	1935: Sold to Arnold Bernstein's Red Star Line.
	1939: Sold to Holland-America Line.
	1940: Chartered by British government, converted to troopship.
	1941 (25 April): Sunk by German planes in Gulf of Athens.

THE 'PAPER FLEET'

In the highly competitive, late-Victorian business world, pragmatic realism ruled. The bottom line — the only line — was a ledger's profit or loss. There was no room for fantasy. Sir Edward Harland, founder and chairman of Harland and Wolff, had a dream. During the 1880s he designed a 1,000 ft ocean liner suitable for his principal client, White Star. Sir Edward died in 1895, never having achieved his dream. But his idea persisted well into the 20th Century.

Harland's successor, Lord William Pirrie, kept the dream alive as a goal toward which all ship-building efforts, not only Harland and Wolff's, should be set. To keep pace with advances in materials, design and engines, Harland and Wolff's original design was updated periodically. But restrictions on materials, inadequate docking and repair facilities and harbour- and channel depths prevented the dream's realization for decades. Other, lesser White Star vessels also were planned, but fell victim to economic conditions and ledger balances.

Gigantic (1892)

Even before Sir Edward Harland's dream was sketched, journalists frequently speculated about prospective ocean liners' sizes. Builders' designs almost invariably contained length, machinery and furnishings specifications which exceeded requirements. Owners then scaled the plans down to size.

Thus, it most likely was a preliminary plan for *Oceanic* (launched 14 January 1899) that inspired a *New York Times* reporter whose 17 September 1892 story said,

'The White Star Company has commissioned the great Belfast shipbuilders Harland and Wolff to build an Atlantic steamer that will beat the record in size and speed.

'She has already been named *Gigantic*, and will be 700 ft long, 65 ft 7½ in beam and 4,500 horsepower. It is calculated that she will steam at 22 knots an hour, with a maximum speed of 22 knots. She will have three screws, two fitted like *Majestic*'s, and the third in the centre. She is to be ready for sea in March 1894.'

A 1 June 1893 article in *The Shipping World* examined the press's role in perpetuating gossip.

'Some curious rumours are now floating around the newspapers with regard to new vessels for the White Star Line. The name, dimensions and detailed particulars of a vessel, to be called the *Gigantic*, have from time to time been published in various shipping newspapers. Gradually the dimensions have grown, and now, according to the latest rumour, Messrs. Harland and Wolff are about to build a steamer of no less than 800 ft long

'At the White Star offices the rumours are said to be positively idle canards, probably based on plans and suggestions which are continually passing between Messrs Harland and Wolff and the White Star Company, and knowledge of which must have been acquired by draughtsmen and others engaged on the work.'

When completed, *Oceanic*, at 705 ft overall, was first to exceed *Great Eastern*'s 690 ft length; *Celtic* (1901) at 20,880 tons, the first to exceed *Great Eastern*'s 18,915 tons. Triple-screw propulsion had to wait until the Allan Line's *Victorian*, 1904. While a 700 ft *Gigantic* was never built, the name was to persist in subsequent White Star history.

Olympic (1899)

Thomas H. Ismay, White Star's owner, wished *Oceanic* to have a consort. Preliminary plans were discussed with Lord Pirrie. But Ismay wished to have his family financially able to meet death-duty benefits (introduced in 1894) should he die suddenly. So plans for the vessel, provisionally named *Olympic*, were abandoned.

Gigantic (1911–12)

Once again Sir Edward Harland's speculative 1889 plans surfaced, this time referring to the vessel planned to sail with *Olympic* and *Titanic*. Her sisters' luxurious appointments and technical advances during their construction caused conjecture about this liner — assigned yard number 433 — even before her keel was laid. A 25 November 1911 *New York Times* story stated:

'Remarkable details are now known of the thousand foot liner, the *Gigantic*, which the White Star Line has commissioned Harland and Wolff to build at Belfast.

'The beam will measure between 111 and 112 ft; the displacement will be 70,000 tons, the gross tonnage over 50,000. The levels [decks] will be a dozen or thirteen, with the highest over seventy-five feet above the water line. The passenger accommodation will be increased in the first class from 800 to 1,000 or more, and the total passengers carried will number over 4,000.

'The *Gigantic*...will have both reciprocating and turbine engines...She will have a cricket field, a tennis court, golf links and reception and ball rooms, and a restaurant and verandah café, which will be placed forward instead of aft. There will also be a plunge and all kinds of baths, and a gymnasium.'

Most authoritatively, the name *Gigantic* appears in a Liverpool *Journal of Commerce* article dated, coincidentally, 15 April 1912, which added speculation:

'The *Gigantic*, Another World's Largest Vessel — Our Belfast correspondent telegraphs last night - With the departure of the *Titanic* attention is now being centred in the great ship for the White Star Line, the keel of which was laid last week [*sic*] in Messrs. Harland and Wolff's Belfast yard. The monster, which will be fittingly named *Gigantic*, will, it now transpires, be 924 ft long, 84 ft broad, and nearly 54,000 tons gross register. The *Gigantic* will thus be considerably larger than either the new Cunarder *Aquitania* or the Hamburg-American *Imperator*. But for the lack of dry dock accommodation and the Belfast channel depth she would have been much larger.

Following *Titanic*'s loss, White Star, through owner Bruce Ismay, denied the name *Gigantic* had been considered for the new liner. It was not until 1 September 1912 that yard number 433's name was announced officially...*Britannic*.

Ceric (1913–14)

Intended as replacement for *Titanic*, *Ceric* was given yard number 391, originally assigned to Hamburg-America's *Europa*, whose contract had been cancelled in 1906. Edward Wilding, Harland and Wolff's chief designer, drew up the new vessel's plans. It is not certain whether he used the 'thousand-foot ship' plan prepared by Sir Edward Harland, but one of the projected liner's measurements matches one in Harland's plan: the 60,000 gross tonnage.

War ended the project. Yard number 391 was reassigned to Red Star Line's *Belgenland*, temporarily renamed *Belgic* soon after launch.

Germanic (1913–18)

Shown in White Star's 1913 list of new tonnage, plans for yard number 470, the 33,600 ton *Germanic* were suspended because of the war. At war's end, planning resumed and in June 1919 her keel was laid. Renamed *Homeric* and redesigned as 40,000 gross tons, the ship was to replace the lost *Britannic*.

With 1921 acquisition of North German Lloyd's *Columbus* (1913), herself renamed *Homeric*, plans for the new vessel were dropped. Yard number 470 was subsequently assigned to the 18,700 ton *Laurentic*, launched 16 June 1927 after having been originally designated yard number 615.

Oceanic (1925–30)

With Lord Pirrie's death in 1924, Harland and Wolff's chairmanship passed to Lord Kylsant, also chairman of the Royal Mail Group. Kylsant had shared Harland's and Pirrie's dream of a 1,000 ft liner. When Royal Mail acquired White Star in January 1927, Kylsant set out to make it reality.

In midsummer 1925 White Star had already quietly ordered plans for a 60,000-ton liner. It may be that Harland's original 1880s' design was the basis for the new ship. Work on the plan began, and berth 14 in the Musgrave ('South') yard was extended and reinforced to accommodate her.

Design work ceased in 1926 while Kylsant tried to find funding. In August, White Star's American director P.A.S. Franklin reported the great new ship would embody the best features of *Majestic* and *Olympic*, and would bear a 'family resemblance' to the latter, with a speed around 25 knots.

The new liner's cost was estimated at £3,500,000 ($10,500,000). When it appeared that funding would be forthcoming, design work resumed early in 1927. On 18 June 1928 White Star publicly announced it had placed the order with Harland and Wolff for a 60,000-ton, 1,000-ft long ship, to be named *Oceanic*. Assigned yard number 844, her first keel plates were laid on 28 June.

White Star's announcement said nothing of the new vessel's propelling machinery. At first, it was reported that 'long and anxious' deliberation was being given to the choice between turbine and diesel power, subsequently providing Kylsant with an excellent public excuse for construction delays. That all was not well regarding *Oceanic*'s construction was apparent almost from the start. After the media splash surrounding the keel plate's laying, construction proceeded slowly and intermittently. All work ceased on 23 July 1929 and on 26 September, the *Times* reported,

'The White Star Line announce that it has been decided to defer work on the *Oceanic* and to give priority to a new motor vessel of 27,000 tons. The keel plate of *Oceanic* will remain undisturbed on its present slip until the problems that face both owners and builders, primarily with regard to the propelling power to be adopted, have been solved.'

Early in 1930 it was reported that Kylsant had delayed *Oceanic*'s construction while he examined the design and, especially, the machinery of *Bremen* (launched 16 August 1928). In reality, his financial empire verged on collapse. There simply was no money to continue work on the immense vessel. When pressed at a May 1930 stockbroker's meeting to explain delays, he told them,

'Though preparing as far as possible our plans and arrangements for the construction of the new *Oceanic*, we have decided to defer actively proceeding with the vessel for the present. In the existing shifting phase of marine engineering science, the progress and development of varying types of engines is so rapid that it is naturally of the utmost importance to give the fullest and maturest consideration to the design of the propulsive machinery for so large and costly a vessel...'

In June 1930, the government imposed reorganization on the Royal Mail Group. During the next three years, as it became apparent Kylsant's group could not survive, the British Government prepared to support Cunard, whose financial structure was more sound. Negotiations ended in December 1933 with agreement to merge Cunard and White Star.

Work on Cunard's number 534, *Queen Mary*, resumed. Work on White Star's number 844, long in abeyance, was brought finally to an irrevocable end.

The dream — White Star — was over.
White Star. Bright Star. Falling Star.

Ships of dreams that sail on seas of the mind's
   making,
Ships that will never know the winds, the surging
   waves,
The gentle water in safe harbours, or the breaking
   of gold and rosy dawn after the storm;

Ships of dreams that sail beneath strange constellations
—
Gods and heroes that, like you, could never be —
Strange stars and oceans, even stranger nations
   between whose ports you roam unceasingly...

Dreams, seen only through your creator's eye:
Ships never born that can never die.

— John P. Eaton

INDEX

WHITE STAR LINE FLEET CHRONOLOGY

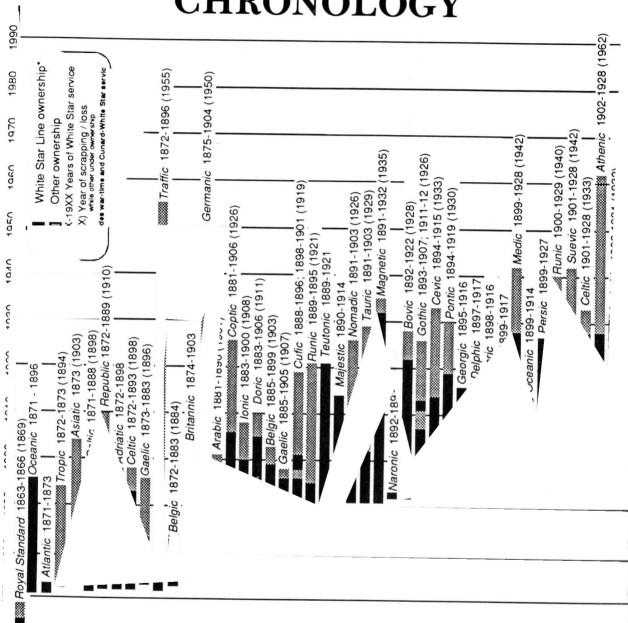

Legend:
- White Star Line ownership*
- Other ownership
- (-19XX) Years of White Star service
- X) Year of scrapping / loss while other under ownership
- * des war-time and Cunard-White Star servic

Royal Standard 1863-1866 (1869)
Oceanic 1871 - 1896
Atlantic 1871-1873
Tropic 1872-1873 (1894)
Asiatic 1873 (1903)
...tic 1871-1888 (1898)
Republic 1872-1889 (1910)
...driatic 1872-1898
Celtic 1872-1893 (1898)
Gaelic 1873-1883 (1896)
Belgic 1872-1883 (1884)
Britannic 1874-1903
Traffic 1872-1896 (1955)
Germanic 1875-1904 (1950)
Arabic 1881-1890 (...)
Coptic 1881-1906 (1926)
Ionic 1883-1900 (1908)
Doric 1883-1906 (1911)
Belgic 1885-1899 (1903)
Gaelic 1885-1905 (1907)
Cufic 1888-1896; 1898-1901 (1919)
Runic 1889-1895 (1921)
Teutonic 1889-1921
Majestic 1890-1914
Nomadic 1891-1903 (1926)
Tauric 1891-1903 (1929)
Magnetic 1891-1932 (1935)
Naronic 1892-189...
Bovic 1892-1922 (1928)
Gothic 1893-1907; 1911-12 (1926)
Cevic 1894-1915 (1933)
Pontic 1894-1919 (1930)
Georgic 1895-1916
Delphic 1897-1917
...ric 1898-1916
...99-1917
...ceanic 1899-1914
Persic 1899-1927
Medic 1899-1928 (1942)
Runic 1900-1929 (1940)
Suevic 1901-1928 (1942)
Celtic 1901-1928 (1933)
Athenic 1902-1928 (1962)